QUALITY AND ACCOUNTABILITY IN HIGHER EDUCATION

QUALITY AND ACCOUNTABILITY IN HIGHER EDUCATION

Improving Policy, Enhancing Performance

E. GRADY BOGUE
and
KIMBERELY BINGHAM HALL

PRAEGER

Westport, Connecticut
London

Library of Congress Cataloging-in-Publication Data

Bogue, E. Grady (Ernest Grady), 1935–
Quality and accountability in higher education : improving policy, enhancing performance / E. Grady Bogue and Kimberely Bingham Hall.
p. cm.
Includes bibliographical references and index.
ISBN 0–89789–883–4 (alk. paper)
1. Educational accountability—United States. 2. Education, Higher—United States—Evaluation. I. Hall, Kimberely Bingham. II. Title
LB2806.22.B637 2003
378.1—dc21 2002028760

British Library Cataloguing in Publication data is available.

Library of Congress Catalog Card Number: 2002028760
ISBN 0–89789–883–4

First published in 2003

Praeger Publishers, 88 Post Road West, Westport, CT 06881
An imprint of Greenwood Publishing Group, Inc.
www.praeger.com

Printed in the United States of America

The paper used in this book complies with the Permanent Paper Standard issued by the National Information Standards Organization (Z39.48–1984).

10 9 8 7 6 5 4 3 2 1

Copyright Acknowledgment

The authors and publisher gratefully acknowledge permission to reprint W. Edwards Deming's "14 Points for Management" (pp. 165–66, this volume) from W. Edwards Deming, *Out of the Crisis* (Cambridge: MIT Press, 1986), pp. 23–24.

We dedicate this book to Dr. Joseph E. Johnson, President Emeritus of the University of Tennessee and Trustee of South College, who in 40 years of service to Tennessee and American higher education exemplified, and continues to exemplify, a devotion to standards of quality and integrity.

Contents

Preface

Among the more visible policy accents in American higher education in the latter half of the twentieth century were access and accountability. While there were any number of other issues on the table concerning higher education, the policy concerns over increasing access and assessing performance were highly visible. The quest for quality remains a central issue of high visibility as we enter the twenty-first century.

The evidences for both academic and public concern over higher education quality and performance are plentiful. They include the rapid and widespread emergence of rankings and ratings in public media; new accreditation criteria featuring educational effectiveness information as compared to the older process accent; position statements and papers issued by regional and national higher education associations; frequent book-length critiques; public statements of faculty leaders and college presidents; policy papers such as *Policy Perspectives* issued by the Higher Education Research Program sponsored by the PEW Charitable Trust and the Higher Education Report Card *Measuring Up 2000* evaluating higher education in each of the states and released by the National Center for Public Policy and Higher Education in California; and finally various state laws and regulations mandating assessments and performance indicator reporting. All these evidences point to a more intensified and widespread academic and civic occupation with quality in our colleges and universities.

Where lies the impetus for this more active quest for quality and for the movement of performance curiosity from inside the campus, with faculty as premier players, to outside the campus, with various other stakeholders in government and the media? Some responsibility may be properly assigned to those within the academy who are doing what leadership in any enterprise should be doing—asking questions of purpose and performance. What are we trying to achieve, a curiosity of purpose? How good a job are we doing and how do we know, a curiosity of performance? Perhaps another impulse may be assigned to civic and political leaders who, seeing the large investments that had been made in higher education over fifty years, were no longer willing to "leave the money on the stump" without asking questions of performance and quality. Another source may rest in revenue reduction and cost-containment challenges that lead to intensified curiosity over public priorities and a probing of the conventional wisdom that cost and quality are always positively and directly related.

And it seems fair to say that public curiosity with the performance of colleges and universities may certainly be expected to grow more intense when both individuals and institutions depart from paths of integrity in their academic duty and responsibility. The sad and disappointing record of duplicity in colleges and universities invited increased scrutiny, and understandably so. Whatever the origins of the emerging national interest in collegiate quality and accountability, the conversation has opened for public and professional inspection a range of issues on the definition, the development, and the demonstration of quality in our colleges and universities:

- Is quality in limited supply? By definition, can only a few institutions hope to achieve excellence? Are we to have pyramids of prestige based on size and selectivity, or will we expect and honor excellence of performance among a diverse range of institutional missions?
- Are the premier guarantors of quality in colleges and universities our systems of quality assurance, such as accreditation and assessment, or is there a place for moral and ethical engagement as well?
- Is the quality of a program or institution to be expressed in a single performance indicator or evidence such as a ranking or rating, or does it take more than one data point to circumscribe the richness of both individual and institutional performance?
- How are the *evidences* on quality to be tried? That is, what standard of performance will be deemed acceptable and who will decide?
- What is to be the primary decision motive for quality assurance efforts—improvement or stewardship? To whom are colleges and universities accountable?
- To what extent should information on quality be disclosed in public domain?
- What is the proper partnership relation between campus and external actors on the quality stage? How can the principles of autonomy and accountability be constructively balanced?
- What complications do marketplace pressures—students as consumers, degrees as products—add to the challenge of quality assurance?

In some ways, one could believe that American academics and civic friends speak facilely about collegiate quality, as though everyone clearly understood what the term meant. Much lively dissent over issues regarding performance, however, can be traced to a lack of clarity or consent over mission and purpose and further philosophic complications reflected in the above questions.

THE PURPOSE OF THIS BOOK

This book is designed to bring historical, technical, and philosophical engagement to these questions, to advance the cause of both clarity and understanding. It has its origins in a 1992 work entitled *The Evidence for Quality,* for which one of the current authors was also an author and also the copyright holder. Material in original chapters has been updated and additional chapters have been added to more fully engage the theme of quality assurance.

We intend this book, as in the antecedent volume, to be descriptive, furnishing a synthesis of contemporary practice and policy in collegiate quality assurance. We intend it to be evaluative, probing the strengths and liabilities of each system and approach to quality assurance. We intend it to be assertive, emphasizing that quality assurance in colleges and universities is a partnership journey of caring and daring, of perseverance and risk. And we intend it to be prescriptive, introducing a framework of principles and practices designed to enhance the effectiveness of quality assurance efforts.

Certainly a first aspiration for this work is that the descriptive treatment of quality assurance systems and practices will prove informing and that each chapter will promote enhanced understanding. We expect, however, that the book will also stimulate curiosity and dissent, an outcome that would sustain our conviction that quality assurance should be (1) a venture in decision and discovery, one leading to renewal of programs, policies, and persons, and (2) a discovery exercise that challenges our understanding of purpose and performance and the nature of the collegiate enterprise.

We also accent the promise of quality assurance for strengthening a sense of community and nurturing an agenda of common caring. Too often questions of teaching and learning are privately engaged in professorial isolation and loneliness. Other questions of responsibility and reward, of reconciling tensions in professional duty are often analyzed and acknowledged but remain organizationally disengaged while individual faculty members struggle to negotiate the tensions in their careers.

The search for quality as portrayed in this book should affirm faculty members in standing responsible for their individual impact on campus life and students and for their collective impact on the community and culture that they help create. Neither in corporate nor in collegiate settings will quality emerge unless conversations breach departmental barriers and link all partners in common commitment.

Not all the outcomes of a college education, not all that is important to what happens in our classrooms and studios, not all that is precious in the interaction between teacher and students, not all the value-added impacts of college can be or should be captured by numbers and measurement. Where is the instrument powerful enough and sensitive enough to translate every beautiful moment of learning transaction into numbers?

We can, however, ascertain whether we are elevating the vision of our students from the poverty of the commonplace. And we can know whether we are cheating our students of their promise and potential. The first call on our accountability in higher education, then, is not to governing boards and legislatures and not to accrediting agencies and the media. The first call on our accountability is to our students. To know that our students have been exposed to low-quality climates requires no great philosophical agony in defining quality nor any technological feat in measuring quality but only the simple passions of caring and daring.

And on that point, we argue that quality assurance is not just an intellectual exercise. To be sure, it is an exercise that should call for our best thought and the engagement of our best minds. But it is an adventure that must tap our passion and our integrity as well. Failing to acquire and to apply information on quality is to confirm that we lack both caring and daring, a lamentable flaw of character in a community of curiosity.

How can we possibly give meaningful leadership to program and service improvements without data on quality? How can such timidity deserve the respect of our students? How can we teach our students the role of risk, courage, discipline, and perseverance in learning if we do not model these same values in learning about purpose and performance? Learning by doing, harnessing reflection and action—our search for quality offers an unparalleled instrument of learning, an opportunity to demonstrate the power and the character of a learning community.

Audience

Quality and Accountability in Higher Education is designed for a range of readers interested in quality—in its definition, its measurement, and above all, in the way information about quality can and should be applied to inform decision. Faculty and staff interested in developing and improving quality assurance programs will find the book useful. We also hope that friends in government and civic affairs who are interested in collegiate quality—governing board members, legislators, journalists, and other media representatives—will find the book of value in honing their knowledge of and sensitivity to questions of collegiate quality. Experience with the precursor volume *The Evidence for Quality* suggests that the book will prove of value for graduate students enrolled in graduate programs in higher education.

Friendly critics are of mixed opinion about another possible audience for the book. We believe, however, that the book may also prove of interest to friends in corporate sector enterprise who certainly have serious engagement with questions of quality. We learn from them, and we believe there is room for two-way traffic here. Collegiate and corporate—we share common challenges in definition and decision, in evidence and standards, in timing and judgment. A lively and learning conversation is possible as our entire society looks for ways to tone up our performance, from both individual and institutional perspectives. Whatever the nature of the enterprise, asking questions of ends inevitably forces us to ask questions of beginnings.

Finally, we hope that international colleagues in higher education may find the book informative. The ways in which American higher education nurtures and assures quality will differ in part from those of other cultures and countries. Again there is merit in bridges of learning that carry two-way traffic, and there is an increasing and encouraging international flavor to the conversation on higher education quality assurance.

Overview of Contents

Chapter 1 furnishes the background for the growing interest in collegiate quality and then offers a serious examination of current issues on how quality is defined and measured and how information on quality can and should contribute to academic decision making. In this chapter, we also propose a definition of quality that takes into account both technical and ethical aspects. The definition allows us to link our presentation and evaluation of quality assurance systems and approaches in succeeding chapters.

Described in chapters 2 through 8 are current approaches to quality assurance: accreditation, colleges' rankings and ratings, follow-up studies, professional licensure, academic program reviews, college outcome studies, total quality management. These approaches are presented in the approximate chronological order of their emergence. For example, accreditation is clearly one of the oldest approaches to quality assurance and one distinctive to the history of American higher education. Program reviews, outcome studies, and total quality management, on the other hand, are more recent developments in higher education quality assurance. We present the strengths and limitations of each approach and attempt to identify the philosophic anchors on which each quality assurance system is constructed.

Chapters 9 through 11 move more into the realm of accountability, how quality assurance systems are employed to demonstrate stewardship to interested stakeholders. Chapter 9, for example, portrays the emergence of performance indicator and performance funding systems as exemplars of accountability approaches. Chapter 10 accents the importance of ethical commitments as complement to our technical systems for quality assurance. And chapter 11 explores the tensions often found between civic and collegiate accountability cultures and offers a principled framework for the formation of more effective accountability partnerships.

Chapter 12 is the concluding chapter and attempts to pull from previous chapter discussions a set of governing ideals, or guiding principles, designed to yield a more effective approach to quality assurance in higher education. It proposes a more integrated and strategic vision for our quality assurance ventures and highlights the renewal outcomes that may flow from those who take the journey of discovery. This closing chapter accents the need for quality commitments that penetrate the heart of a campus, that engage the active allegiance of all who give voice and meaning to the collegiate enterprise, that reveal the presence of a culture of caring and daring.

ACKNOWLEDGMENTS

There are many to whom gratitude is due for this work. We express our appreciation to our spouses, Linda and Ronnie, and to our children for their support; to the University of Tennessee and to South College for affirmation of our efforts in bringing this work to reality; to graduate students at the University of Tennessee for their comments on drafts of the manuscript; to Dr. Fred Harcleroad, Dr. Cameron Fincher, and Dr. Robert Saunders (deceased) for their encouragement and contribution to the foundations of this work and a predecessor volume; to able editors of the Greenwood Publishing Group; and to administrative and faculty colleagues who in daily acts of caring and competence stand to duty on the call to quality and accountability in American higher education.

E. Grady Bogue
Kimberely Bingham Hall

Chapter 1

Introduction

Defining Academic Quality

College quality: Is it measurable or mysterious? Is it to be found in reputation or results? Is it carried in the perceptions of our academic colleagues and our students, or does it exist independently of their opinion? Is it purchased at the expense of other principles important to American higher education—access, equity, autonomy, diversity—or does it enrich and support those principles? Is it directly related to cost or does it run independently of financial support levels? Is it found in media rankings or in the knowledge and skill of our graduates? Is it expressed in test scores or does it evade capture by existing performance measures?

Quality: Can you improve quality if you cannot define it? Can you measure it if you cannot define it? And if you cannot define it, does it really exist? This is where Robert Pirsig left us several years ago when he noted that "obviously some things are better than others ... but what's the 'betterness'? ... so round and round you go, spinning mental wheels and nowhere finding any place to get traction. What the hell is quality? What is it?"[1]

In this book, we hope to reveal something of the ways in which American higher education has opened its search for quality. It will be the story of an unfinished journey, indeed of an ongoing journey. In this chapter, our aspiration is to engage some of the fundamental questions that must be confronted in that search—questions of definition and decision, of dreams and evidence, of meaning and measurement. We do not subscribe to the notion that every worthy and desirable outcome of American higher education will yield to measurement. But we do hold the conviction that quality can be defined, that quality can be measured, and that results of such measurement can be used to improve our impact on students and their growth as well as to enhance programs and services.

Would any college president or faculty member be willing to admit that he or she was producing a low-quality college graduate? Not likely. Would any president or faculty member be willing to admit that quality could not be improved at his or her college or university? Also not likely. But what does he or she have in mind when talking about quality? Whatever the definition (and we will venture a definition in this chapter), on one point a consensus appears to be emerging. If we are to judge by frequency and intensity of public commentary, colleges and universities should be more active in obtaining, using, and communicating data on quality.

Almost twenty years ago, the 1984 publication of the National Institute of Education entitled *Involvement in Learning* recommended that to enhance excellence in higher education, "institutions of higher education demonstrate improvements in student knowledge, capacities, skills, and attitudes between entrance and graduation."[2] Later in the monograph, a further recommendation appears: "Faculty and academic deans should design and implement a systematic program to assess the knowledge, capacities, and skills developed by academic and co-curricular programs."[3]

In the 1985 publication *Higher Education and the American Resurgence,* Frank Newman, then president of the Education Commission of the States (ECS), advanced the opinion that "higher education is entering a period of questioning of its purposes and quality."[4]

A major ECS paper, *Transforming the State Role in Undergraduate Education,* suggested that the "need to use assessment to improve teaching and learning is not reflected in current policies and practices."[5]

To Secure the Blessings of Liberty, a 1986 report of the American Association of State Colleges and Universities, recommended that "public colleges and universities should respond to these concerns by agreeing on and adopting a set of minimum academic skills and levels of proficiency that all students should attain, preferably by the end of the sophomore year."[6]

In the June 1988 *Special Advisory for College and University Presidents,* the National Task Force on Higher Education and the Public Interest carried the recommendation that "higher educators must communicate to on- and off-campus constituencies: improvements that are being made in the quality of instruction; and what reliable assessment tools are in place."[7]

One of the major goals expressed in the *1989–90 Annual Report* of the Southern Regional Education Board was that "by the year 2000 the quality and effectiveness of all colleges and universities will be regularly assessed, with particular emphasis on the performance of undergraduate students."[8]

A report entitled *State Priorities in Higher Education: 1990* reported that accountability and effectiveness ranked in the top tier of issues related to higher education.[9]

A February 1991 issue of *Policy Perspectives,* published by the Pew Higher Education Research Program, University of Pennsylvania, suggested that revenue reductions and cost containment may cause institutions to develop more strategic visions of mission and that some national universities, the University of Michigan, for example, now admit that in some areas there may be an inverse relationship between cost and quality. *Policy Perspectives* notes that such observations are "hardly music to an industry accustomed to equating quality enhancement with increases in funding."[10]

In more recent years, the theme of collegiate quality assurance has remained front and center. A 1996 issue of *Policy Papers on Higher Education* published by the ECS features the title "Priorities, Quality and Productivity in Higher Education."[11] The 1998 Southern Regional Education Board publication *Educational Benchmarks* continued to carry the regional goal that "the quality and effectiveness of colleges and universities will be regularly assessed, with particular emphasis on the performance of undergraduate students."[12] A range of books and other works on the themes of assessment and accountability have emerged over the past decade. These we will feature in later chapters.

Questions of purpose and performance are just as central—no, perhaps more central—in collegiate enterprise as corporate enterprise, though the engagement may be more challenging and complex given the nature of the enterprise. What do we hope to accomplish and how good a job are we doing? These are premier leadership questions in any organized enterprise, corporate or collegiate. As we just noted, however, such questions are perhaps more important to those holding the leadership of colleges and universities in trust, because we are expected to nurture leadership for every sector of our nation. In an essay entitled "First Glimpses of a New World," Robert Hutchins noted that "the most embarrassing question that can be raised in a university is what are we trying to do? . . . The administrator of an educational institution is to be forgiven if he evades this question and announces that education is what goes on in an educational institution."[13] Evasion of these leadership questions of purpose and performance—quality questions—is not a leadership option, however, for today's college educator, as this commentary suggests.

WITHOUT CONSCIENCE AND COMPETENCE

Why do we need a definition of quality, a means of measuring quality, a system to improve quality? Clearly, two of the major policy accents in American higher education over the last half of the twentieth century were access and accountability. The accountability motive often will be cited as a basis for attending questions of quality—accountability to governing boards, to state agencies, to legislatures, to taxpayers, and so forth. But our first accountability allegiance rests elsewhere, as the following illustration will show.

A thirty-year-old student enrolled in a graduate course has submitted a major paper. This paper is not just grammatically incorrect; it is incoherent! The student's performance in the course has been marginal on every dimension, culminating in this disappointing and heartbreaking final paper. Any reasonable standard of acceptable performance for graduate study would not encourage a passing grade for this paper, much less for the course. It might be argued that each person contributing to the meaning of this student's bachelor's degree has committed an act of malpractice, cheating this student of potential and dignity. The student has adequate intelligence and talent for good work, but has been denied the full use of that intelligence and talent by low and empty expectations. This is not a hypothetical illustration.

How could this happen? This student is a graduate of an institution that is regionally accredited and of a program that is professionally accredited. Think of the simplicity of attitudes and actions it would have taken to discover whether this student could write a grammatically correct sentence, a coherent paragraph, or a sensible essay. Think of the prescriptive and corrective action that could and should have been taken early in the student's collegiate career. This example illustrates a mind left wasted, a mind left dispirited and disengaged. To know that this student has been exposed to a low-quality climate requires no great philosophical agony in defining quality nor any technological feat in measuring it. In a 1985 book, one of the authors noted that "We know when we are challenging talent and when we are not. We know when teaching is demeaning to bright and lively spirits. We know when classroom climates are never sparked by the exhilarating and exciting clash of minds and ideas. We know when we are treating our students with arrogance unworthy of those who hold the human spirit and mind in trust. And we know when programs are cheating students of their potential."[14]

At the risk of troubling some readers with an opening illustration of this tone, we believe that a modest display of passion is both legitimate and appropriate as we open our book-length conversation on quality. And although some might argue that our notions of quality should not be built on exceptional cases, we can counter with the proposition that the exceptions constitute powerful and pertinent evidence on collegiate quality. The concepts of "zero defects" and "do it right the first time" are as important to what takes place in our classrooms, studios, playing fields, and rehearsal halls as they are to what takes place in our manufacturing and service enterprises in the profit sector. Peters and Waterman made clear in their widely read work *In Search of Excellence*[15] that passion and commitment are as important (perhaps more so) to quality as rational models for quality assurance. In this book, we intend to accent the idea that quality assurance is more than a work of systems and technique. It is a work of conscience and competence.

A precious work is the work that unfolds in our collegiate classrooms. Without conscience and competence, it is a work that can carry our students and our institutions in harm's way. Just one mind cheated of its potential is adequate justification for reasonable efforts in quality definition and assurance. Just one such example accents the most basic reason for our quality search: the effective nurture of human talent, spirit, and potential.

One of the reasons that students like the one cited in the preceding example slip through our quality nets is that we are too often preoccupied in arguing about the philosophical and technical complexities inherent in quality definition and measurement. The arguments have an unfortunate tendency to immobilize our quality assurance efforts. Let us have a look at some of the conceptual challenges by exploring first the multiple definitions and theories of quality.

THEORIES AND DEFINITIONS OF QUALITY

Certain conventional assumptions about quality are often widely held by academics and civic friends:

- Only high-cost colleges have quality.
- Only large and comprehensive colleges have quality.
- Only highly selective colleges have quality.
- Only nationally recognized colleges have quality.
- Only a few colleges have quality.
- Only colleges with impressive resources have quality.

These assumptions tend to produce what some call a pyramid of prestige. Residing at the apex are larger public and private colleges and universities, the "national" universities. Making up the lower levels are the regional and "directional" state and community colleges (Northeast U, Southwest U, Central U, etc.). Community colleges often are perceived to occupy the bargain basement in this flawed vision of quality. Another unfortunate consequence of these assumptions—bigger is better, expensive is excellent—is that some colleges raised their fees not so much because of financial needs as in response to the belief that students and their parents equate price with quality. See, for example, Ted Marchese's editorial appearing in the May/June 1990 issue of *Change* magazine.[16]

Some state college and university systems assert that the state can afford only one "flagship" university—usually the largest university in the state and most often the research university. (Should the term "flagship" be returned to the navy and left there?) Some states can (and obviously do) afford more than one research university, whereas others cannot. No matter what its Carnegie classification or size, no college or university can be completely comprehensive in any exhaustive sense—that is, have programs and services in every conceivable field of inquiry. Thus, the word "comprehensive" will always have a limited meaning, and every college and university—no matter what its mission, its size, or its Carnegie classification—will always have a limited mission.

These assumptions also suggest that quality is in limited supply. This idea, indeed, constitutes the philosophic cornerstone for college rankings and ratings, and we have more to say on this point in chapter 3. Are quality and excellence in limited supply? They certainly are if you subscribe to a definition of quality based on assumptions of size, cost, and selectivity. However, a good argument can be made that one can find large, high-cost, and selective colleges of mediocre quality. And one would not have to search very long to find graduates of these institutions whose behaviors, skills, and values constitute occasional and unfortunate evidence of this mediocrity.

The philosophy of limited supply argues with the conviction that quality is not only attainable but essential to every campus. It also argues with the assertion that quality can and should be found within limited mission—*because every campus will have a mission that is ultimately limited.* And it argues with the belief that any campus without quality in its mission has no reason to exist!

Governors, legislators, board members, media, and civic friends—these are not the only members of the educational partnership who need to engage the question of definition. We watched recently as a newly designated doctorate-granting university ("doctorate" as defined in the Carnegie classification system) celebrated its new quality status and launched media campaigns to carry the celebration. The difference between a comprehensive university and a doctorate-granting university, as defined in the Carnegie classification system, turns on the level and number of degrees granted and the number of fields in which these degrees are granted. These are descriptive criteria and not quality criteria—unless one subscribes to the idea that bigger is better and more is better.[17]

Stripped to the raw essential of expression, the question for state systems is whether academics and civic friends will persist in viewing their system of higher education as one in which there is a quality pecking order—an order of prestige built on size, selectivity, and program diversity—or whether members of the partnership are willing to see quality potential in each campus mission, and, more importantly, whether they are willing to insist on quality in each mission.

The challenge of quality definition is certainly a premier challenge for American higher education. But is it a challenge unique to the collegiate sector of our national life? We think not. A book published by the American Management Association entitled *I Know It When I See It: A Modern Fable About Quality* constitutes a venture into the definition of quality in the corporate and profit sector. The book concludes with this observation: "Customers aren't interested in our specs. They're interested in the answer to one simple question: Did the product do what I expected it to do? If the answer is yes, then it's a quality product. If the answer is no, then it isn't. At that point our specs and tolerance aren't wrong, they're just irrelevant."[18]

Another authoritative writer on quality in the corporate sector is Philip Crosby. His definition of quality does involve a match to specifications. In *Quality without Tears,* Crosby offers this simple definition: "Quality is conformance to requirements."[19] Crosby goes on to suggest that establishing requirements is essentially an exercise in addressing the question of what we want the product or service to do. More important, conformance to requirements can be used to define more clearly the expectations for those involved in production or service delivery. We note here that conformance to requirements can embrace some specification on customer acceptance and satisfaction. We are attracted to the simplicity and the power of this definition and will be returning to it shortly as we offer our definition of collegiate quality.

In his 1988 book *Managing Quality,* David Garvin traces four stages in the evolution of quality management in the corporate sector: inspection, statistical quality control, quality assurance, and strategic quality assurance. He identifies multiple dimensions of quality as follows:

- Performance, the "fitness for use" test: Does the product do what the consumer wants?
- Features, the "bells and whistles" that supplement product basic functions and add competitive edge.
- Reliability: How long till first failure or need for service?
- Conformance, the extent to which the product meets established specifications and manufacturer standards.
- Durability, closely related to reliability but addresses the question of length of product life.
- Serviceability, speed, cost, ease of repair.
- Esthetics, a highly subjective but measurable aspect of product sense appeal.
- Perceived quality: Is a Honda built in America perceived as a Japanese car? Of higher quality?[20]

Garvin's book is helpful reading to anyone interested in quality definition, measurement, and improvement. He goes on to cite the differences in quality perspective and interests among design engineers, service technicians, and customers and then produces an informative analysis of the home air-conditioning industry between the best and worst performers. At the end of his book, Garvin says about a major goal of his analysis: "An equally important goal has been to test the conventional wisdom about quality, for a vast mythology surrounds the subject. It takes many forms: the belief that quality is undefinable and impossible to discuss objectively; that high quality is always associated with high costs; that automation is the key to Japan's superior quality; and that vice presidents of quality are required for superior results. None of these assumptions was supported by the results."[21] Sound familiar? There are good and parallel lessons for collegiate leadership in this book, which brings us to a series of questions to which we will turn in a moment: questions of evidence and performance standard, questions of analysis and judgment, and questions of decision application and timing.

Let us restate our conviction that each college and university has the potential for excellence within its own mission. With organizations and with individuals, however, the question of whether excellence is realized depends greatly on accessories of emotion—on investments of daring and discipline, caring, and courage. These emotional elements that contribute to quality are also not in limited supply, but neither is their potential always realized in individuals or organizations. For concrete illustration of this point, see Peters and Austin's 1985 book *A Passion for Excellence.*[22] What were those lines from Emerson's essay "Man the Reformer"?: "Every great and commanding moment is the triumph of some enthusiasm. The victories of the Arabs who, after Mahomet, established a larger empire than that of Rome, is an example. They were miserably equipped, miserably fed. They conquered Asia, and Africa, and Spain on a bag of barley."[23] An illuminating commentary on resources and results!

In the above note, we used the word "excellence," so it will probably be helpful to say that we view the words "excellence" and "quality" as conveying the same meaning and that the varying definitions reveal the different ways in which these two concepts can be seen.

Certainly one of the more informing and stimulative works on excellence is John Gardner's book by that title.[24] Gardner suggests that excellence is to be found in our striving—whether individual or organization—to reach the far edge of our circle of promise and potential:

> Our society cannot achieve greatness unless individuals at many levels of ability accept the need for high standards of performance and strive to achieve those standards within the limits set for them ... And we are not going to get that kind of striving, that kind of alert and proud attention to performance, unless we can instruct the whole society in a conception of excellence which says that whoever I am or whatever I am doing, provided that I am engaged in a socially acceptable activity, some kind of excellence is within my reach.[25]

In a later chapter, we will comment on Scandinavian Airlines President Jan Carlzon's book *Moments of Truth* in which he suggested that the quality and reputation of an organization was conveyed and nurtured in those thousand "moments of truth" that exist every day between the customers/clients of an organization and those employees who give voice and meaning to a company or a college.[26]

Not content, however, to center attention totally on this interaction, Carlzon also talks about measuring results: "We thought we were doing very well on precision; our cargo people reported that only a small percentage of shipments did not arrive at their destination on time. But we decided to try a test anyway. We sent 100 packages to various addresses throughout Europe. The results were devastating. The small parcels were supposed to arrive the next day; however, the average was four days later ... Clearly we needed to start measuring our success in terms of our promises."[27] Is there a message in that finding for American higher education? We believe there is, and it will also play a part in our definition. It is a central theme of this book that higher education quality requires a culture of evidence and a culture of caring. Quality is to be found in the numbers and in the spirit.

Let us come back to higher education and see what we can find on the definition of quality. Among the more thoughtful and helpful of those who have written on the issue of quality and excellence is Alexander Astin. We count

Achieving Educational Excellence[28] and *Assessment for Excellence*[29] as books that can be read with profit by educator and layperson. Astin contends that there are four conventional views of excellence in collegiate quality: excellence as reputation, excellence as resources, excellence as outcomes, and excellence as content. After examining the limitations of each of these views, Astin offers a "talent development" definition of excellence: "The most excellent institutions are, in this view, those that have the greatest impact—add the most value, as economists would say—on the student's knowledge and personal development and on the faculty members' scholarly and pedagogical ability and productivity."[30] There is an appealing simplicity to Astin's definition. It focuses on results. It asks the question, "What difference did we make in student knowledge, skill, and attitude?" His thought and his books merit review by collegiate educators, by board members, and by other civic friends, such as legislators.

A different definition is offered by Lewis Mayhew, Patrick Ford, and Dean Hubbard in *The Quest for Quality.* Mayhew and his colleagues argue for a more limited view on higher education mission, suggesting that some of the affective hopes that are assumed in Astin's definition are unlikely to be realized in colleges. They state that "colleges and universities, for example, can have little effect on the fundamental character traits such as honesty, optimism, or sense of humor."[31] They anticipate a more limited definition of quality with this preamble: "The emergence of an information-based, technologically-driven economy requires citizens who are facile with the higher order cognitive skills of analysis, synthesis, and evaluation and who can express themselves clearly in verbal, written, or numerical form."[32] Their definition of quality, then, is as follows: "Quality undergraduate education consists of preparing learners through the use of words, numbers, and abstract concepts to understand, cope with, and positively influence the environment in which they find themselves."[33]

This vision of college purpose and quality definition may argue with the view that teaching is a moral enterprise. We are inclined to the perspective expressed by John Goodlad, Roger Soder, and Kenneth Sirotnik in *The Moral Dimensions of Teaching.*[34] In their view, teaching at every level is a normative venture. We agree. Our policies and practices in collegiate education convey moral posture and value; in the classroom and out, our behavior as faculty and administrators conveys a moral model.

Not even in science, known for its commitment to objectivity, are we without value principles that support inquiry, as Jacob Bronowski makes clear in *Science and Human Values.*[35] Thus, in the content of what we teach, we are anchored to a philosophy of values. Later in this book, in chapter 7 on college outcomes, we will report how one state publicly committed its system of higher education to a set of values.

This preliminary exchange on the definition of quality anticipates a principle that we hope to celebrate throughout this book: The definition and meaning of quality is a venture in decision and discovery.

THE EVIDENCE OF QUALITY

A 1990 issue of *World Magazine* featured a lead article by George Fisher entitled "Measuring the Unmeasurable," the story of a major quality assurance effort at the Motorola Corporation. The article lead-in begins with the note that "everyone knows that quality is impossible to define. But that didn't stop Motorola."[36] Though the program for Motorola is a multistep process, it also involves some relatively simple approaches to evidence and measurement. The article reports that chairman Bob Galvin encouraged the posing of these two questions at all levels of the organization and with its customers: "What do you like about Motorola and what don't you like?"[37] At the collegiate level, we are inclined to expend considerable energy in debating the merits of measurement. If we just took the time to ask these same simple questions of our students and our civic supporters, we might be surprised how much we would learn.

Several questions associate with the measurement of quality. What evidence or indicators will we accept as appropriate operational expressions of quality? What evidence can we assemble, should we assemble, to reflect the performance and quality of institutions as diverse in their mission, their history, and their environment as Dallas County Community College, the Ohio State University, the University of Montevallo, and Rhodes College? Surely the evidence of quality at these colleges and universities will require more than one data point.

Once the evidences and indicators of performance are identified, the question of performance standard arises. What level of performance will be accepted or required as demonstrating an appropriate level of quality? Will we employ in these judgments a standard that is criterion based or norm based? Are we going to gauge program or personnel performance against a standard of predetermined acceptability or against the performance of other programs and personnel? Actually, we have three possible choices for performance standards:

- A criterion standard, in which performance is compared to a predetermined criterion level
- A comparative normative standard, in which performance is judged against the performance of another program or person (or group of persons)
- A connoisseurship standard, in which performance is judged against the opinions and values of a panel of judges

One final question turns on who will make these judgments. For example, is it reasonable to assume that every college and university would like its students to communicate effectively in written form? One evidence for that quality goal could be an essay written by all students at some appropriate point in their college careers—at the end of the freshman year, the end of the sophomore year, or as a major paper in the senior year. Assume that an institution fashions a consensus on the form of such evidence. Who will evaluate or grade the essay: professors in the English department, professors from all departments, or civic friends and/or alumni? And what will constitute an acceptable performance level?

An array of quality indicators might be offered as evidence of collegiate quality: peer reviews as expressed in accreditation and program reviews, student and alumni opinion and satisfaction indices, reputation and ranking studies, student performance profiles on entrance and exit tests, professional licensure results, faculty research and publication productivity. One difficulty is that the variety of possible indicators constitutes an embarrassment of riches from which it is difficult to choose. In chapter 12, however, we will suggest a profile of quality indicators that we think should constitute a fundamental information base on quality.

Is there something to commend a medical analogy here? When we go to our physician, he or she does not plug us up to a healthometer that in a single reading or data point tells about the condition of our health. No. There are many data points to be obtained—blood pressure, blood chemistry, x-rays, EKG, PET SCAN, and so on—from which the physician will make an informed assessment and prescription.

A second problem of quality assurance is that any one of these indicators—whether reputational and satisfaction studies or value-added and outcomes studies—can be and will be criticized for some philosophical or technical imperfection. Indeed, in the chapters to follow, one of our goals is to probe the strengths and the limitations of the major expressions of quality assurance now used by American higher education.

Because there are so many evidences of collegiate quality and because any single evidence may be criticized, there is often a proclivity to debate without action. We are immobilized by argument. We are like a confused centipede, not knowing which foot to put down next. We can, however, employ a useful principle—the principle of multiple evidences—to combat the tendency to do nothing. What might be the mood of an accounting department chairman and his or her dean as they contemplate the following performance profile?

- Of the last thirty accounting graduates, all but two passed all parts of the Certified Public Accountant (CPA) exam on first sitting. This rate is six times the state pass rate and twice the national pass rate.
- A recent alumni follow-up survey revealed that the graduates in this department accorded the department one of the highest satisfaction ratings of department graduates in the university and was the highest in the College of Business.
- The dean's office has received a dozen letters of commendation from firms hiring the graduates and only one letter offering a constructive criticism.
- The department's upper-division students have the highest scores in the university on the Educational Testing Service Academic Profile Test of general education skills, when compared to students from other departments and colleges, and all sophomore majors successfully passed the written essay part of the Academic Profile Test.

- A recent visitation team assembled by the state coordinating board reviewed the academic program in accounting and ranked the program as "outstanding" on a scale of four descriptors: low quality and should be terminated, marginal quality and should be improved, adequate quality, and outstanding quality.

Cogent arguments can be advanced about the limited power for any one of these performance/quality indicators taken in isolation. What is less debatable, however, is that these indicators offer a useful and happy performance profile for this program and its students. Refusing to judge the quality of student, program, or campus performance on the basis of a single indicator or evidence is, we believe, an important principle of quality assurance.

The measurement of quality, then, embraces a good bit of complication—selecting evidences and indicators of performance, making provision for both acquisition and analysis of data, setting an appropriate standard of performance, and identifying who will make the judgments of performance and how. Scientists will want an experiment and philosophers a logical argument. Lawyers will want an adversarial hearing, sociologists an opinion poll, and artists a panel of judges. Engineers will want a systems study and economists a cost-benefit or regression analysis. Appraising quality is an exercise in evaluation, an adventure in the pursuit of truth.

THE DECISION APPLICATION OF QUALITY INFORMATION

Quality: What is it and how do we measure it? Why do we need information on quality? One could well argue that this discussion of decision utility should have been placed first in our discussion. From the perspective of campus partners involved in quality assurance, there should be little argument that the primary motive for any effort is that of improvement—of enhancing the instructional and learning climate of educational policy and practice.

A Faculty-Friendly Approach: We want to emphasize early in our presentation the importance of designing a quality assurance system and adopting a quality assurance philosophy that will have root in the heart of an institution—its classrooms and studios, its laboratories and faculty offices—and that will engage the active allegiance of its faculty and staff. A strategic approach is one characterized by long-term perspectives on the nature of quality; one built on the willing and active involvement of every member of the academic community; and one where the impact on instruction, research, and service is clear. We try to emphasize this perspective in each chapter, but we give the strategic perspective special treatment in chapter 12.

As for the accountability motive, we restate a point made earlier. Certainly, an aggressive quality assurance effort at the campus level enables a college or university to offer evidence of performance accountability to graduates, to boards, to legislatures, and to other civic friends. However, the first call on accountability belongs not to external groups but to our students.

A Decision and Discovery Mindset: A decision-based quality assurance program is going to affirm the idea that the journey in definition and measurement of quality should also be a journey in learning and discovery. Action and decision inform thought, and vice versa. Knowledge and technology interact. Knowledge enables us to invent technology, and the technology in turn opens up additional avenues of inquiry. Knowledge advances by design, accident, and serendipity. Elements of both reflection and action, of theory and raw empiricism, are involved in the search for truth. We believe "Acting on the possible while awaiting perfection" is a useful motto in developing programs of quality assurance. We need the creator and the critic. And this brings us to a final matter on the decision application of quality assurance information—the question of public disclosure.

Many years ago, the Ohio Board of Regents published a monograph, *Management Improvement Program,*[38] in which the regents posed these planning and performance questions for campuses in Ohio: What is the distinctive mission of the institution, the reason it exists? What are the things the institution wants to do or to see happen? What will count as evidence for or against the claim that the goal or objective has been reached? How will an individual outside the institution be able to determine whether the institution is attaining its goals or objectives? This last question poses an intriguing test and suggests another useful, albeit debatable, performance principle, the principle of public disclosure.

Public disclosure of performance results is not a suggestion received with uniform comfort by faculty members and administrators, even though we are already exposed to such public displays as reputational rankings, about which we will say more in chapter 3. Complaints about public disclosure are often prefaced with the recitation of real and imagined dangers:

- Educational goals are necessary for any assessment. However, by the time consensus is reached, goals may be trivial and unimportant.
- Not all variables contributing to quality are under institutional control, for example, funding levels, licensure standards, employment opportunities, and so on.
- Narrow definitions of quality and effectiveness will cause perversions in the educational process—the teaching-to-the-test syndrome.
- There is a tendency to believe that what can be measured is the only thing that is important.

Of course, colleges and nonprofit-sector organizations are not alone on this issue. American Airlines, for example, at one time featured itself as the "On-Time Machine," centering on on-time departures and arrivals, which is one of the performance variables monitored by the airline transportation industry. Delta Airlines preferred to use "Scheduled Flights Completed," a reliability performance indicator. Ford Motor Company once featured its corporate philosophy as one in which "Quality Is Job One." Chrysler touted its "Customer's Quality Bill of Rights." And General Motors sold cars on its safety record. Each company chose a different quality indicator for public disclosure and accent.

We like what editor Ted Marchese had to say in the May/June 1990 issue in a *Change* magazine article entitled "Costs and Quality." He cited three characteristics of an effective quality effort: "External peer review of the undergraduate function; impacts on student learning as the first criterion for judging quality; and a process that results in public reports, with students and funders as intended audiences."[39] Here is a call for public disclosure that we believe to be important and appropriate.

With this impressive array of interrogatories related to the issues of definition, measurement, and decision application of quality, it is easy to understand why there is mixed progress in quality assurance ventures among American colleges and universities. More impressive, however, are those faculties and institutions that take to heart that little motto we mentioned earlier: "Acting on the possible while awaiting perfection." These institutions and their forward-thinking faculties offer splendid models of action and discovery, and we will look at some of them in the chapters to follow.

VARIETIES OF EXCELLENCE

Earlier in this chapter we promised to present a definition of quality, and we need to deliver on that promise. The philosophic and technical complexities cited in our discussion up to this point make clear that anyone who dares to offer a definition of quality for higher education agrees to become an academic target of high visibility. However, we believe that the debate and tension that inevitably surround any discussion of quality are part of the discovery process that should be associated with any college or university as a learning community. Our proposal is that educational quality be defined as follows: *Quality is conformance to mission specification and goal achievement—within publicly accepted standards of accountability and integrity.*

The first advantage of this definition is that it respects and affirms diversity of institutional missions and their historical and environmental settings. Consider, for example, the sweep of mission as one looks at the role of the Juilliard School of Music, the U.S. Naval Academy, the Emery Aeronautical Institute, Bemidji State University, Austin College, and the University of California, Berkeley. Add to this list the University of Phoenix and Maricopa Community College. Each of these institutions makes a contribution to the development of human talent in our nation, and a single-factor quality exercise hardly suffices to describe or define that quality.

A second advantage is that the definition requires an operational expression of mission and goals. Here is the "promise and deliver" challenge for colleges and universities. From those grand statements of intent that can be found in catalogs, the definition asks that institutions outline more clearly and specifically those knowledges, skills, and values they expect to be associated with their credentials and degrees. "What difference did we make?" is a question encouraged by this definition. Also assumed is that the multiple stakeholders—faculty, governing board, state agencies, and so forth—are involved in the specification of mission and goals and in the assessment of institutional achievement and progress.

The third advantage of the definition is that it focuses debate on purpose—what the institution intends—so that arguments on quality—what it achieves—are not confounded over dissent that is actually related to purpose. Consensus building and partnership efforts are encouraged, we believe, by this definition. Asking questions of ends will drive the partners to ask questions of beginnings.

A fourth advantage of the definition is that it encourages public disclosure of institutional mission, goals, and performance results. The effect of public disclosure should be, as we previously noted, to open debate on purpose but to narrow debate on performance. Each of the questions associated with any quality assurance exercise—questions of decision, of evidence and indicators, of performance standards and modes of judgment, of who will judge and when—becomes a part of the public forum on quality. To that extent, then, the definition also promotes quality assurance as an exercise in learning and discovery.

A fifth advantage, at least in the authors' judgment, may elicit mixed reaction. The definition contains an ethical test. Contemporary media stories and book-length reports continue to highlight a brace of integrity issues in both corporate and collegiate sectors of our nation—ranging from deliberately diluted juice for babies, defense contract rip-offs, and check kiting by major accounting firms to acts of wrongdoing in the savings and loan, tobacco, asbestos, energy, and communications industries. In the collegiate sector, we find padded enrollment figures traced to unenforced retention policies and fraudulent enrollments and prostitution of integrity in a host of other educational and administrative areas. Even though any one of these acts may be counted an exception to the general reality of integrity, can we claim, in either a corporate or collegiate setting, to produce quality while we are busy stealing from ourselves, our government, and our customers and clients? We think not. We will say more on the ethical environment in higher education in chapter 10.

One of the more obvious disadvantages of this definition is that colleges and universities could become quite proficient in achieving shallow and unworthy purposes, in serving missions of dubious distinction. Our conviction, however, is that the public-disclosure feature would offer protection against this potential liability and likewise would offer some "consumer protection" to potential students.

In summary, this definition affirms the idea that there are varieties of excellence in both individual and institutional performance. Who can look at Harvard on the East Coast and Mills College on the West Coast, the University of Michigan in the North and the College of Charleston in the South and not realize the range of missions, each with the potential for quality.

A JOURNEY OF CARING AND DARING

Reflecting that peculiar yet constructive lack of neatness that characterizes so much of our national life, Americans have fashioned a complex pattern of practices in our search for quality. Among them are the following:

- Accreditation: the test of goal achievement and improvement
- Rankings and ratings: the test of reputation
- Outcomes: the test of results
- Licensure: the test of professional standards
- Program reviews: the test of peer review
- Follow-up studies: the test of client satisfaction
- Total quality management: the test of continuous improvement

In addition to these more conventional approaches to quality assurance, there are emerging models that bear the imprint of imagination and boldness. The partners involved in the definition, measurement, and application of quality are also becoming more numerous. To the historical and premier roles of faculties, we must add the interests of system and governing board staffs, coordinating agencies, regional compacts, legislative and executive officers. For public institutions, the state has become an active partner in both regulatory and incentive roles, and, of course, the federal government continues to be a player. In the chapters to follow, we will explore the strengths and limitations of each of these approaches to quality assurance and the roles of the partners in the process.

This book, therefore, is about the definition of quality, the measurement of quality, the decision application of quality information, and the renewing outcomes of quality assurance efforts. We intend it to be descriptive, furnishing an outline of contemporary practice and policy. We intend it to be evaluative, probing the advantages and the liabilities of each approach to quality assurance. We intend it to be explorative, searching for new approaches that might offer promise of improving our search and examining the issues of theory and practice that surround the search for quality.

In this first chapter, we have pointed to some of the convictions on which the book is constructed. The first of these is that our search for quality is a renewing and learning adventure in the best spirit of higher education. The second is that our willingness to risk, to try (to act on the possible while awaiting perfection) offers an opportunity to harness the power of reflection and action, which also respects an important principle of learning.

In an essay we cited earlier—"First Glimpses of a New World"—Robert Hutchins opened with this reflection: "I have been plagued all my life by two obsessions, the search for standards and the search for community."[40] The search for standards, for community, for quality—here is a magnificent obsession for those entrusted with the care of our colleges and universities. Failing to acquire and apply information on quality is to confirm that we lack both caring and daring. How can we possibly give meaningful leadership to program and service improvement without data on quality? How can we honor our responsibilities to the growth and nurture of our students without knowing what impact we have on their knowledge, their skills, and their values? How can timidity in the search for quality command the respect of our students and our publics? How can we teach our students the role of courage, of discipline, of risk, of perseverance in learning and living unless we are willing to model these same qualities in learning about our performance and ourselves?

However, the challenge for colleges and universities to be exemplars in the quest for quality is not a small challenge. One of the authors has characterized this challenge as follows:

> Conserving the past, criticizing the present, constructing the future—this is a complex mission that destines colleges and universities to remain always in the crucible of public conversation. It also guarantees a continuing tension between civic expectation and evaluation of higher education mission and performance. For organizations that are established to honor our social, economic, political, and scientific heritage even as they criticize that heritage, that hold hands with the past even as they reach for the future, quality assurance is a majestic and complex challenge.[41]

The dimensions of quality assurance in American higher education are complex in origin and structure. To outline those dimensions more clearly, this book will first examine the major quality assurance systems already in place. Probably the best-known quality assurance approach is that of accreditation, to which we now turn in chapter 2.

NOTES

1. Pirsig, R. (1974). *Zen and the Art of Motorcycle Maintenance.* New York: Morrow, 184.
2. National Institute of Education. (1984). *Involvement in Learning: Realizing the Potential of American Higher Education.* Washington, DC: National Institute of Education, 15.
3. Ibid., 55.
4. Newman, F. (1985). *Higher Education and the American Resurgence.* Princeton, NJ: Carnegie Foundation for the Advancement of Teaching, xiii.
5. Education Commission of the States. (1986). *Transforming the State Role in Undergraduate Education.* Denver, CO: Education Commission of the States, 17.
6. American Association of State Colleges and Universities. (1986). *To Secure the Blessings of Liberty: Report of the National Commission on the Role and Future of State Colleges and Universities.* Washington, DC: American Association of State Colleges and Universities, 35.
7. Council for Advancement and Support of Education.(1988). *Special Advisory for College and University Presidents.* Washington, DC: Council for Advancement and Support of Education, National Task Force on Higher Education and the Public Interest, 5.

8. Southern Regional Education Board. (1990). *1989–90 Annual Report.* Atlanta, GA: Southern Regional Education Board, 11.

9. Lenth, C. (1990). *State Priorities in Higher Education: 1990.* Denver, CO: Joint Project of the State Higher Education Executive Officers and the Education Commission of the States.

10. Pew Higher Education Research Program. (1991). "The Other Side of the Mountain." *Policy Perspectives,* February, 1–2.

11. Wallhaus, R. (1996). "Priorities, Quality and Productivity in Higher Education: the Illinois P*Q*P Model." Denver, CO: Education Commission of the States, September.

12. Southern Regional Education Board. (1998). *Educational Benchmarks, 1998.* Atlanta, GA: Southern Regional Education Board, 44.

13. Hutchins, R. (1966). "First Glimpses of a New World." In *What I Have Learned.* New York: Simon and Schuster.

14. Bogue, E. G. (1985). *The Enemies of Leadership.* Bloomington, IN: Phi Delta Kappa, 63.

15. Peters, T., and Waterman, R. (1982). *In Search of Excellence.* New York: Harper Collins.

16. Marchese, T. (1990). "Costs and Quality." *Change,* 22(3), 4.

17. Carnegie Foundation for the Advancement of Teaching. (2000). *A Classification of Institutions of Higher Education: 2000 Edition.* Princeton, NJ: Carnegie Foundation for the Advancement of Teaching.

18. Guaspari, J. (1985). *I Know It When I See It: A Modern Fable About Quality.* New York: AMACOM, 68.

19. Crosby, P. (1984). *Quality without Tears.* New York: McGraw Hill.

20. Garvin, D. (1988). *Managing Quality.* New York: Free Press, 49–68.

21. Ibid., 221.

22. Peters, T., and Austin, N. (1985). *A Passion for Excellence.* New York: Random House.

23. Emerson, R. W. (1929). "Compensation." In *The Complete Writings of Ralph Waldo Emerson.* New York: Wise, 75.

24. Gardner, J. (1984). *Excellence.* New York: W. W. Norton.

25. Ibid., 119–120.

26. Carlzon, J. (1987). *Moments of Truth.* Cambridge, MA: Ballinger.

27. Ibid., 107–108.

28. Astin, A. (1985). *Achieving Educational Excellence.* San Francisco: Jossey-Bass.

29. Astin, A. (1993). *Assessment for Excellence.* Phoenix, AZ: Oryx Press.

30. Astin, op. cit., 1985, 61.

31. Mayhew, L., Ford, P., and Hubbard, D. (1990). *The Quest for Quality: The Challenge for Undergraduate Education in the 1990s.* San Francisco: Jossey-Bass, 24.

32. Ibid., 22.

33. Ibid., 29.

34. Goodlad, J., Soder, R., and Sirotnik, K. (eds.). (1990). *The Moral Dimensions of Teaching.* San Francisco: Jossey-Bass.

35. Bronowski, J. (1956). *Science and Human Values.* New York: Harper Collins.

36. Fisher, G. (1990). "Measuring the Unmeasurable." *World,* 2, 4.

37. Ibid., 4.

38. Ohio Board of Regents. (1973). *Management Improvement Program.* Columbus: Ohio Board of Regents.

39. Marchese, op. cit., 4.

40. Hutchins, op. cit., 177.

41. Bogue, E. G. (1998). "Quality Assurance in Higher Education: The Evolution of Systems and Design Ideals." In Gaither, G. (ed.). Quality Assurance in Higher Education: An International Perspective [Special issue]. *New Directions for Institutional Research,* No. 99, Fall.

Chapter 2

Accreditation

The Test of Mission Achievement

To many, having a degree from an accredited college is tantamount to having a product with the collegiate "Good Housekeeping Seal of Approval." Indeed, accreditation is probably the most widely known and respected form of quality assurance among parents, government officials, and other civic friends of American higher education. It could even be said that in such a diverse educational system, this flexible process that promotes both internal and external evaluation may be the most effective way to judge the quality of colleges and universities and the extent to which they meet their stated missions. Paradoxically, it may be one of the most widely criticized.

This chapter will reveal just how extensively accreditation is used as an instrument of quality assurance. A brief history of accreditation is followed by a classification of accrediting agencies by type and function. Also included is a description of the improvement and accountability functions of accreditation and recent changes in philosophy, criteria and standards, and methodology—including the important shift in emphasis from process orientation to results or performance orientation. The chapter concludes with an analysis and evaluation of current problems and issues related to accreditation.

THE NATURE AND FUNCTION OF ACCREDITATION

Though our community college system is distinctly American in design, many aspects of the American senior college and university system were patterned after features of European higher education. A major difference in American and European systems, and other systems as well, is the degree of government control. Many European and other countries have ministries of education that exercise direct control over universities. In some countries, for example, professorial appointments are made through a national system. In the United States, the jurisdiction over universities is primarily invested in state governments, which grant operational charters to both private and public institutions. The complex pattern of these institutions and the complexity in campus governance patterns can be a source of confusion to some foreign educators. It probably would not be inaccurate to say that governance patterns can confuse Americans as well, including those who work within colleges and universities.

The federal government's role in American higher education has historically been somewhat distant and limited. Obvious historic exceptions have been the Land-Grant Act of 1862 and the GI Bill for financial support following World War II. The federal government has continued to focus on support—scholarship, research, facilities, and so on—but has only somewhat increased its focus on quality assurance, relying on accreditation and state agencies for these procedures. The federal part in litigation surrounding the Fourteenth Amendment is an example of activity that has had a sharp and direct impact on America higher education. Even so, higher education in the nation still remains comparatively free of quality assurance control by the federal government.

This historical laissez-faire policy resulted in a wide variation among colleges and universities with respect to mission, organization, curriculum, and quality. Accreditation was invented as a way to "bring a semblance of order out of an increasing variation among institutions . . . a phenomenon peculiar to the United States."[1] For example, the Association of Colleges and Preparatory Schools of the Southern States (ACPSSS), later changed to the Southern Association of Colleges and Schools, was formed in 1895. Though not originally created to serve as an accrediting agency as we know them today, the association initially established a threefold purpose:

1. To organize Southern schools and colleges for cooperation and mutual assistance.
2. To elevate the standard of scholarship and to effect uniformity of entrance requirements.
3. To develop preparatory schools and cut off this work from colleges.[2]

The South's educational system was hardly what should be considered a "system" at that time. "Impoverished and lacking in resources in so many areas of its life, the South's educational deficiencies seemed especially striking to those who believed that educational improvement was the key to all other economic, social, and cultural progress. While problems were myriad, the issue that focused the attention of the Association's founder was how to bring order to the relations between the region's colleges and secondary schools."[3] Due to the need for students, those who were considered somewhat more advanced were enticed by colleges to leave the secondary schools in order to enter college early. In most cases, the colleges were then structuring their curricula to include preparatory classes that were much more appropriate for the secondary level. In 1899, President F. C. Woodward of South Carolina College articulated that the subtraction of the secondary schools' best students weakened those schools and diminished the quality of education for those who remained. He also added that the addition of insufficiently prepared students was hardly a blessing for the colleges. In his opinion, a college's preparatory department functioned as "a sort of collegiate hospital for intellectual weaklings and scholastic delinquents."[4] Because of these activities and the lack of standards and organization, standards of discipline and scholarship were most often lowered at all levels.

The Southern Association's founders recognized this vicious cycle of disorganization and sought to form an association with the task of facilitating an atmosphere for the discussion and debate of issues such as these. What resulted from this association's early efforts was the beginning of standards for the admission of students into higher education in the South and, consequently, concentrating colleges and universities on their legitimate role of providing higher, not secondary, education. The association was later forced by necessity, and the lack of any other organization, to establish requirements for members, as well as standards by which members and applicants for membership would be evaluated.[5]

Accreditation in the United States "typically consists of certification by a regional or professional accreditation body that a program or institution has a generally recognized and appropriate set of goals and objectives that are being achieved."[6] Another definition is "a process by which an institution of postsecondary education evaluates its educational activities, in whole or in part, and seeks an independent judgment to confirm that it is substantially achieving its objectives and is generally equal in quality to comparable institutions of postsecondary education."[7] Ratcliff, Lubinescu, and Gaffney (2001) identify the purposes of the accreditation process as follows:

- Fostering excellence through the development of criteria and guidelines for assessing effectiveness
- Encouraging improvement through ongoing self-study and planning
- Ensuring external constituents that a program has clearly defined goals and appropriate objectives, maintains faculty and facilities to attain them, demonstrates it is accomplishing them, and has the prospect for continuing to do so
- Providing advice and counsel to new and established programs in the accrediting process
- Ensuring that programs receive sufficient support and are free from external influence that may impede their effectiveness and their freedom of inquiry.[8]

The word "accreditation" is often, and incorrectly, used interchangeably with "certification" and "licensure." Whereas accreditation is a status ascribed to an institution or one of its parts, certification usually applies to an individual or connotes a process that determines that he or she has fulfilled requirements set forth in a particular line of work and may practice in that field of work.

Licensure is also a term applicable to an individual rather than an institution. Often related and sometimes linked to both accreditation and certification, licensure is the process by which an individual is granted the authority to practice in a particular field. It runs the gamut from vehicle operation to brain surgery, from barbering to flying jumbo jets. Chapter 5 describes how in several professional programs the concepts of accreditation, certification, and licensure are interrelated, but each has a distinctive nature and purpose. In this chapter, however, we differentiate between them and focus on how and why accreditation serves as an indicator of quality.

Of the several beneficial purposes of accreditation, the two considered to be most fundamental are to ensure the quality and to assist in the improvement of the institution or program. Specifically, the accreditation of an institution or program says to the public in general and to institutional constituencies in particular that it has appropriate mission and purposes, resources necessary to achieve those purposes, and a history and record implying that it will continue to achieve its purposes.[9]

The needs of several constituencies are served when accreditation fulfills its purposes of quality assurance and institutional or program improvement. The general public is served by being assured that the institution or program has been evaluated internally and externally and conforms to general expectations in higher education. The public benefits when it can be assured that the accredited institution has ongoing and explicit activities deemed adequate to enable the institution to improve itself continuously and to make necessary modifications to accommodate changes in knowledge and practice in various fields of study. Accreditation decreases the need for intervention by regulatory agencies because accredited institutions are themselves required to provide for the maintenance of quality.

Accreditation benefits students in several ways. It assures them that an accredited institution has been found to be satisfactory and capable of meeting their needs, facilitates the transfer of credits among institutions, promotes admission to graduate degree programs, and serves as a prerequisite, in some cases, for entering professions.

Institutions also benefit from accreditation. There is first the stimulus for periodic self-evaluation and continuous improvement. Accreditation enables institutions to gain eligibility for themselves and their students in certain programs of government and private aid to higher education and helps institutions prevent parochialism by setting expectations that are national in scope. But the benefit most relevant to the theme of this chapter is the enhanced reputation of an accredited institution, primarily because of the generally high public regard for accreditation.

Admittedly, accreditation is based on the evaluation of institutional or program performance against a set of minimal standards. There may be, therefore, an understandable variance among accredited institutions—a perceived deficiency that we will treat at the end of this chapter. Here we only note that without accreditation the degree of variation would be much greater, and the public's ability to discern the differences between institutions of adequate quality and those of inadequate quality would be seriously damaged. Without accreditation, the vagaries of reputational studies (see chapter 3 on college rankings and ratings) also would be greatly exacerbated.

A value of accreditation not always fully appreciated by the general public can be found in the organized professions. Accreditation benefits professions in three major ways: (1) It provides for the participation of practitioners in setting the requirements for preparation to enter the profession; (2) it enables representatives of the respective professions to participate in evaluating the quality, appropriateness, and effectiveness of professional preparation programs and in weaving together theory and practice; and (3) it increases unity through collaborative activities of practitioners, representatives from the preparing arm, and students seeking entry into the profession. After all, quality assurance is important to the various professional bodies as well as to institutions, students, and the public. Professionals are often highly involved in recommending certain institutions to students and in communicating to students, parents, and the public their perceptions and judgments about institutional quality or the absence of it.

As noted earlier, accreditation is a voluntary, nongovernmental evaluation system devised, in part, to establish and maintain educational standards, a responsibility performed by central governmental authorities in many countries. Although accreditation remains a private and voluntary process, certain conditions and realities have moved it toward a quasi-governmental status. Actions by government funding organizations, foundations, employers, counselors, and professional associations have contributed much to this movement. For example, the Department of Education has established a system of approval for accrediting agencies. In order for institutions of higher education and their students to participate in Title IV Federal Financial Aid programs, accreditation must be attained from an approved accrediting agency. In this regard, an institution electing not to become accredited does so at its own peril.

OVERSIGHT OF ACCREDITATION

Following the merger of the National Commission on Accrediting and the Federation of Regional Accrediting Commissions of Higher Education, the Council on Postsecondary Accreditation (COPA) was established in 1975 as a nongovernmental national accrediting association to coordinate and certify accrediting activities in the United States. COPA attempted to "foster and facilitate the role of accrediting agencies in promoting and insuring the quality and diversity of American postsecondary education."[10] As indicated by Bloland (2001), COPA was "conceived and put together in the face of widely differing and often opposing expectations on the part of the major constituencies involved in accreditation: the institutional accrediting agencies, the specialized accrediting bodies, and the colleges and universities."[11]

The actual accreditation of institutions and programs was not performed by COPA. It recognized, coordinated, and periodically reviewed the work of its member accrediting bodies.[12] The association also sought to provide national leadership for accreditation, to improve the overall understanding of accreditation, to publish research on accreditation, and to monitor state and federal activities regarding accreditation.[13]

In the early 1990s, dissatisfaction with COPA appeared on the horizon. A March 27, 1991, article in the *Chronicle of Higher Education* reported on dissatisfaction with COPA's leadership, as perceived by heads of regional accrediting agencies. They claimed that COPA had furnished little leadership or direction on the major issues facing accrediting agencies and voiced the possibility of withdrawal from the COPA umbrella.[14] Bloland (2001) also states that the "regional accrediting commissions complained of paying too large a portion of the COPA operating funds without a commensurate voice in COPA decision making."[15] Internal dissension was not limited to the regional associations. Specialized accrediting agencies felt as if they were being ganged up on by the regional associations and members who were non-degree-granting trade schools felt the displeasure of many, knowing that some members felt them to be "marginal to the higher education enterprise."[16]

External factors also affected the operation of COPA. The latter quarter of the twentieth century saw various stakeholders, concerned with clear and sustained quality in higher education, begin to more vigorously demand increased evidences of the thoughtful use of monetary allocations given to institutions. Students and parents began to seek greater levels of comfort that completion of a college degree would provide assurance of a bright future. State and federal agencies began requiring increased evidences that colleges and universities were meeting their mission and utilizing increasingly limited state and federal funds appropriately. Ratings and rankings of colleges and universities appeared in magazines and newspapers such as *U.S. News and World Report, Time, Newsweek,* and *Money.* These interventions by state and federal agencies and the impacts of rankings and ratings were "direct competition with the accreditation system in defining and spurring changes in how higher education operated."[17]

So, as higher education continued to be criticized, so did accreditation. The 1992 Amendments to the Higher Education Act provided evidence that Congress felt the role of the accrediting agency should be expanded and more standardized. The requirements that accrediting agencies had to fulfill in order to be eligible for U.S. Department of Education recognition expanded. The amendments included the specification that accrediting agencies would evaluate an institution in twelve areas including curricular offerings, faculty credentials, and job placement rates. In addition, the creation of State Postsecondary Review Entities (SPREs) was included in the amendments. SPREs were to review institutions identified by the Department of Education as having triggered certain predetermined review criteria.[18] Though never funded, the legislative idea that there was a need for the SPREs was a blow for accreditation and its idea of self-regulation. COPA President Kenneth Perrin asserted in 1993 that "Accreditation is now seen as part of the problem, not as part of the solution."[19]

COPA was blamed for not having thwarted many of these issues directed toward accreditation. Dissatisfactions manifested, resulting in the February 1993 withdrawal from membership of the country's six regional accrediting associations (more about these associations in the next section). Faced with the loss of 40 percent of its income, the COPA board voted to dissolve the Council by the end of the year.[20]

Following the COPA dissolution, a twenty-eight-member group comprised of the regional accrediting agency directors, CEOs of the national higher education associations who were members of the President's Policy Assembly on Accreditation, several college and university presidents, and public representatives formed the National Policy Board on Higher Education. It was through this group's lengthy efforts, along with the subsequent work of a twenty-five-member group of college and university presidents and a consultant given the name of the President's Work Group, that a proposal to form the Council for Higher Education Accreditation (CHEA) was formalized.[21] The proposal was then submitted to the various accreditation constituencies for approval.

For the most part, the proposal received very positive endorsement. Of the 1,603 colleges and universities receiving ballots in a referendum, 54 percent returned their ballots and 94 percent of these approved the establishment of CHEA.[22] Four of the six regional accrediting associations endorsed the proposal. The New England Association of Schools and Colleges Commission on Institutions of Higher Education voted against the proposal and the Western Association of Schools and Colleges Commission for Senior Colleges and Universities took no position. Other agencies such as the American Council on Education and the Association of Colleges and Universities approved the proposal.[23] Thus, CHEA was established in 1996 as a private, nonprofit national organization to coordinate accreditation activities in the United States. Currently, the Council represents over 3,000 colleges and universities and 60 national, regional, and specialized accreditors.[24]

Governed by a seventeen-member board comprised of college and university presidents, institutional representatives, and public members, CHEA's purposes include those of advocacy, service, and recognition. As an advocate for accreditation, the Council is the primary national voice to the U.S. Congress and U.S. Department of Education, the general public, opinion leaders, students, families, and international audiences regarding accreditation issues. The Council strives to serve the higher education community and the public by providing a national forum to address issues in voluntary accreditation and educational quality issues. CHEA's recognition process provides scrutiny and certification as to the quality of regional, national, and specialized accrediting organization.[25]

As with most new organizations, and considering the not so recent dissatisfaction with COPA, just the mere establishment of CHEA did not give it the clout needed to effectively provide support and guidance for accreditation in the United States. Formidable tasks such as the establishment of a strong foundation of member support, effective lobbying contacts with the government, and mechanisms to disseminate crucial information on accreditation to a variety of constituencies were included in the organization's early goals. According to Bloland (2001), "As CHEA entered the early years of century 2000, the organization was still in its infancy. However, it was steadily constructing a vital, appropriate, and useful role in enhancing the contribution of accreditation to improving quality in higher education. Continuing its courses should bring the moral and cognitive legitimacy that would move CHEA into a successful maturity, while avoiding a slide into an early obsolescence."[26]

ACCREDITING BODIES

Accreditation of institutions as total entities largely occurs through six national institutional accrediting bodies and six regional accrediting associations. The national bodies are the Accrediting Association of Bible Colleges, the Accrediting Council for Independent Colleges and Schools, the Distance Education and Training Council, the Association of Theological Schools in the United States and Canada, the Accrediting Commission of Career Schools and Colleges of Technology, and the Association of Advanced Rabbinical and Talmudic Schools. The regional bodies include the Middle States Association of Colleges and Schools, the New England Association of Schools and Colleges, the North Central Association of Colleges and Schools, the Northwest Association of Schools and Colleges, the Southern Association of Colleges and Schools, and the Western Association of Schools and Colleges. Within the New England regional body is a specialized body that accredits vocational-technical programs—the New England Association of Schools and Colleges Accrediting Commission on Technical and Career Institutions.

The regional accrediting associations currently include over 3,000 accredited institutions. The six national accrediting bodies list 1,778 accredited institutions, 75 percent by just two of the bodies: the Accrediting Council for Independent Colleges and Schools and the Accrediting Commission of Career Schools and Colleges of Technology.

The forty-five CHEA-recognized specialized accrediting bodies reflect broad coverage and considerable heterogeneity. The specializations range from the accrediting of programs in medical education to programs in music education, from interior design to librarianship, and from journalism to social work. Most of the specialized bodies are national in scope, and a few have multiple program subdivisions (for example, the Commission on Accreditation of Allied Health Education Programs accredits programs in twenty-three subdivisions). As a general rule, the specialized accrediting bodies require institutional accreditation by the appropriate regional or national association as a precondition. Most of them are freestanding except for their affiliation with CHEA.

Difficulties encountered by some institutions in meeting the conditions of this array of accrediting groups are numerous. As an example, one of the authors visited a major health sciences center as part of the university's initial preparation for regional accreditation. That university averages one or more accreditation studies and visits per year. The investment of time, talent, and money to sustain this continuous pattern of visits is considerable. The chancellor of the university observed that folks in the university were about "self-studied out." Here is another issue of accreditation with which we will grapple at the conclusion of the chapter.

Even with the central coordination of CHEA, difficulties exist in the tangled web of accreditation requirements, expectations, and associational politics. Changes in higher education, such as the explosion of distance education and the focus on student outcomes, demand that accreditation processes integrate these new developments rapidly. In addition, CHEA must continue to wage an effective campaign against the increasing skepticism of the public and our state and federal governments toward self-regulation.

THE ACCREDITATION PROCESS

During the accreditation process, institutions are required to examine their goals, policies, procedures, and achievements; to consider the expert advice, suggestions, and recommendations of a visiting team; and to develop strategies for dealing with the visiting team's recommendations. Virtually every accrediting body requires institutions to maintain programs for continuous self-study and improvement in conjunction with the periodic review concept.

Although the various accrediting agencies have their own distinctive features and requirements, essentially the following procedures are employed in an institution's efforts to become accredited, either in whole or for separate programs.[27]

- The faculty, administrators, and staff of the institution or academic program conduct a self-study using the accrediting association's set of expectations about quality (standards, criteria) as their guide.
- A team of peers selected by the accrediting association reviews the evidence, visits the campus to interview faculty and staff, and writes a report of its assessment including a recommendation to the commission (a group of peer faculty and professionals) of the accrediting association.
- Guided by a set of expectations about quality and integrity, the accreditation organization reviews the evidence and recommendation, makes a judgment, and communicates the decision to the institution and other constituencies as appropriate.

A special comment on the site-visit team is appropriate. This evaluation by an on-site team of peer educators constitutes a key element of the accreditation process. In some accreditation processes in fields outside of education—the accreditation of hospitals, for example—full-time paid professional evaluators make these visits and judgments. In colleges and universities, the evaluation team is ordinarily composed of peer faculty and administrators from institutions or programs of similar mission. Thus, the standard of acceptable performance on accreditation criteria resides in the values and judgments of these visiting teams. We should also remember that the original selection and definition of accreditation criteria are done in representative assemblies of institutional delegates. Thus, the concept of "peer judgments" marks the entire accreditation process and constitutes the philosophic foundation for this American approach to quality assurance.

Figure 2.1 furnishes a diagram of the accreditation process. Step 8 in that diagram does not fully describe the different decisions that can be made. Though these decision actions may differ by association, they vary from a completely positive action—original accreditation or reaffirmation—to a "notice" or "probationary" status requiring that the institution or program effect some improvement on particular standards or criteria within a specified time period. The ultimate negative action, of course, would be denial of accreditation or suspension of accredited status for a program or institution. As the figure indicates, an appeals process allows an institution to challenge actions.

Accreditation is normally granted for a specific term, usually from five to ten years, but accrediting bodies can review member institutions or programs at any time for cause or when substantive change has been made, for example, proposed expansion to the graduate level.

It is apparent that the procedures and actions required to attain and maintain institutional and/or programmatic accreditation are exhaustive, time consuming, and expensive, both in actual dollars and in personnel time devoted to the process. The time and money are well spent, however, when educational effectiveness is enhanced by the process of accreditation and when institutional constituencies view accredited status as an assurance of quality.

As indicated, these policies, procedures, and mechanisms are essentially the same whether in the accrediting of the institution as a whole or in the accrediting of programs in areas of professional preparation. So important is accreditation in the medical field that, with only two or three exceptions, both certification and licensure require graduation from an accredited school.[28] Programs in medical education leading to the M.D. degree in the United States and Canada seek accreditation through the Liaison Committee on Medical Education (LCME). Jointly sponsored, staffed, and financed by the Council on Medical Education of the American Medical Association (AMA) and American Association of Medical Colleges (AAMC) and recognized by CHEA, this body has served as the national accrediting agency for programs in medical education since 1942.

Figure 2.1
Steps and Sequences in the Accreditation Process

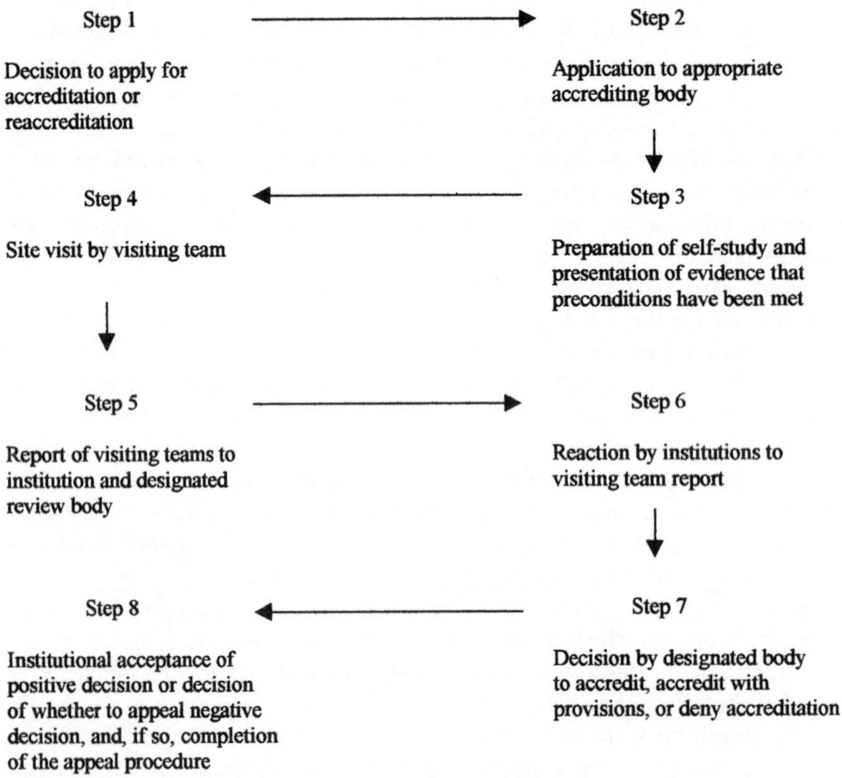

The accreditation process, consistent with the generic process previously outlined, begins with an institutional self-study followed by an on-site team visit. The team prepares a written report that describes the program of education and accounts for the school's compliance with each of the standards of accreditation. The LCME makes the accreditation decision, which is then transmitted to the institution. Provisions exist for institutions to appeal decisions not to accredit. The usual period of full accreditation is seven years.

Two accrediting bodies exist in the field of legal education: (1) the Council on the Section of Legal Education and Admission to the Bar of the American Bar Association (ABA) and (2) the Association of American Law Schools (AALS). Each of these bodies is recognized by CHEA. Although both have similar missions in regard to accreditation, the ABA Council grants accreditation to law schools in the United States, while the AALS recognizes as members programs leading to the professional degree in law (J.D. or LL.B.). The two bodies function separately and have no interdependent relationship; however, all AALS recognized programs are also accredited by the ABA Section of Legal Education and Admission to the Bar. Accreditation by the ABA Council is understandably a first order of business by law schools, because most states will not allow applicants to sit for the state bar examination unless they have graduated from a law school that has been approved by the ABA Council. The accreditation process for both agencies is very similar to the general process described in Figure 2.1.

The accreditation of nursing programs has traditionally been the responsibility of the National League of Nursing (NLN). Established in 1952 through the merger of several national nursing organizations with the National League of Nursing Education, the NLN performs the accreditation role through four review boards, one each for baccalaureate and master's degree programs, associate degree programs, diploma programs, and practical nursing programs. Each board of review is vested with the power to determine the accreditation status of programs being evaluated. The accreditation process consists of an initial staff consultation, an institutional self-study, a team site visit, a team report, staff evaluation of the team report and institution response, review of all materials by an evaluation review panel with specific program expertise, commission decision, and referral to an appeal panel if desired. The NLN and its four review boards are recognized by CHEA and are listed as a nationally recognized accrediting agency by the U.S. Department of Education.

The "new kid on the block" in nursing accreditation is the Commission on Collegiate Nursing Education (CCNE). Conceived in 1996 by the American Association of Colleges of Nursing (AACN), the CCNE began accrediting programs in 1998. While the NLN accredits programs at various levels, the CCNE only accredits programs at the baccalaureate and graduate levels.[29] The accreditation process is much the same as those described previously—a self-study is completed by the institution; an evaluation team of peers visits the program to assess compliance with criteria; the institution responds to the report generated by the evaluation team; the CCNE Board decides whether to grant, deny, reaffirm, or withdraw accreditation; and the Commission periodically reviews accredited programs between on-site evaluations in order to monitor continued compliance.[30] The CCNE is recognized by CHEA and listed as a nationally recognized accrediting agency by the U.S. Department of Education.

As with most specialized accrediting bodies, including the two previously described, nursing programs in institutions of higher learning, for example, must be accredited by the appropriate commission of a regional accrediting body. An additional eligibility requirement is approval without qualification by the state board of nursing.

Since 1954, authority for the national accreditation of programs in teacher education has resided in the National Council for Accreditation of Teacher Education (NCATE). Prior to 1952, a system of quasi-accreditation existed, handled by the American Association of Colleges for Teacher Education (ACCTE), currently a major stakeholder in NCATE. Founding members of NCATE were the National Education Association and the Council of Chief State School Officers.

NCATE is a member of CHEA and is recognized by the U.S. Department of Education as a national accrediting agency. The Council has established an intricate system of nine preconditions that must be met before the accreditation process proceeds further. For example, one of these preconditions requires the unit to present satisfactory evidence that it employs systematic evaluation of its programs (including the evaluation of its assessment systems and of its candidates' performance). Once an institution has met the nine preconditions, the accreditation process is very similar to the ones described in law, medicine, and nursing. A self-study must be completed and a site visit follows. The report of the visiting team and a follow-up report from the institution are submitted to an audit committee of the Unit Accreditation Board, one of NCATE's four governance boards. The audit committee examines the team report and makes a recommendation to the Unit Accreditation Board, which, acting as a whole, considers and acts upon this recommendation.[31]

Despite improvements through the years, accreditation of teacher education at the national level is restricted by factors and circumstances beyond the control of the profession or the accrediting body. A serious restricting factor is the absence of a linkage between accreditation and certification/licensure. This means that for the most part, state certification is not dependent upon an applicant's having completed an NCATE-accredited teacher education program. The absence of this linkage in some cases serves as a disincentive for some teacher education programs to seek NCATE-accredited status.

While accrediting processes appear to be largely uniform for both institutional and programmatic accrediting agencies, there are proposals to deviate from tradition. For example, the Commission on Colleges of the Southern Association of Colleges and Schools has undergone an intensive study of both its *Accreditation Criteria* and accreditation procedures during the past two years. The Commission presented to its membership a proposal for change at its 2001 Annual Meeting. Having been approved by the membership by a commanding margin, the Commission's current accrediting process will be drastically changed, allowing for a much shorter self-study process and more emphasis placed on a plan for institutional improvement. Another example comes from the North Central Association of Colleges and Schools. In 2000, this association implemented a voluntary alternative process to its traditional accreditation process called the Academic Quality Improvement Project. The process for this project is not to measure an institution against a set of minimum standards that are applicable to all institutions, but to help the institution achieve its own unique mission and goals. Every three to five years, institutions participating establish their own goals and the means for measuring their progress. Representatives from peer institutions assist in the process.[32]

Accreditation is by no means a perfect process. But it enables institutions of higher learning to demonstrate to their important constituencies their commitment to quality—for it is the best process we have available today. Moreover, holding accredited status is demonstrable evidence that their programs have met the test of peer review and that graduates of the accredited programs hold "safe-to-practice" status within the appropriate professional world.

THE EVOLUTION OF ACCREDITATION

As noted earlier, accreditation was initiated as a way to achieve reasonable standardization in higher education, thus serving a public need by helping to define institutional missions, to promote articulation among them, and to assist the general public in recognizing and appreciating quality. Voluntary accreditation guidelines and standards are seen as preferable to control and regulation by the central government. The need for some kind of accreditation arose first with problems associated with institutional definition, vast differences in institutional quality with no widely accepted basis for ascertaining quality, and difficulties encountered by students and institutions in the transfer of credit.

An early precursor, sometimes erroneously mentioned as the first accreditation, was legislation enacted in 1787 in New York that required the state board "to visit every college in the state once a year."[33] Although this was an important development and a search for standards, the activity was not accreditation in the best sense of the concept.

Action by the AMA in 1904 also served as a precursor to accreditation, but the very first accrediting action was by the American Osteopathic Association, which began reviewing and approving schools in 1901. In 1904, the AMA established a council on medical education that developed, a year later, a rating system for medical schools. Working rapidly, the council initiated "inspections" in 1906 and published its first list of classifications in 1907. Collaboration with the Carnegie Foundation in a study of medical education produced the famous Flexner Report in 1910. This report paved the way for the designation of the medical school at Johns Hopkins University as a prototype and also set the stage for closing many "inferior schools." Although not "accreditation" as it later came to be known, these actions had a lasting impact on medical education and established a pattern still revered today by other professions, although few have replicated it fully.[34]

Several aspects of Flexner's work merit a quick digression. First and notably, Flexner was not a physician. Indeed, he argued that those external to a field might, with the application of common sense and unfettered experience, be as effectively equipped to judge a field as those experts within: "The expert has his place, to be sure; but if I were asked to suggest the most promising way to study legal education, I would seek a layman, not a professor of law; or for the sound way to investigate teacher training, the last person I should think of employing would be a professor of education."[35] In addition, Flexner was not always inclined to courteous criticisms, euphemistic evaluations, and ambiguous advice in his reviews. His evaluation of one school concluded this: "The school is a disgrace to the state whose laws permit its existence."[36] We will consider the matter of expertise external to a field again at the conclusion of this chapter.

The nation's first true accreditation of an institution of higher learning occurred in about 1910, by the North Central Association of Colleges and Secondary Schools, using standards developed in 1909. The association published its first list of accredited institutions in 1913.[37]

Citing ten significant events during the period of 1862 (and the passage of the Land-Grant Act) to 1914 (and the passage of the Smith-Lever Act and the founding of the Association of American Colleges), Young, Chambers, Kells, and Associates (1983) concluded that "accreditation was therefore born during a time of ferment and hope," sharing "the characteristics of the society that spawned it; idealistic, self-motivated, reform-minded, desiring improvement, believing in individual initiative and voluntary collective action, and distrustful of government (though seeing government as embodying the ultimate power to right wrongs)."[38]

Overcoming problems associated with definition, accreditation quickly moved to concerns and goals of a higher order—establishing, for example, membership requirements for the North Central Association and the Association of American Medical Colleges. A major development occurred in 1929 when the Higher Education Commission of the North Central Association appointed a committee on revision of standards. The work of this committee involved fifty-seven institutions and resulted in a seven-volume report. The report set forth a policy that was to have a lasting impact on regional and professional accreditation, namely, that institutions would be evaluated according to their own purposes, not by arbitrary standards. This action led to the self-study process, which remains embedded in virtually all accrediting efforts.[39]

To describe fully the development and evolution of accreditation since its outset would transcend the purpose of this chapter. Rather, a brief statement of major changes in accreditation during its ninety-year history will be given. Again, the exhaustive work by Kenneth E. Young and his associates (1983) is a major source document.

1. The universe of accreditation has changed as the concept of higher education has changed. It began as one of the degree-granting colleges and universities offering traditional academic programs and serving mainly full-time students immediately upon their graduation from high schools. Now it is more accurately described as postsecondary education comprising an ever-expanding variety of institutions, programs, and delivery systems involving a growing diversity of students of all ages with widely differing educational objectives.

2. The participants in accreditation have increased dramatically since World War II, when they consisted primarily of six regional associations and a few major professional associ-

ations. Today CHEA recognizes six national accrediting bodies, six regional bodies, and forty-five specialized bodies. Over 3,000 institutions hold accredited status in one or more of these bodies and many programs within these institutions have approved status by one or more of the specialized bodies.

3. During the past seventy-five years, both the philosophy and practice have changed: from a quantitative approach to one relying more on qualitative factors; from regarding institutions as if they were all alike to recognizing and encouraging institutional individuality; from heavy dependency on external review to an emphasis on self-evaluation and self-regulation; and from a focus of judging (accepting or rejecting) to a goal of encouraging and assisting institutions to continuously improve their educational quality.

4. Accreditation has changed through the years as society's expectations have changed. In retrospect, the initial expectations of accreditation seem rather mundane, for example, developing a consensus on the meaning of a high school, a college, or a professional school. Today, society places rather high expectations on accrediting bodies; in fact, accreditation helps to determine eligibility for certain funds, to define licensure requirements in several professions and occupations, and to help make decisions about the employment of graduates and the awarding of funds to institutions.

5. Accreditation began with a mixture of support and suspicion, but with little or no governmental involvement. As time has passed, and increased demands for accountability from colleges and universities have occurred, accreditation has also been highly scrutinized and even questions raised as to the appropriateness of accreditation to determine institutional quality. Thus, governmental involvement has increased.

As in the beginning, however, the general public still has less than a full understanding of the importance and value of accreditation. The average citizen probably has an abiding faith that an "accredited institution" is more likely to be a quality institution than if it were not accredited, but he or she may understand few of the complexities and nuances involved in an institution's becoming and remaining accredited.

Stimulated by increased demands for institutional accountability, a seemingly welcome change in accreditation has been the shift in focus from quantitative standards to qualitative standards—a shift from inputs to outputs—and the determination of institution-specific assessment processes to assist in meeting these standards. Concerted efforts have been made in recent years, particularly in the regional accrediting associations, to require institutions to set forth goals and objectives in a clear and measurable fashion, to describe procedures to be employed in seeking those goals and objectives, to identify indicators to be used in determining the degrees of attainment, and then to present evidence that the goals were, in fact, attained. This transition suggests that institutional and programmatic conversations on quality should be linked to a simple yet powerful question: How do we know we have quality? Where is the evidence?

The Southern Association of Colleges and Schools (SACS) initiated this movement in 1984 when it adopted a new criterion on institutional effectiveness as part of its effort to link outcomes assessment to the process of accreditation. Noting that institutional quality is dependent not only on an institution's educational processes and resources but also on its successful use to achieve established goals, SACS believes that all "institutions have an obligation to all constituents to evaluate effectiveness and to use the results in a goal-based, continuous planning and evaluation process.[40]

The action by SACS was followed rather quickly by the Western Association of Schools and Colleges, which revised several standards to accommodate the new emphasis on assessment and provided member institutions with implementing guidelines.[41] The Commission on Institutions of Higher Education (North Central Association of Colleges and Schools) approved a statement of assessment and student academic achievement that made explicit the position that student achievement is a critical component in assessing overall institutional effectiveness.[42] The Commission on Institutions of Higher Education of the New England Association of Colleges and Schools revised its standard on evaluation and planning to explicitly require the institution to systematically collect and use data necessary to support its planning efforts and to enhance institutional effectiveness.

Increased focus in these areas is not limited to regional accrediting bodies. Many specialized and national accrediting agencies have implemented evaluative criteria relating to planning and assessment as well. The Accreditation Board for Engineering and Technology's (ABET) *2000–2001 Criteria for Accrediting Engineering Programs* includes the requirement that "Each program must have an assessment process with documented results. Evidence must be given that the results are applied to the further development and improvement of the program."[43] The Accrediting Council for Independent Colleges and Schools requires each of its accredited institutions to construct an Institutional Effectiveness Plan that is a working document to include institutional assessment, evaluation, and planning steps to be taken by the institution to ensure optimum effectiveness of all educational programs and services. Each institution is subsequently required to present the assessment data collected, information relating to those involved in its evaluation, and evidence that the data were utilized to make decisions relating to improvement of educational effectiveness—close the loop, so to speak.

Clearly, accrediting bodies have responded to the challenge of requiring better demonstration of institutional effectiveness, including student achievement. And the process has continued. As mentioned earlier, the Southern Association of Colleges and Schools is in the midst of a major accreditation criteria revision project. The goal of the association's highly participative endeavor has been to maintain an emphasis on quality through evidence of compliance with established standards, but to (1) increase efficiency by decreasing the number of criteria, decrease the time that is currently required for the comprehensive self-study, and increase reliance on institutional integrity, and (2) improve effectiveness in the focus of accrediting reviews by increasing the opportunities for the institutions to examine issues that directly relate to their quality enhancement with particular attention to student learning outcomes.[44]

The North Central Association of Colleges and Schools (2001) has also initiated a similar process, which they have entitled "Restructuring Expectations: Accreditation 2004." The association endeavors to "move the focus of accreditation from description and evaluation of resources to educational effectiveness, improvement, and commitment to renewal."[45]

We cannot end this discussion on the evolution of accreditation without briefly discussing a somewhat recent but continually expanding issue in higher education that has given rise to a healthy degree of attention from most accrediting agencies—distance education. There is considerable reason for this attention. In 1997–98, almost 44 percent of all institutions of higher education offered distance-based courses, a one-third increase since 1994–95. Total enrollments in postsecondary, credit-granting distance learning courses in 1997–98 were 1,363,670.[46]

Distance education challenges many of the core assumptions surrounding quality higher education. Can quality educational courses be delivered without face-to-face interaction with qualified instructors and peers? If we subtract the brick and mortar and requirements for student attendance, can desired student outcomes still be achieved? As stated by Judith Eaton (2001), president of CHEA, "Whether the emergence of distance learning spells the end of traditional campuses, as some maintain, or whether distance learning instead represents a particularly powerful addition to a growing array of delivery options for higher education, the fact remains that distance learning is already having a very real impact on higher education operation."[47] Examples of these impacts include the emergence of new providers of education, employment of alternative instructional techniques, revisitation and revision of faculty job descriptions, and inclusion of technologically qualified individuals as a key component of the educational delivery team.

Therefore, distance education brings new challenges to accreditation endeavors. The federal government has traditionally looked to accreditation to best ensure the presence of institutional administrative capability in the administration of federal financial aid funds for students attending institutions of higher education. But that is the key component—those in physical attendance. With the advent of distance education, this key component, if not disappearing, is at least changing definitions from physical presence to cyber presence. Can the federal government become comfortable that self-regulation will continue to be adequate in this changing environment—comfortable enough that additional federal controls will not be implemented?

In the face of this changing environment, accreditation must address and act on certain key questions. How can quality in distance education courses/programs best be determined? Are the current accreditation criteria and standards utilized for courses and programs offered on campuses appropriate for distance education programs/courses? Eaton (2001) suggests that there are five responsibilities of the accrediting community that will assist institutions and programs offering distance education:

1. Identify the distinctive features of distance learning delivery, whether within traditional settings or supplied by one of the new providers.
2. Modify accreditation guidelines, policies, or standards to assure quality within the distinctive environment of distance delivery.
3. Pay additional attention to student achievement and learning outcomes in the context of distance learning.
4. Work with government to adjust current policy understanding about the use of federal funds and about quality assurance in a distance learning setting, while sustaining shared commitment to self-regulation through voluntary accreditation and preserving the autonomy of institutions.
5. Assume more responsibility for addressing public interest in the quality of higher education as distance learning opportunities and providers diversify and expand.[48]

Many accreditors and associated organizations have already attempted to address many of the tasks that Eaton suggests and have, in many cases, indicated required and/or suggested guidelines for distance education courses/programs. The six regional accrediting associations have agreed on certain guidelines for distance education courses/programs. "Any institution offering distance education is expected to meet requirements of its own regional accrediting body and be guided by the Western Interstate Commission for Higher Education (WICHE) Principles."[49] These guidelines address the areas of evaluation and assessment, curriculum and instruction, library and learning resources, student services, and facilities and finance. Institutions are expected to address each of these guidelines in their self-studies.

CHEA and the National Center for Higher Education Management Systems (NCHEMS) have designed and tested what they feel is an alternative to accreditation standards and review—a set of competency standards that places significant emphasis on student outcomes and delivery via distance education. The standards address student outcomes and attainment, responsiveness to students, and organizational alignment and support. The identified competencies include: "each degree or credential requires successful student completion of a defined assessment or set of assessments that covers the learning outcomes identified" and "criteria for evaluating student performance on assessment are clearly established, as stated in the institution's publications, and are generally understood by students and staff."[50]

In a study conducted by the Institute for Higher Education Policy, twenty-four benchmarks for distance education were formulated based on practical strategies being used by institutions considered to be leaders in this area. These benchmarks are clustered in areas addressing institutional support, course development, teaching/learning, course structure, student support, faculty support, and evaluation and assessment.[51]

The American Academy for Liberal Education (AALE) has received funding from the Fund for the Improvement of Postsecondary Education's (FIPSE) Learning Anytime Program to conduct a project entitled "Accreditation Based Upon Evidence of Student Performance and Educational Effectiveness in Distance Learning Degree Programs." This project, to be completed over a three-year period, seeks to answer the questions of what procedures should be used in the accreditation of distance education courses/programs and who should be responsible for this accreditation. The AALE has established "a distinguished national board of advisors composed of distance learning providers and national education and assessment experts to address the problem of accreditation."[52] Heads of the regional accrediting agencies are also being involved. At the end of the three-year project, AALE states that "we will have achieved a working consensus on what the accreditation standards are, suggested how and by whom they should be applied, and applied them successfully to a number of programs."[53]

Accreditation has certainly evolved substantially since its beginnings, but for the most part, at a somewhat cautious pace. Historically, changes in standards and philosophies have involved much participation from colleges and universities and other experts in higher education. As higher education continually evolves and diversifies, it can certainly be expected that accreditation evolution will keep pace.

PROBLEMS AND ISSUES IN ACCREDITATION

The preceding discussion refers to various problems and issues associated with the accreditation of colleges and universities. In this concluding section, a more direct presentation is made of several problems and issues that are of concern to leaders in both accrediting organizations and institutions seeking reaccreditation or initial accreditation.

Young, Chambers, Kells, and Associates[54] caution that accreditation will not survive "just because it is a good idea." Future success, they suggest, will depend on how well individual institutions and organizations address problems carried over from the past and how well current and future leaders in the field enable the accreditation process to accommodate rapid and significant changes in education and society. Confidence in our ability to accommodate the changes is enhanced by the progress made in the past forty years in responding to the seven issues identified in 1960 by Selden[55] as critical to the future of accreditation:

1. Development of criteria that place less emphasis on minimum standards and more on continued reevaluation, experimentation, and improvement,
2. Making accreditation more stimulating for institutions of high quality,
3. Accrediting increasing numbers of graduate schools without impairing independent research and individual scholarship,
4. Meeting the need for quality assurance in specialized and professional programs without increasing the number of professional accrediting bodies,
5. Simplifying the accreditation process without decreasing its effectiveness,
6. Providing more information about the degree of quality of individual institutions attaining accreditation and what it means to be accredited,
7. Meeting the government's increasing interest in accreditation without increasing its involvement and control.

Few will argue that each of these issues has been satisfied completely, but many will contend that on balance the progress has been substantial, in fact, rather remarkable, considering the fact that accreditation is a voluntary matter.

Mahew, Ford, and Hubbard[56] identify several issues associated with regional accrediting bodies.

1. Safeguarding the public interest, a stated goal of accreditation, cannot be met truly until a definition of comparability is established and accrediting associations clearly state that one institution barely meets minimum standards while another far surpasses them.
2. The claim that accreditation influences quality by withholding accredited status from institutions until they meet minimal standards has little basis because relatively few institutions have been so denied as long as their financial base appears reasonably sound.
3. Whereas the shift from rigid standards to judging institutions according to purposes they have set for themselves has many benefits, this shift sometimes leaves institutions totally adrift when they are cited with obvious deficiencies. This problem is exacerbated by the lack of success by accrediting bodies in forcing institutions to cease questionable activities, as, for example, in the case of many nontraditional off-campus programs.
4. The ability of accreditation, using historic instruments, to provide obvious benefit to strong, high-quality, prestigious institutions can be seriously questioned.

Despite the weaknesses and shortcomings cited by these authors, they conclude that "voluntary accreditation is still the best mechanism for certifying undergraduate quality."[57]

We believe that there are several additional accreditation concerns, problems, and issues, perhaps less sophisticated than those cited above, but no less troublesome to college and university leaders as they endeavor to achieve and maintain accreditation of their institutions and programs. These concerns are presented as criticisms or shortcomings of accreditation that, if unattended, might reduce both the attractiveness and the effectiveness of accreditation—and thus its value as a quality assurance.

One of these criticisms suggests that accreditation is little more than "professional back-scratching." University faculty frequently hold greater loyalty to their particular discipline or profession than to their respective employing institutions. Serving on a visiting team for an accreditation agency is sometimes used as an opportunity to help a group of disciplinary colleagues achieve higher salaries, lower teaching loads, and increased support services. "I'll help you now," the argument goes, "with the expectation that you or some other disciplinary colleague will return the favor when evaluating my institution." Some critics contend that this occurs all too often, even when discipline or professional kinship does not exist.

This criticism may be more imagined than real, and it is perhaps overdrawn. Members of visiting teams are not as free to sort out and act upon their own particular concerns (or ways to help a colleague) as this criticism implies. Rather, team members are expected to review information surrounding prescribed standards, to validate that information, and to clarify any points of conflict or inconsistency with what the self-study presented and what they see and hear during the site visit. Critics who subscribe to the fear of professional back-scratching often fail to appreciate both the nature and purpose of peer review in light of evidence produced and professional judgments rendered rather than opinions held. It is also suspicion and hearsay. In any event, there is little evidence to support the criticism as a significant shortcoming of accreditation.

A second criticism charges that, despite considerable progress in the direction of results versus process, the progress is too little and too slow, pointing to standards that continue to stress numbers, procedures, and processes at the neglect of results—student achievement, goal attainment, and so forth. Performance of graduates, for example, seems to be more clearly associated with the concepts of certification and licensure, dealt with in chapter 5, than with accreditation.

Closely aligned with this shortcoming of accreditation is the presumption or belief that the general public has neither a good understanding nor a deep appreciation of the importance of institutions' policies, processes, and practices. What the public wants, especially those that have a stake in a particular institution, is an answer to the ever-present and troublesome question: So what? What difference does accreditation mean to graduates, to their employers, to their communities?

It is probably true that the public has little appreciation of the advantages that accrue from accreditation, as noted earlier in this chapter. These advantages are more likely to be understood and appreciated by individuals and agencies whose work and responsibilities enable them to genuinely appreciate the importance of accreditation vis-à-vis self-renewal, the relationship between goal identification and goal attainment, and institutional and program assessment, to mention just three of the advantages. Efforts to answer the "so what" question by citing the several genuine advantages are not likely to convince skeptics, however, especially those who want one-liners.

A fourth frequently cited criticism of accreditation is that it is more a self-serving mechanism for professionals than a public benefit. Too much emphasis is placed on salaries, teaching loads, support services, and employee benefits, for example, and too little on indicators and determinants of quality. A part of the problem here is, again, the public's perception of quality and what makes it happen. Institutions must provide salaries, working conditions, and support services that enable them to attract and retain competent faculty. Not to do so would have deleterious effects on the quality of teaching and learning and on research and service. Perhaps more effort should be made to help the public understand how student achievement is so closely intertwined with faculty competence, favorable working conditions, and adequate support services.

Another dimension of this criticism involves an accreditation strength that can be a liability. Throughout this chapter we have emphasized the constructive contribution of the peer review process. We may want to remember, however, the posture taken by Flexner concerning the merit of reviewers outside the field. It might be argued, as a point of criticism, that accreditation undertaken only by those who are practitioners within the field promotes a limited and predetermined perspective on what might constitute quality performance of a program or an institution. Those outside a field may not have been socialized to the "conventional wisdom" of an academic specialty or to higher education in general. Thus, they may be more inclined to ask those naive and obnoxious questions that could produce more effective evaluations. Having celebrated the merit of the peer review process, we run the risk of being accused of contradicting ourselves in acknowledging some validity to this criticism. This is not an either-or issue, however. We believe that inclusion of external members on both professional and regional accreditation teams has some merit. The inclusion of someone from a discipline outside the one being studied, in the case of professional accreditation, and the inclusion of a layperson outside education, in the case of regional accreditation, we believe is a practice worthy of salute—and a practice whose potential outcomes outweigh the risks.

This conviction does not come without an experience base that would suggest a contrary posture. Years ago, one of the authors received a regional accreditation team in which one of the visiting committee members was a lay member (owner and operator of a chain of retail business outlets). After only one day on campus, this lay member offered a number of snap judgments on several university personnel—including multiple recommendation on personnel termination. His confidence was undeterred by his ignorance of the complex history of both the institution and the affected staff, and his arrogance was a source of severe discomfort to the remainder of the visiting committee members. In the life of education institutions, as in the life of many other organizational forms, the theory of practice must be interpreted in the attitudes and behavior of individuals operating on the theory. The choice of the individual is as important as the theory on which his or her behavior may ride. On a point of theory, what we are saying is that the inclusion of external accreditation team members may constitute a useful counterpoint to this criticism.

A fifth criticism, referred to earlier in this chapter, is the rapidly escalating cost of accreditation, both direct and indirect. Fees paid to accrediting bodies and the costs of visiting teams are rising rapidly. Preparing for the visiting team, conducting the self-study, and maintaining liaison with the accrediting agency require substantial cash expenditures as well as many hidden costs, such as faculty and administrative time and energy. These problems are exacerbated by the proliferation of accrediting bodies, particularly in the specialized domain. They are troublesome to all institutions, but acutely so to those with weak or marginal financial resources, those who are reluctant to voice this concern for fear that it would constitute prima facie evidence that the institution has insufficient funds. Those in institutions with better resources are increasingly tempted to risk the penalty of not seeking accreditation—especially in those programs where the penalty for nonaccreditation would not be great.

This criticism minimizes, if not ignores, the fact that many of the activities associated with the efforts to gain and maintain accreditation are essential to institutional effectiveness, even if accreditation were not involved. The recent emphasis on assessment, for example, should be an ongoing part of institutional life. The fact that it is required by accreditation agencies is not a good reason to label money and energy spent in these efforts as accreditation costs. In fact, few of the costs of accreditation are unique to accreditation but, rather, are expenditures good institutions make in the course of maintaining high quality.

A sixth criticism pertains again to public perception and understanding—and to the troublesome side effects of basing accreditation on the concept of minimal standards. It is not uncommon for institutions held in low prestige, both by their constituencies and fellow institutions, to achieve accreditation—sometimes national, regional, and specialized altogether. Often the attainment of accreditation leaves constituents and colleagues convinced that the achievement is indicative of weak standards of the accrediting body. Indeed, in some specialized fields of accreditation in which graduation from an accredited school is not a precondition for certification and/or licensure, high-prestige institutions often deliberately avoid accreditation. Their rationale is that more harm than good results from being accredited by an agency that will accredit institutions widely believed to be inferior.

Greenberg (2000) contends that accreditation should be used as a means for America's colleges to rank themselves. He states that "Perhaps instead of criticizing *U.S. News,* we should consider following its example. Instead of treating accreditation as an insider game, we should make public use of our official peer-review system—not just in response to the *U.S. News* challenge, but also to meet higher-education's responsibility for public accountability."[58] However, accreditation was never intended to bring all institutions into a single, monolithic band of like institutions, all of pristine quality. Rather, it was intended to set standards beneath which institutions could not fall without signaling to their constituencies and publics that serious questions exist about the appropriateness of their mission, the extent to which it is being achieved, and the likelihood that its purposes will continue to be achieved. Obviously, all institutions meeting minimum standards are not of the same quality. Some barely meet the standards; others greatly exceed them. Critics who expect all accredited institutions to be of equal and superior quality hold unrealistic expectations. These critics may be insensitive to the vagaries of reputational rankings, described in chapter 3, and may be making their own assessment without specifying the criteria or information used. In any event, as noted earlier, the concept of minimum standards reduces the variation in institutional quality and assists the public in discerning the differences in institutions with adequate quality and those without.

A seventh criticism centers on the question of whether accreditation is meaningful to the larger, research-based, "national" universities. Some argue that accrediting associations would never deny such leading institutions accreditation. Why, therefore, should they be put through a process whose outcome is never much in question? What real benefit accrues to these institutions? At least one answer to this criticism rests in the original statement of two accreditation purposes: accountability and improvement. It could well be true that the "accountability" judgment might not be in serious question for these institutions (though arrogance on this point is not warranted). Surely, however, a learning community asserting that it could never benefit from the renewing scrutiny of its own faculty and staff and the external evaluation of peers would be a formidable and unhappy curiosity in American higher education.

In line with this criticism is the concern by some that regional accreditors use sanctions both rarely and inconsistently. A *Chronicle of Higher Education* review of actions taken by the six regional accrediting associations from 1997 through 2000 "found that only 52 institutions were placed on probation, issued an order to show why they should not have their accreditation revoked, or had their accreditation terminated. ..."[59] McMurtrie also pointed out that small, private colleges were most often targeted with sanctions. This same review noted great variety in the types and frequency of use of penalties. Perhaps some reluctance is present in the imposition of sanctions due to the link of federal funding to accreditation status—no accreditation by a Department of Education approved accrediting agency, no access to federal financial aid funds. The McMurtrie article contains an acknowledgement from the executive director of the North Central Association of Colleges and Schools's higher education commission that "the federal link makes accreditors reluctant to take that last drastic step."[60]

This idea of reluctance brings us to our eighth criticism—Is accreditation still a voluntary process or an increasingly mandatory one? When an institution's eligibility for federal funding is attached to its accreditation status, it seems that the institution has little choice. Federal funding is an essential operating aspect for most institutions—many students attending colleges and universities could not do so without assistance from some sort of Title IV Federal Financial Aid program.

With this question of voluntary versus involuntary is also the question of how much government involvement there is in higher education. Not only does an institution have to be accredited to receive federal funds; it must be accredited by a Department of Education approved accrediting agency. And the department has influence over these agencies in the processes and standards they utilize in the evaluation of institutions. For example, the 1992 Higher Education Act included twelve institutional areas that accrediting agencies should review.

A ninth criticism concerns the persisting problem of standards: their adequacy, their uniformity and comprehensiveness, their relevancy to quality, and their applicability to the exceedingly diverse nature of colleges and universities in this country and the diverse mechanisms for educational delivery. The matter of relevancy to quality and to student achievement was touched on earlier. It is difficult, however, to fashion standards that apply equally and evenly to all institutions that may justifiably seek accreditation. For example, standards that require faculty to be productive in research and publication are germane to graduate and research institutions, but their relevancy is questionable when applied to institutions that are primarily undergraduate and have no doctoral program. Standards that are appropriate for traditionally delivered educational programs may or may not be appropriate for programs delivered via distance education. The concept of mission achievement is deeply embedded in the accreditation process, yet standards often mitigate the concept by having a single set of standards that apply to all institutions irrespective of type, size, or mission.

This note on mission statements and mission achievement encourages our attention to yet another criticism of accreditation, which strikes at one of the foundations of the accrediting process. Readers may recall that accreditation was cited as "the test of mission achievement." One of the often cited strengths of accreditation is that it is designed to nurture diversity of campus missions, and, as we will note in other places in the book, notably in our final chapter, there are few national reports today that do not call for campuses to formulate more realistic and limited mission statements.

Two scholars at Mississippi State University, however, have conducted research that leads them to conclude that campuses may spend a lot of time fussing with their mission statement, but too few of these mission statements offer anything very distinctive about the campuses they are supposed to describe. In the winter 1990–91 issue of *Planning for Higher Education,* Walter Newsom and C. Ray Hayes note that "the mission statement should be a declaration of the special purposes of an institution and whom it intends to serve. It is a revelation of the college's reason for being."[61]

The authors surveyed 142 institutions in eleven southeastern states and received replies from 114. In reviewing and evaluating mission statements from these campuses, the authors found "that when we hid the institution's name, most of the colleges or universities could not be identified from their statements because they read alike, full honorable verbiage signifying nothing. Not surprisingly, few colleges find much use for their mission statements. They are usually not guidelines for serious planning."[62]

In 1997, Delucchi analyzed the mission statements of over 327 colleges that published mission statements relating only to liberal arts education. He then analyzed the programs offered by those institutions. If 60 percent or more were considered liberal arts, the criteria of a true liberal arts institution were met—his own definition. If less that 60 percent of the offerings were considered liberal arts, Delucchi considered the mission statement of the institution to be misleading. His findings were that over two-thirds of the mission statements published were misleading.[63]

If information such as that presented in these studies is true and widespread, then our definition of quality, as offered in chapter 1, may be in some difficulty. How can any organization evaluate how good a job it is doing if it does not know or say what it is supposed to be doing? The solution, we believe, is not to abandon our definition of quality but to urge each campus to construct a mission statement that makes a more specific case for the distinctiveness of that campus. Newsom and Hayes outline a set of mission dimensions that includes target clienteles, intended outcomes and their priorities, region to be served, commitments for survival and growth, values and philosophical priorities, and matters of public image.

The standards and criteria of most regional and specialized accrediting agencies call for a well-developed and well-publicized mission statement, at both campus and program levels. Why, then, do we still find so many mission statements empty of meaning? Perhaps accrediting bodies need to be more specifically serious about one of the foundations of their own work. This would make a major contribution to the cause of quality.

An eleventh issue centers on the question of whether a review every five or ten years constitutes sufficient pressure for a college or university to maintain and enhance its quality. Is there, in this long-term time frame, an incentive for an institution to float for years and then to engage in frenetic activity as the imminent arrival of the self-study period looms? Certainly, the activity of some campuses would suggest a "yes" to that question. Increasingly, however, the institutional effectiveness standards of accrediting associations require that institutions build their quality assurance efforts over a period of years. Campus faculty and staff awaiting the self-study stimulus for quality assurance action find themselves "behind the quality eight ball," inviting the hoisting of a red flag on their accreditation flagpole.

A CONCLUDING PERSPECTIVE ON ACCREDITATION

Most of the ways colleges and universities have devised to assure their publics that quality programs exist are relatively new inventions. Accreditation, however, has been with us most of this century. From its understandably meager beginning in 1910 when the process consisted of little more than evaluating a handful of institutions according to developed criteria, accreditation has evolved into a sophisticated process that, in addition to serving the quality assurance role, promotes the continuous improvement of member institutions and their movement toward a time when accreditation will become the true test of both effectiveness and quality.

That accreditation is a valued way to ensure quality can be seen by the impressive number of organizations and agencies that place credence in the concept. Students, their counselors, and their parents pay attention to accreditation when selecting a college or university. Institutions of higher learning have reciprocal articulation agreements based on respect for accreditation. Employers, philanthropic foundations, and governmental funding agencies increasingly require accreditation as a condition of eligibility for funding, grants, and employment. Additionally, the general public is more likely to perceive accreditation as a quality assurance than they are the more recently devised ways, such as program reviews and alumni surveys, which, in a general sense, go unnoticed.

Perhaps the greatest support for accreditation as a quality assurance is use by several professions. The fields of medicine and law serve as good examples for the importance attached to graduation from an accredited program, without which applicants for licensure and entry into the profession cannot even begin. Several other professions have virtually the same requirements, and still others desire such a condition.

During its eighty-year history, accreditation has undergone changes in philosophy and process that parallel and accommodate changes in society and in higher education. Examples of changes can be seen in the way specialized accreditation has kept pace with the specialization movement in American society, both among institutions and within them. A further example is the creation of citations designed to handle the accreditation needs of vocational and technical institutions and programs.

Currently, accreditation places great importance on goal formulation and attainment, a heavier emphasis on results obtained than on meeting externally prescribed standards and criteria. The concept of minimal standards still prevails, however.

Despite great improvement in accreditation, several issues and problems still surround the process. Noteworthy among the issues are the increasing costs of obtaining and maintaining accredited status; the proliferation of accrediting agencies and the inherent difficulty in articulating and coordinating with them; and the belief that professional fraternalism frequently invades the evaluation of institutions.

Accreditation has a long and rich history as a quality assurance instrument. Despite its imperfections, it remains the best-known signal and perhaps the most effective instrument for nurturing and guaranteeing collegiate quality. As Kenneth Young and his associates remarked, "the genius of accreditation is that it began with the impossible task of defining educational quality and in just 25 years evolved, by trial and error, into a process that advances educational quality."[64]

NOTES

1. Mayer, J. (1965). *Accreditation in Teacher Education—Its Influence on Higher Education.* Washington, DC: National Commission on Accreditation, 11.
2. Miller, J. D. (1998). *A Centennial History of the Southern Association of Colleges and Schools: 1895–1995.* Decatur, GA: Southern Association of Colleges and Schools, 14.
3. Ibid., 15.
4. Woodward, F. C. (1899). "The Correlation of Colleges and Preparatory Schools." *Proceedings,* 5, 55. (In Miller, *A Centennial History of the Southern Association of Colleges and Schools.*)
5. Miller, *A Centennial History of the Southern Association of Colleges and Schools.*
6. Gaither, G. H. (1998). "Quality Assurance in Higher Education: An International Perspective." In Gaither, G. (ed.). Quality Assurance in Higher Education: An International Perspective [Special issue]. *New Directions for Institutional Research,* No. 99, Fall.
7. Young, K., Chambers, C., Kells, H., and Associates. (1983). *Understanding Accreditation: Contemporary Perspectives on Issues and Practices in Evaluating Educational Quality.* San Francisco: Jossey-Bass, xi.
8. Ratcliff, J. L., Lubinescu, E. S., and Gaffney, M. A. (2001). "How Accreditation Influences Assessment." *New Directions for Higher Education,* No. 113, Spring.
9. Young, Chambers, Kells, and Associates, *Understanding Accreditation.*
10. Council on Postsecondary Accreditation. (1986). *A Guide to COPA Recognized Accrediting Bodies, 1986–88.* Washington, DC: Council on Postsecondary Accreditation, v.
11. Bloland, H. G. (2001). *Creating the Council for Higher Education Accreditation (CHEA).* Phoenix, AZ: Oryx Press, 26.
12. Young, Chambers, Kells, and Associates, *Understanding Accreditation,* 296–297.
13. COPA. (1987). *The Balance Wheel for Accreditation,* Washington, DC: Council on Postsecondary Education, 6.
14. Leatherman, C. (1991). "Leaders of Regional Accrediting Agencies Voice Dissatisfaction with National Organization: Some Say Defections are Possible." *Chronicle of Higher Education,* 37(32), A13–A14.
15. Bloland, *Creating the Council for Higher Education Accreditation,* 41.
16. Ibid.
17. Ibid., 36.
18. Ibid.
19. Perrin, K. L. (1993). "Accreditation at the Crossroads." President's Address to the Membership, Council on Postsecondary Accreditation (COPA) Spring Semi-Annual Meeting, San Francisco, April 6. (Cited in Bloland, *Creating the Council for Higher Education Accreditation.*)

20. Magner, D.. (1993). "19-Year-Old Accrediting Group Disband." *Chronicle of Higher Education,* April 14.

21. Bloland, *Creating the Council for Higher Education Accreditation.*

22. Council for Higher Education Accreditation. (2001). "Why Did CHEA Come into Being?" Available on-line: http://www.chea.org.

23. Bloland, *Creating the Council for Higher Education Accreditation.*

24. Council for Higher Education Accreditation. (2001). "What Is the Council for Higher Education Accreditation?" Available on-line: http://www.chea.org.

25. Council for Higher Education Accreditation. (2001). "Recognition." Available on-line: http://www.chea.org.

26. Bloland, *Creating the Council for Higher Education Accreditation,* 206.

27. Council for Higher Education Accreditation. (2001). "What Is Accreditation?" Available on-line: http://www.chea.org.

28. Jewett, R. (1985). *Interview with Task Force on Teacher Certification.* Washington, DC: American Association of Colleges for Teacher Education.

29. Commission on Collegiate Nursing Education (2002). Available on-line: http://aacn.nche.edu.

30. Ibid.

31. National Council for the Accreditation of Teacher Education. (2001). Available on-line: http://www.ncate.org.

32. North Central Association. (2001). Available on-line: http://www.nca.org.

33. Selden, W. (1960). *Accreditation: A Struggle Over Standards in Higher Education.* New York: Harper Collins, 30.

34. Young, Chambers, Kells, and Associates, *Understanding Accreditation.*

35. Flexner, A. (1960). *Abraham Flexner: An Autobiography.* New York: Simon and Schuster, 71.

36. Flexner, A. (1910). *Medical Education in the United States and Canada* (Bulletin No. 4). New York: Carnegie Foundation for the Advancement of Teaching, 190.

37. Pfnister, A. (1959). "Accreditation in the North Central Region." In *Accreditation in Higher Education.* U.S. Department of Health, Education, and Welfare.

38. Young, Chambers, Kells, and Associates, *Understanding Accreditation,* 5–6.

39. Ibid.

40. Commission on Colleges. (1984). *Criteria for Accreditation.* Atlanta, GA: Commission on Colleges, Southern Association of Colleges and Schools.

41. Ewell, P. (1990). "Implementing Guidelines for Western Association of Colleges and Schools Standards." Paper presented at the meeting of the accrediting liaison officers for the Western Association of Colleges and Schools, Oakland, CA.

42. Farnsworth, S., and Thrash, P. (1990). Memorandum to Chief Executive Officers of Commission Institutions, Commissioners, Accreditation Review Council Members, Consultant-Evaluators, and Friends of the Commission. Chicago: North Central Association of Colleges and Schools, February 1.

43. Accreditation Board for Engineering and Technology. (2001). *2000–2001 Criteria for Accrediting Engineering Programs.* Available on-line: http://www.abet.org.

44. Southern Association of Colleges and Schools. (2000). Memorandum to Member Institutions of the Commission on Colleges and Other Interested Parties, December 5.

45. North Central Association. (2001). Available on-line: http://www.nca.org.

46. Council for Higher Education Accreditation. (2000). "Distance Learning in Higher Education." CHEA Update No. 3.

47. Ibid., 5.

48. Council for Higher Education Accreditation. (2000). "Distance Learning: Academic and Political Challenges for Higher Education." CHEA Monograph Series, Number 1, 11.

49. Oblinger, D. G., Barone, C. A., and Hawkins, B. L. (2001). "Distributed Education and Its Challenges: An Overview." American Council on Education Center for Policy Analysis, 33.

50. Ibid., 35.

51. Ibid.

52. American Academy for Liberal Education. (2000). "Accrediting for Educational Effectiveness in Distance Learning Degree Programs." Project Proposal, 1.

53. Ibid, 7.

54. Young, Chambers, Kells, and Associates, *Understanding Accreditation,* 380.

55. Selden, *Accreditation,* 32–34.

56. Mayhew, L., Ford, P., and Hubbard, D. (1990). *The Quest for Quality: The Challenge for Undergraduate Education in the 1990s.* San Francisco: Jossey-Bass, 222–224.

57. Ibid., 231.

58. Greenberg, M. (2000). "America's Colleges Should Rank Themselves." *Chronicle of Higher Education,* July 16.

59. McMurtrie, B. (2001). "Regional Accreditors Punish Colleges Rarely and Inconsistently." *Chronicle of Higher Education.* January 12.

60. Ibid.

61. Newsom, W., and Hayes, C. (1990–91). "Are Mission Statements Worthwhile?" *Planning for Higher Education,* Winter, 19, 28.

62. Ibid., 29.

63. Delucchi, M. (1997). "Liberal Arts Colleges and the Myth of Uniqueness." *Journal of Higher Education,* May/June.

64. Young, Chambers, Kells, and Associates, *Understanding Accreditation,* 13.

Chapter 3

College Rankings and Ratings

The Test of Reputation

In the fall of 1983, *U.S. News and World Report* first brought to newsstands across the nation a report and rating of "America's Best Colleges." Although there have been a number of scholarly ratings published since 1911, the *U.S. News'* journalistic exercises, which are now published annually, may have become the nation's most widely known quality reports. They have certainly become the most intensely debated approach to quality assurance among college educators.

After describing a range of quality indicators, McGuire and others concluded that "given a universe of unsatisfactory output concepts, reputation—with all its flaws—is probably as good or better because it is broader and more representative of the range of important output components that are produced."[1] In contrast, Robert Zemsky and William Massey offered this comment on the fall 1989 *U.S. News and World Report* ratings: "The rankings of colleges and universities in *U.S. News* are as meaningless as the calculations spewed by Dustin Hoffman's character in 'Rain Main'." [2] Graham and Thompson (2001) agree with this assessment and elaborate that *U.S. News* pays little attention to measures of learning and effective educational practices, but enormous attention to "a school's wealth, reputation, and the achievement of the high school students it admits."[3] Those within academe often criticize and denounce published ratings, but are quick to advertise their inclusion. The News Bureau of the University of Illinois at Urbana-Champaign touted its 1997 eighteenth ranking in the nation in *Money* magazine by stating that it was by far the highest ranked Illinois and Big Ten institution. Its news release even listed the rankings of other schools in Illinois and the Big Ten to illustrate the superior ranking.[4]

The entire process of rating and ranking is built on the philosophic premise discussed in our opening chapter, that quality is in limited supply. In other words, there can never be more than ten in the top ten or twenty-five in the top twenty-five, no matter that the actual performance level of a program or an institution or what impact the program or institution has on its students. Whether there is a definitive relationship between reputation and results is yet another issue to be engaged in this chapter.

Most organizations are concerned with both the perception and the reality of quality—that is, the public perception of and the hard data on product performance. One is not surprised then to see full-page advertisements in the *Wall Street Journal*, *USA Today*, or weekly magazines such as *Time* or *U.S. News and World Report* in which auto or airline industry executives pitch the quality theme. Indeed, in a 1988 *Time* magazine advertisement, Chrysler executive Lee Iacocca outlined a "quality bill of rights" to which customers of Chrysler are supposedly entitled.[5] Ford Motor Company has advertised today that "Quality Is Job One." Is there a lesson here for American higher education? It may not be enough for quality to show through in whatever indicator or evidence we may select to demonstrate quality. It may be equally important for us to attend to public perceptions of quality as well.

Do rating and ranking exercises make a meaningful contribution to quality assurance? We begin the engagement of that question by exploring first some of the more significant reports on both graduate and undergraduate rankings.

RATING GRADUATE PROGRAMS—THE ORIGINS OF COLLEGE RANKING

In his 1964 book *The Academic Man*, Logan Wilson said that rating colleges has a history as early as 1911, when the Bureau of Education published a list, a rating of 344 institutions by the Association of American Universities. The leading institutions were, in order, Harvard, Chicago, Columbia, California, Yale, Michigan, Cornell, Princeton, Johns Hopkins, Wisconsin, and Minnesota.[6]

The study most often cited as the original study of graduate quality was reported by Raymond Hughes in 1925. As rationale for this early rating of graduate programs and schools, Hughes offered the opinion: "It has seemed that such a rating would be of distinct value to the college president or dean who is seeking men to fill vacancies on this staff. Such a rating also seems proper and desirable in printed form, so that any one interested can turn to it readily for a rough estimate of the work in a given field."[7]

The ratings began by securing from members of the Miami University (Ohio) faculty "a list of the universities which conceivably might be doing high grade work leading to a doctor's degree."[8] The Miami faculty also furnished a "list of from forty to sixty men who were teaching his subject in colleges and universities in this country, at least half of the names on the list to be those of professors in colleges rather than universities."[9] Rating forms were returned, according to Hughes's report, from about half the respondents.

Hughes chaired a second study of graduate schools for the American Council on Education, and the results were reported in the April 1934 issue of the *Educational Record*.[10] Whereas the 1925 study included a rating of about twenty fields, this one encompassed fifty different fields of study. Identification of the institutions offering different graduate work was derived from a study of catalogues and reports of graduate deans. Learned societies in each of the fields were asked to supply a list of 100 scholars in that field, to whom the rating forms were circulated.

At the end of his introduction to the results, Hughes commented: "There was marked evidence of a lag in the estimate of departments. A department which has been strong, but which has lost good men and is really on the decline, has in several cases been rated too high. On the other hand, several departments that have recently developed much strength seem to be underrated. If this type of study could be repeated every few years, such errors would be corrected."[11] The time-lag liability of ratings and rankings is thus well identified. However, the next comprehensive rating was not to occur within the time line suggested by Hughes.

In 1959 Hayward Keniston reported a ranking of graduate departments and institutions undertaken as part of an evaluation of the program at the University of Pennsylvania. Keniston describes the study's approaches as follows: "A letter was addressed to the chairmen of departments in each of twenty-five leading universities of the country. The list was compiled on the basis of (1) membership in the Association of American Universities, (2) number of Ph.D.'s awarded in recent years, and (3) geographical distribution. The list did not include technical schools like Massachusetts Institute of Technology and the California Institute of Technology, nor state colleges, like Iowa State, Michigan State or Penn State, since the purpose was to compare institutions which offered the doctorate in a wide variety of fields."[12]

These rather important caveats notwithstanding, a review of the results will prove of interest. Appearing in the Keniston list of top twenty institutions are Harvard, California, Columbia, Yale, Michigan, Chicago, Princeton, Wisconsin, Cornell, Illinois, Pennsylvania, Minnesota, Stanford, University of California, Los Angeles (UCLA), Indiana, Johns Hopkins, Northwestern, Ohio State, New York University (NYU), and Washington. With the exception of UCLA, NYU, and Washington, all remaining institutions had appeared in Hughes's 1925 ranking. There had been, then, a considerable stability over the thirty-two-year history of the ratings. North Carolina and Iowa were not in the Keniston list, although they appeared in 1925. Can it be that the actual quality of these two universities declined during this thirty-two-year period? We will have more to say about this feature of collegiate rankings later in the chapter.

Two of the most frequently cited and best known of recent quality ratings of graduate departments and institutions are the 1966 study by Allan Cartter and the 1970 study by Roose and Anderson. Logan Wilson's foreword in Allan Cartter's report contains an arresting opening line: "Excellence, by definition, is a state only the few rather than the many can attain."[13] With this definition, Wilson supports the philosophic position of "limited supply" to which we earlier referred, which assumes a standard of performance that is comparative and relative rather than criterion based. The Cartter study is cited as the fourth such quality rating following Hughes's study of 1925, the American Council of Education Study of 1934, and the Keniston study of 1957.

Cartter offers these introductory notes on the concept of quality: "Quality is an elusive attribute, not easily submitted to measurement ... In an operational sense, quality is someone's subjective assessment, for there is no way of objectively measuring what is in essence an attribute of value."[14] Arguing for the contributions of rankings and ratings, Cartter points to the limitations of diversity. "Diversity can be a costly luxury if it is accompanied by ignorance. Our present system works fairly well because most students, parents, and prospective employers know that a bachelor's degree from Harvard, Stanford, Swathmore, or Reed is ordinarily a better indication of ability and accomplishment than a bachelor's degree from Melrose A&M or Siwash College."[15] As an editorial note, we find it interesting that Cartter had no difficulty naming top institutions but fudged on his public disclosure of the supposedly lower-quality schools by resorting to pseudonyms and poorly disguised racial identification. Cartter then states this rationale for quality ratings: "Just as consumer knowledge and honest advertisement are requisite if a competitive economy is to work satisfactorily, so an improved knowledge of opportunities and of quality is desirable if a diverse educational system is to work effectively."[16]

To avoid criticisms of the earlier studies, Cartter used three panels of raters—department chairpersons, senior scholars, and junior scholars—in twenty-nine different fields of study.

In a replication of the Cartter study in 1970, Roose and Anderson published yet another rating of graduate programs. In a synopsis of the findings, they noted: "There is an increase in the rated quality of faculty of graduate programs, moving from 69.8 percent rated adequate plus or better in 1964 to 80 percent in 1969. Second, there is evidence of regional improvement. The south, for example, had only 59 percent of it faculties rated 'adequate plus' or better in 1964 but this percentage rose to 73 percent in 1969."[17]

In a section entitled "policy implications of the findings," Roose and Anderson warn of the limitations: "The superficiality of exclusive reliance on reputation as a measure of quality was well illustrated in a comment made to us by the former chief academic officer of a top rated institution about one of his distinguished faculty members: '________' is highly regarded in his profession and has contributed importantly to the reputation of his department, but what has he done for students? In twelve years be has not turned out a single Ph.D."[18]

While we are reviewing the Cartter and Roose-Anderson reports, we note one of the more vigorous assaults on these two reports. In a monograph entitled *The*

Ranking Game: The Power of the Academic Elite by W. Patrick Dolan (1976), we were drawn not so much to the body of the monograph as to the preface. William A. Arrowsmith begins this preface by labeling the reports as "quantified gossip" and "formidable professional sanctions against daring, diversity, and openness." Arrowsmith's prefatory remarks include the following judgement: "The Cartter report and the Roose-Anderson reports are monstrosities, not simply because they are the patent product of reflex, bad faith and suboptimization, but because they are the regressive instruments of standardization which has no valid cultural or human purpose; which serves merely governmental, professional, administrative, or bureaucratic convenience. They simply have no educational purpose which is compatible with the needs of our culture or with the life of the mind."[19]

Of this we may be certain: The person who dares to evaluate anything in higher education invites evaluation. We will never be without lively argument when it comes to the purpose and performance of American collegiate education.

In 1976, Mary Jo Clark, Rodney Hartnett, and Leonard Baird of the Educational Testing Service (ETS) reported on an extensive study of quality indicators in three graduate fields. The opening pages of their report carry these warnings about the contributions of program rating and give a rationale for multidimensional study of graduate quality: "Ratings of the reputation of a program among faculty members in the same field have a place in program evaluation; but they are not very helpful to those who may be seeking to improve their program, are highly related to program size and visibility, and only occasionally reflect recent changes (good or bad) in a program."[20] Their study involved an extensive review of the variety of evidences that should be examined to ascertain program quality: faculty, students, resources, and curricular characteristics.

As another example of graduate study ranking, we explore a five-volume study that attempts to take advantage of the multidimensional approach advocated by the previous ETS study by Clark and others. The 1982 study edited by Jones, Lindzey, and Coggeshall, conducted under the aegis of the Conference Board of Associated Research Councils and published by the National Academy of Sciences, is by far the most ambitious of contemporary efforts—reviewing programs at 228 institutions (compared, for example, to 130 in the Roose-Anderson study). Within these 228 institutions, almost 2,700 programs in thirty-two disciplines are evaluated.

In their preface to Volume 1, the editors noted that at the time of the study American universities were producing over 20,000 research doctorates a year but "what might surprise us, however, is the imbalance between the putative national importance of research-doctoral programs and the amount of sustained evaluative attention they themselves receive."[21] They claim that collegiate educators are poorly informed about the quality of graduate programs and offer their study as a logical but improved continuance of the Roose-Anderson tradition.

This study employed sixteen measures for most of the fields reviewed: mathematical and physical sciences, humanities, biological sciences, engineering, and social and behavioral sciences. These sixteen variables were clustered in six groups: program size (three measures), characteristics of graduates (four measures), reputational survey results (four measures), university library size (one measure), research support (two measures) and publication records (two measures). Many of the measures are of dubious qualitative linkage. The number of faculty members in a program (program size measures) and the median number of years from first enrollment of a doctoral student to receipt of the doctorate (characteristics of graduate measures) may be of interest but hardly qualify as hard evidence on quality.

The qualitative heart of this study is embraced by the four "reputational survey results," in which participating faculty were asked to evaluate these factors: the scholarly quality of program faculty on a scale from 0 to 5, the effectiveness of the program in educating research scholars, and the improvement in program quality in the last five years. Then the faculty evaluators were asked to indicate their familiarity with the programs they were evaluating. In Volume 1 of the evaluation of programs in mathematics and physical sciences, the comments of the editors are instructive: "It should be pointed out that the evaluators, on the average, were unfamiliar with almost one-third of the programs they were asked to consider."[22] Is this a condition designed to enhance confidence in the outcomes of the evaluation? We think not.

Under the measure of publication records, the editors report that a program was evaluated on the number of published articles attributed to it. The qualitative limits of this measure are reasonably obvious, but it ignores other major evidences of scholarship and also tends to bias the evaluation toward large departments.

In the May/June 1983 issue of *Change,* David Webster furnishes an informing review of the 1982 study. He is both complimentary and critical and describes the study as "the biggest, best, most expensive, most thoughtfully conceived, and carefully carried out academic quality rating ever done."[23] Unlike what one might expect from a study of this nature, one searches in vain for systematic rankings of programs based on any one of the sixteen measures or combinations of measures. Webster criticizes the authors for this approach: "By publishing endless columns of figures for institutions in each discipline it covers, without summarizing, combining, or averaging these figures, or ranking the institutions in any way, this most reluctant of all academic quality ratings is like the bible for some religious sects. Of which anyone is welcome to make any interpretation he or she wishes."[24]

Webster then undertakes to remedy this difficulty by a numeric routine designed to portray shifts in institutional rankings from the earlier rankings (by Hughes, Keniston, and so on) to the Jones study. He publishes a table of results showing, among other movements, that Johns Hopkins had slipped twenty-three positions and MIT had gained fourteen positions from the 1925 Hughes study. Webster admits, however, that the results of this comparison cannot be considered very accurate for the simple reason that different groups of judges used different criteria with different groups of departments and different groups of universities.

Returning now to the original 1982 study, we find on page vi of the preface to Volume 1 that the three purposes of this massive study were to assist students in seeking the best match of graduate programs to their interests, to serve scholars in higher education, and to inform the judgement of those responsible for protecting quality. As an interesting and perhaps questionable commentary on these purposes, the copy of the study that we reviewed had never been checked out of the research university library in which we found it.

Webster cites this 1982 study as one of the more expensive ones undertaken. Given the general liabilities of previous studies and the specific liabilities of this 1982 study, we wonder if funding agencies ever bother to obtain hard evidence on whether the three purposes above were well served and whether the study had any significant decision utility. It would be a simple matter, for example, to evaluate the achievement of the first purpose just cited by simply asking a random sample of students enrolled in research-doctoral programs whether they had ever heard of the study.

In 1995 the National Research Council (NRC) released *An Assessment of Research-Doctorate Programs in the United States.* According to Webster and Skinner (1996), the NRC release covers 41 disciplines, 274 institutions, 3,634 programs, and the reputational judgements of 7,876 faculty members.[25] Not only does this rating of programs include reputational rankings by faculty but also objective statistics relating to the seniority, research productivity, and productivity in conferring doctoral degrees of program faculty.[26] "Institutions were ranked if they offered even one program from among the 41 disciplines the *Report* covered that met the Committee's eligibility criteria."[27] Top institutions in the arts and humanities included the University of California, Berkeley (receiving a rating of 4.36 on a 5.0 scale) and Princeton University (rating of 4.28). The following categories also yielded other first-place recipients: biological sciences—the University of California, San Francisco (4.67), engineering—the Massachusetts Institute of Technology (4.65), physical sciences and mathematics—the University of California, Berkeley (4.74), and social and behavioral sciences—Harvard University (4.61). According to Rogers and Rogers (1997), this publication has been criticized because it does not include master's and doctoral-level programs in fields such as law, medicine, business, dentistry, nursing, social work, architecture, library science, journalism, education, and public administration. In addition, NRC only conducts its study every ten years and it is very expensive. This time frame limits the usefulness of the ratings.[28]

The Roose and Anderson or NRC studies did not involve, by the way, major rankings of professional programs, other than engineering. Perhaps we should examine some of the work that has been done in such rankings. In 1973 Margulies and Blau ranked professional schools in such fields as medicine, law, and so forth. The authors sent questionnaires to deans in 1,180 schools offering degrees in seventeen different professional program fields. A comment on response rate in this study is instructive: "A look at the response rates shows that one explanation for the differences (in response rates) between types of schools is the prestige of the profession. The largest proportions of deans who did not respond are in those professions that research has shown to have the highest prestige. Inasmuch as the ratings of expert judges are of interest, even if they are statistically unreliable, we present the rating of the eight types of professional schools with fewer than 20 respondents in the lower part of the table."[29]

The authors seem to suggest that we should be interested in ratings of these programs even though the representative participation of raters cannot be assured. It is no small curiosity that we are invited to find these results of interest even though they are statistically meaningless, and professionals in these high-prestige fields did not care enough to participate.

A second example is the *U.S. News and World Report* rating of graduate and professional programs. Not content with their venture into the rating of colleges and universities, *U.S. News and World Report* entered the field of graduate school rating in March 1990. This issue offered ratings in four graduate and professional fields: business, law, medicine, and engineering.[30] *U.S. News and World Report* now publishes rankings for more than 1,000 graduate programs surveyed each year in the five primary fields of law, education, business, engineering, and medicine. However, the issue is of interest for more than the ratings. With the publication of the first graduate schools rankings is an accompanying article entitled "Why U.S. News Ranks Colleges" and it opens with this lead: "The sad truth is that it is easier to learn about the relative merits of compact disc players that it is to compare and contrast America's professional schools. And some educators prefer to keep it that way."[31]

Here is the closing comment of *U.S. News* editors: "The editors expect that like our study of undergraduate education, now going into its sixth edition, it will evolve, change and eventually merit the active cooperation of all the leaders of the graduate and professional community. We trust they will come to understand that the 'light of public scrutiny' often can be as valuable a tool for improving higher education as it is for informing the reading public."[32]

Discomforting though it may be to some collegiate educators, *U.S. News and World Report* makes a good point. We cannot continue to talk about quality without operational evidence of what we are talking about, and that is going to mean public disclosure. It is difficult to reduce the quality of an institution to a single number, but what other methods have been developed? We are inclined to see the test of public disclosure—whether on ratings, outcomes assessments, results of peer reviews, or other evidence—to be a helpful trend. We encourage readers to review the rating results of graduate and professional schools in the five fields cited: business, education, law, medicine, and engineering.

In summary, what can we say about the reputational ratings and rankings of graduate programs and institutions having graduate programs? We certainly have to note an important consistency and stability in the results. One is hard pressed to find any list of top-rated institutions in which some of the national universities of the land cannot be found. The visibility and prestige of these universities, and the primary basis of these ratings, rest heavily upon the eminence of their faculties; and the eminence of the faculties resides heavily in their publication and research records. We are not surprised, then, that the top-rated universities and graduate programs are those whose faculties are publication productive and research oriented. Institutional size, history, and resources play important roles in this stability.

REPUTATIONAL RATINGS OF UNDERGRADUATE PROGRAMS

Although the rating of graduate programs in the United States has a history reaching back to the early part of the twentieth century, the rating of undergraduate programs is of more recent origin. Of special interest is that a good portion of activity and initiative for such ratings has occurred not so much in scholarly studies, such as those previously discussed in this chapter, but in media and journalistic reviews.

A good lead example for the ratings of undergraduate programs is furnished by Lewis Solmon and Alexander Astin, who conducted a pilot study to rate undergraduate programs in seven fields in four states—California, Illinois, North Carolina, and New York. A more complete record of their study can be found in the September and October 1981 issues of *Change* magazine.[33]

Respondents were all department members, approximately 1,000 in number. Rating criteria included these factors:

- Overall quality of undergraduate education
- Preparation of student for graduate school
- Preparation of student for employment
- Faculty commitment to undergraduate teaching
- Scholarly accomplishments of faculty
- Innovativeness of curriculum

Here is one interesting, and perhaps disturbing, result of the study. Princeton University appears in the top ten departments of business on each of the six criteria above even though Princeton does not offer an undergraduate program in business. Solmon and Astin comment as follows: "The finding underscores the need to interpret the results of any reputational survey with care, since strong halo effects appear to be operating. In this report, we have not presented the results for business programs because of the confounding halo effects."[34]

In the follow-up article entitled "Are Reputational Ratings Needed to Measure Quality?" Solmon and Astin conclude: "In short, while our analysis suggests that reputational ratings of undergraduate programs may indeed be unnecessary because they seem to be redundant with other known information about institutions, we must defer final judgment about the value of such ratings until additional ratings covering more fields and possibly more diverse quality criteria can be obtained, and until longitudinal value-added studies can be carried out to test the validity of such ratings."[35] The last comment merits more thought because it offers a good lead-in to chapter 7 on student outcomes assessment. Does attending a highly rated institution result in a demonstrated impact on student learning?

Other dimensions of the Solmon and Astin study also deserve attention. In their opening commentary, the authors point out that many raters chose not to respond for a variety of reasons: burdensome time commitments, lack of knowledge about departments to be rated, confusion over institutions included in the lists, and so on. The response rate is not cited in the article.

Another provocative finding of the Solmon and Astin study was that the position of an institution on the two lists of institutions provided to raters—a national list and a state list—did affect how raters responded. Indeed, the results were in opposite directions in two different fields. "California sociologists tended to rate the 'scholarly or professional accomplishments of faculty' in California institutions lower when those institutions were included in the national list rather than the California list. Chemistry faculty in New York tend to rate chemistry departments in their own state more favorably when they are included on the national list rather than a separate list, whereas sociology faculty in New York tend to rate their department more poorly when they are included in a single list along with the other national institutions."[36]

What can we say about this study of ratings in undergraduate departments? The simplest answer may be that if one knows something about the admissions selectivity and size of a campus, then one can reasonably expect that institution to be viewed as a high-quality institution. Second, a variety of variables can affect the reliability and validity of these rankings—size of response, composition and arrangement of institutional lists, and so on. And finally, one cannot know from reputational rankings what direct educational benefit is conferred on a student; that is, whether the institution does, in fact, make a value-added difference. Our common sense is rewarded in this case. Many have experienced graduates of highly prestigious schools whose minds seem empty of meaning and hearts empty of caring. And many have seen graduates from "Melrose A & M and Siwash College"—to borrow pseudonyms from Cartter—whose minds and hearts are making a difference.

As stated earlier, easily the most visible and widely known rating activities related to undergraduate programs in recent years are the surveys conducted by *U.S. News and World Report*. In 1983, 1,308 presidents were asked to name the nation's highest-quality undergraduate schools. Fifty percent responded. Commenting on the fact that only five of the seventy-six schools mentioned were public institutions, *U.S. News and World Report* writers observed: "Educators point to conditions found at many taxpayer supported institutions—among them larger class sizes, more graduate students serving as instructors for undergraduates and less selective admissions standards based on serving state residents than on attracting the nation's top students—as reasons for the predominance of private schools on the lists."[37]

Four years later, in the 1987 survey, 16 of 144 schools would be public, an increase from 6.5 percent to 11.1 percent of public institutions in the ratings. Can we suppose that quality conditions in public colleges changed that dramatically in four years?

Included in the 1985 survey were 1,318 institutions that offered liberal arts programs, with professional schools and military academies excluded. As in 1983 and 1987, the raters were college presidents, each of whom was asked to select the top five undergraduate schools from a list of colleges and universities similar to his or her campus in mission. Of the 1,318 presidents surveyed, 788 or 60 percent responded.

One of the best features of the *U.S. News and World Report* 1985 rating is the focus on diversity and innovation. For example, Evergreen State College in Washington was cited for its innovative curriculum in which students study special topical courses in small student-faculty settings. Evaluation of students at Evergreen takes the form of narrative entries rather than grades. Alverno College in Milwaukee, a smaller Catholic school for women, was cited for its development and evaluation of general education competencies in communication, analysis, problem solving, valuing, social integration, responsibility for global environment, responsible citizenship, and esthetic responsiveness. And Trinity University, a private liberal arts school in San Antonio, Texas, was cited for its aggressiveness in fund-raising and the attraction of top scholars with endowed chairs.[38]

For the 1987 survey, 1,329 presidents were asked to rate colleges with missions similar to their own, as in the 1985 survey. Of the 1,329 polled, 650 responded—a 60 percent response ratio, as in 1985. Authors of the article indicate that "a small number of the presidents declined to participate in the survey and wrote to the magazine to say they felt that neither they nor their peers were in a position to judge the academic quality of institutions other than their own."[39] For 1987, the presidents were asked to rate the top ten institutions, rather than the top five as in the 1985 survey.

Once again, the writers of the story emphasize the curricular innovations that draw attention to the diversity of American higher education: the great books curriculum at St. John's, global education emphasis at Earlham, value-added assessment at Northeast Missouri State University, freshman humanities seminars at Wofford College in South Carolina, one-course-at-a-time at Colorado College.

An informative addendum to the 1987 study is entitled "How the Rankings Changed: 'The Ups and Downs'." It begins with this lead-in statement: "It doesn't take long for new college presidents to discover an essential truth about their vocation: Academic reputations are like campus trees, slow to grow, but once established slow to die."[40]

However, a number of schools dropped out of the 1987 ratings, and the authors felt an explanation was in order. They explain that the disappearance of schools like Mills College in California, Wheaton in Massachusetts, Austin College in Texas, Old Dominion in Virginia, and Tennessee Tech came about because they were victims of their own success. These institutions and others had moved into more competitive Carnegie classifications.

Explaining why Harvey Mudd College, which ranked first among small comprehensive institutions in the 1985 survey, dropped completely out of the rankings, the writers said: "Harvey Mudd's slide into seeming academic oblivion is more apparent than real. Earlier this year, Carnegie reclassified Harvey Mudd, which emphasized engineering, chemistry, math, and physics courses, as a specialized institution of engineering and technology. Because the *U.S. News and World Report* survey does not include a category for ranking specialized schools, Harvey Mudd did not even appear on this year's ballot. In brief after 1985, there was change in Harvey Mudd's category, not its quality."[41] (This conclusion, both descriptive and evaluative, we should remember, is not the consensus of presidential raters but of the authors.)

In October 1988, *U.S. News and World Report* departed from the practices of its three previous surveys, revealing what was done and why: "This year, however, after extensive consultation with college presidents and other academic experts, *U.S. News and World Report* has made two major changes in its study. First, because academic deans and admissions officers often see education from rather different perspectives than do college presidents, they also have been included in the survey of more than 1,000 college officials. Second, because the expert opinions are just that, opinions, *U.S. News and World Report* has based its largest academic rankings on objective data as well as on the subjective judgments in the survey."[42] The authors then indicated that these data included five measures of quality: admissions selectivity, faculty strength and instructional budget per student, resources for educational programs, graduation rates, and school reputational studies.

What happens to the reputational quality of a college or university when one changes both the rater and the criteria? Table 3.1 contains the rankings for national universities in the 1987, 1988, 1989, and 1990 surveys. In 1988, four state institutions dropped out of the top twenty-five: the University of Wisconsin, the University of Illinois, the University of Texas, and the College of William and Mary. And how can we explain the wide swings in position for an institution such as the University of California, Berkeley, which in successive years occupied rank positions of five, twenty-four, thirteen, and thirteen among the national universities?

Did the real quality of these schools change that much in one year? Perhaps they would have liked to return to the more "global and subjective ratings" of college presidents rather than the more "objective ratings" rendered by deans

Table 3.1
Reputational Ranking of National Universities by U.S. News and World Report

Rank 1987	*1988*	*1989*	*1990*	*School (State)*
3	1	1	3	Yale University (Conn.)
4	2	2	4	Princeton University (N.J.)
21	3	4	5	California Institute of Technology
2	4	3	1	Harvard University (Mass.)
11	5	7	6	Massachusetts Institute of Technology
1	6	6	2	Stanford University (Calif.)
6	7	8	8	Dartmouth College (N.H.)
18	8	12	10	Columbia University (N.Y.)
14	9	10	16	Rice University (Tex.)
8	10	9	11	University of Chicago (Ill.)
16	11	14	15	Johns Hopkins University (Md.)
7	12	5	7	Duke University (N.C.)
10	13	15	12	Brown University (R.I.)
11	14	11	9	Cornell University (N.Y.)
19	15	20	13	University of Pennsylvania
17	16	19	23	Northwestern University (Ill.)
*	17	25	19	Georgetown University (D.C.)
*	18	23	*	University of Notre Dame (Ind.)
23	19	22	24	Washington University (Mo.)
15	20	21	18	University of Virginia
*	21	16	17	University of California, Los Angeles
25	22	*	*	Emory University (Ga.)
11	23	18	20	University of North Carolina, Chapel Hill
5	24	13	13	University of California, Berkeley
8	25	17	21	University of Michigan, Ann Arbor
23	*	*	*	University of Wisconsin
20	*	*	*	University of Illinois
25	*	*	*	University of Texas
22	*	*		College of William and Mary (Va.)
*	*	24	*	Vanderbilt University (Tenn.)
*	*	*	22	Carnegie Mellon (Pa.)
*	*	*	25	University of Rochester (N.Y.)

*Not ranked this year.

Source: "America's Best Colleges," *U.S. News and World Report*, 1987, pp. 49–87; 1988, pp. C3–C32; 1989, pp. 53–82; 1990, pp. 103–134.

and admissions officers. At the very least, four universities felt the frustration of other schools that had not appeared in any of the *U.S. News and World Report* rankings, and perhaps they too were scratching their heads about the meaning and value of reputational studies of quality.

Modifications to the methodology used for determining the rankings of colleges and universities continued in the ten years to follow. In 1996, rankings of approximately 4,200 college presidents, deans, and admissions directors counted for 25 percent of the overall ranking total, admissions selectivity 5 percent, faculty resources 20 percent, financial resources 10 percent, retention 20 percent, and alumni giving 5 percent. A new indicator was added in this year: value added. The authors explained that this indicator counted for 5 percent of the overall ranking and accounted for the educational value added by individual colleges.

"Developed in consultation with academic experts, it focuses on the difference between a school's predicted graduation rate—based upon the median or average SAT or ACT score of its students and its educational expenditures per student—and its actual graduation rate."[43] By 1999, the value-added indicator was no longer used in the rankings.

In 1999, the methodology was changed once again. According to Graham and Morse (1999): "One key change we made was to employ a procedure, known as 'standardization,' that brought our calculations more into line with accepted statistical practices. In doing so, we dropped a step we had used for national universities that tended to flatten out large disparities between schools in their performance on each indicator of quality."[44] An example used by these authors to illustrate this change involved three universities. "School A might have spent $200,000 per student, School B $100,000, and School C $50,000. If they were the leaders in spending, we would have recognized them as first, second, and third without giving them credit for the size of the disparities among them. This year our weighting system takes into account the sizes of their differences."[45] As a result of this change the California Institute of Technology moved into first place in this year, ahead of Harvard, Yale, and Princeton. "Caltech's spending on instruction and education-related service works out to far more per student ($192,000) than at any other institution."[46] Johns Hopkins is an example of another institution that moved up in the rankings, to number seven, as a result of this methodological change.

Though thought to improve the methodology, in the September 11, 2000, issue of *U.S. News and World Report*[47] the authors acknowledged that the change still did not reflect how funds spent on students affected undergraduate programs—many large research institutions spend a large portion toward graduate programs. So, for the rankings published in this 2000 issue, the methodology was once again adjusted—"we adjusted each school's research spending according to the ratio of its undergraduate to graduate students."[48] As a consequence, Caltech and Johns Hopkins scaled back to fourth and fifteenth, respectively.

No new methodological changes were announced in the September 17, 2001, issue of *U.S. News and World Report.*[49] This issue included the magazine's most recent rankings of institutions. A total of 4,087 university presidents, provosts, and deans of admission participated in the survey. Princeton and Harvard Universities received top honors.

This exploration of media rankings would not be complete without reference to *Money* magazine's annual publication of "America's Best College Buys," which ranks the top 200 schools for the money. "If assessing academic quality is tough, trying to calculate a school's value—its quality relative to price—is an even more difficult task."[50] The magazine used statistical analysis to determine how much each school might be expected to cost, based on sixteen measures of academic performance, including entrance exam scores, class ranks and high school grades of entering students, faculty resources, quality of instruction, student-faculty ratios, library resources, graduation rates, retention of first-year students, money spent on instruction and student services, and the academic and career success of alumni. Then, that figure is compared to actual cost. According to the September issue, the top ten schools in 2001 were:[51]

1. California Institute of Technology
2. Rice University
3. University of North Carolina-Chapel Hill
4. SUNY-Binghamton
5. Spelman College
6. New College of the University of Southern Florida
7. College of New Jersey
8. Truman State University (Mo.)
9. SUNY-Geneseo
10. University of Florida

Time, *Newsweek*, and *Business Week* also publish special issues or guides that analyze various types of educational institutions.

To this point, we have made no mention of a cluster of rating reports that can be found in most collegiate libraries: *The Gourman Reports* offers a rating of both undergraduate and graduate programs to two decimal places. "Gourman has been unofficially evaluating post-secondary educational institutions since 1955 and publishing his rankings since 1967."[52] In the 1983 rating of undergraduate programs in Louisiana, for example, the top three schools were Tulane, with a rating of 4.53; Louisiana State University and Agricultural and Mechanical College, with a rating of 4.35; and Louisiana State University in Shreveport with a rating of 3.38. Centenary College, which has appeared in the *U.S. News and World Report* lists of best liberal arts colleges for more than one year, was ranked thirteenth in the state with a rating of 3.06. What do these ratings mean? Not much.

The Gourman Reports are filled with puffed-up rhetoric about their own importance, and there are grammatical inaccuracies throughout. Nowhere in these reports are we told precisely what data were gathered, by whom they were obtained, by what means, or on what date. Nor are we told who rendered the judgments that led to the ratings expressed to the hundredths of a decimal point. Yet *The Gourman Reports* have been used by economists and other scholars studying the relationships between college quality and a host of other variables, such as alumni earnings, student choice, and so on.

In a devastating critique of *The Gourman Reports*, Webster concluded that "Jack Gourman is not a reasonable arbiter of educational quality. Students, librarians, book reviewers, and scholars need to reexamine his reports and pronouncements on college and university performance. And more importantly, we need to look again at our willingness to accept such rankings from an individual who simply has the power of the printed page behind him."[53] Our fondness for numbers and our search for "number one" can lead even academics down unhappy paths.

What role do these rankings play in American higher education? We will visit that question again at the conclusion of this chapter. In terms of one of the principal purposes of quality assurance—improvement—the rankings by *Money* magazine, *U.S. News and World Report,* and *The Gourman Reports* are relatively empty. They may prove of some value to those who have the financial capacity to afford these top-ranked colleges and to those who can move from where they are to where these schools are. For those who live within service and financial range of these schools, the rankings may be of some understandable pleasure. For the schools appearing in the rankings, there is the pleasure of national recognition, perhaps accompanied by enhanced enrollment attraction, though we want to say more of that in a moment.

Returning to the discussion on quality definition of chapter 1, it may help to remember the complexity of variables associated with the definition and measurement of quality. To the customer who cannot afford a high-priced luxury automobile, its quality is irrelevant. To the student of modest means living in rural Tennessee or Texas, America's best college buy may be Columbia State Community College or Kilgore Junior College. (It is of some interest that this entire sector of American higher education—community colleges—is omitted in both the *Money* guide and the *U.S. News and World Report* rankings.)

Americans love numerical shorthand, as noted by Robert Hutchins: "He (the American) is not at home with anything he cannot count, because he is not sure of any other measure. He can not estimate or appraise quality. This leaves him with quantity."[54] The competitive edge in our national personality leads us to label rather than understand, to prefer averages rather than depth. There is something highly satisfying about the weekly polls that describe who is on top in collegiate football and basketball. Stories on recruiting violations, ethical misconduct of both coaches and alumni, or misuse of drugs by players will not stay our pleasure in finding out who is in the top ten or twenty.

QUALITY RATINGS AND QUALITY REALITY

Here, then, is a brief glimpse of the history of ratings and rankings as an instrument of quality assurance. Do these ratings make a substantive contribution to quality assurance? What are the limitations? Let us begin our summary by posing a few questions suggested by a review of the studies previously cited.

Who is an effective judge of program and institutional quality? A variety of raters has been employed by these studies. It certainly seems important to know who is doing the rating and whether the rater has reasonable knowledge and authority on which to base his "informed opinion." The earlier graduate rankings used department chairpersons as raters, but Allan Cartter criticized this approach, suggesting that chairpersons were not always the most distinguished scholars in their fields. Later the studies used deans and faculty in departments and programs being rated. The *U.S. News and World Report* ratings of undergraduate programs first used presidents as raters. To what extent might the judgments of these presidents be as much influenced by their knowledge of other presidents as their knowledge of the institutions in question? In few if any of the studies do we find graduates as raters, with the exception of the study by Clark, Hartnett, and Baird (1976).

What criteria are used by the raters to judge quality? Earlier studies obviously touched on the criteria of faculty accomplishments and library holdings. Later studies, such as those in *U.S. News and World Report,* asked for more global assessments. The study of undergraduate quality by Astin perhaps utilized the most extensive list of criteria. Astin's findings, however, lead to the next question.

To what extent do reputational ratings contribute information not already available from other sources? A number of these studies suggest that if one already has knowledge about program size, selectivity, library holdings, and number of graduates, one can predict program and institutional standing in the ratings.

Is there a relation between perceived prestige, as reflected in ratings, and perceived influence? In a study sponsored by and reported in *Change* magazine, Richard Johnson stated: "There are at least three senses in which the term 'leading' can be used: (1) prestige—the degree to which an institution is looked up to or admired; (2) innovation—the frequency with which an institution is first in generating new ideas or programs; and (3) influence—the degree to which other institutions follow the leading institutions' example. Here then is a paradox: All institutions tended to agree on a set of leading institutions which influences other colleges and universities. But when reporting on the influence on their own institutions, they also agreed that these national influential institutions do not influence them."[55]

How extensive is the "halo" effect? We recall the finding in Astin's study of undergraduate programs in which Princeton University was identified as a leading institution in undergraduate business, even though it did not have an undergraduate program in business. Do strong departments and programs tend to bathe weaker programs in a positive light? The evidence suggests that this is so.

Is the philosophy of limited supply of excellence justified? The use of ratings as an instrument of quality identification assumes, as we have shown, that excellence is indeed in limited supply. As additional schools develop high performance records on any criterion of quality—student growth and performance, faculty research and publication, library holdings, or curricular innovation—there can still be only five in the top five or ten in the top ten.

What about the stability of ratings? There appear to be mixed results on this question. One cannot argue with the apparent stability of the national universities' profile in the ratings of graduate programs. However, there are movements in and out of those ratings, suggesting that quality is a fleeting condition, and our common sense suggests otherwise. In the first *U.S. News and World Report* ratings of undergraduate institutions, only 6.5 percent of the institutions were public. Just four years later that percentage had almost doubled to 11.1 percent. Had the quality of public institutions changed that much over four years?

In this chapter, we have pointed to other equally puzzling illustrations of instability. For example, we noted the positioning in the *U.S. News and World Report* ratings for the University of California, Berkeley—from fifth place in 1987 to twenty-fourth place in 1988 and then back up to thirteenth place in 1989 and 1990. Surely the quality of this national university cannot be that mercurial in actuality. And what can we say about the May 2001 number one ranking of Dartmouth College in the business-school ratings published by the *Wall Street Journal* and the number 10 rating in the September *U.S. News and World Report* list?

What effect does the structure of rating studies have on the response? We have evidence that the way in which questions are posed and studies structured can have an effect on the results. Harvey Mudd College was ranked first in the 1985 *U.S. News and World Report* study but, because of a classification fluke, did not even appear in the 1987 study. Astin found that raters responded differently in their ratings depending on whether an institution appeared on a national list or a state list. In 2001, *U.S News* recategorized many institutions due to the change in the Carnegie classification system. As a result, approximately fifty new schools were added to the rankings.

What can we say about rate of response and confidence in ratings? We have seen that ratings are offered as a justifiable expression of quality because they constitute an aggregation of informed opinion. Yet most of the studies report response rates of 50 to 60 percent. Although these response ratios are respectable for questionnaire research, there is little discussion on the margin of error in conclusions occasioned by these response ratios.

Do ratings make meaningful contributions to program and quality improvement? In their informative monograph *A Question of Quality: The Higher Education Ratings Game,* Lawrence and Green (1980) point out that the "results of such studies contribute little to a program's self-knowledge or its efforts toward improvement."[56] Global ratings simply do not offer the specific information necessary for improvement, although program improvement is cited by most educators and evaluators as the principal reason for any venture in educational evaluation. Thus ratings must be counted as making a relatively empty contribution to this important goal.

Do ratings tend to encourage labeling? In their widely read book *The Academic Marketplace,* Caplow and McGee used the terms "major league, minor league, and academic Siberia" as florid terms often used to describe various sectors of American higher education.[57] The mixed use of metaphors from baseball and political geography describes an assumed pyramid of prestige topped by the national universities, which, as we have seen, everyone is willing to identify. There are no ratings, however, of the five or ten worst institutions or programs, and no one is willing to venture their names. They remain covered by Cartter's barely disguised terms "Melrose A&M and Siwash College."

To what extent do ratings encourage a limitation of esteem as well as mission? Reputational studies have succeeded in identifying the diversity existing in American higher education. Read again, for example, the rich descriptions of undergraduate programs found in the *U.S. News and World Report* studies. Whether these studies promote a diversity of esteem and respect for the variety of missions in American higher education is not clear.

One of the finest books ever written on the subject of excellence is Gardner's *Excellence*, first published in 1961 and revised in 1984. In perhaps the most often quoted line from that book, Gardner advocated a diversity of esteem and high expectations in these words: "The society which scorns excellence in plumbing, because plumbing is a humble activity, and tolerates shoddiness in philosophy because it is an exalted activity will have neither good plumbing nor good philosophy. Neither its pipes nor its theories will hold water."[58]

Do ratings make a significant contribution to consumer choice decision? This argument has been advanced by more than one source cited in this chapter. The essence is that a college education is a product (similar to a compact disk or an automobile), that potential students and their parents need to know something about the quality of that product, and that ratings furnish this discriminating evidence. One has to ask, however, whether potential students have been noting the wild swings in the rankings, the disappearance of some universities, and the in-and-out placement of some as carried in two different journalistic publications.

On this topic of consumer choice, we repeat an observation made earlier in this chapter. When almost 40 percent of those attending undergraduate schools in this nation attend two-year colleges, and those two-year colleges are not included in the media rankings, a legitimate question can be asked about the value of the rankings to the majority of college students in this nation. We wonder whether the variable most closely correlated with these rankings is the sales volume of the issue; if you are in the business of selling magazines, that is of legitimate and keen interest.

Thus, we have some questions concerning the decision value of ratings to potential students. Here, however, is a good topic for a useful thesis or dissertation. To plot the history of enrollments, gifts, and other benefits that supposedly follow discriminating student choice based on ratings might help bring speculation on this topic to heel. What would the facts tell us about these relationships?

To what extent do ratings recognize the occasional "maverick" character of American higher education? One of the conventional quantitative signals of academic quality is the number or percentage of the faculty with a doctoral degree. Although few would argue with the general validity of that indicator, is there room in our reflections and ratings for the power of exceptions? Webster carries the point in this comment: "One frequently used 'objective' measure of rankings of institutions and individual departments was by the percentage of their faculty, or senior faculty, who possessed Ph.D.'s. Around 1970, one well-known department would have been ranked quite low in such a quality ranking—fully three of its senior professors had no Ph.D. One had a law degree, one had only an M.Ed., and the third had only a B.A. yet these three members of Harvard's social relations department—David Riesman, Christopher Jencks, and Erik Erikson—might possibly have been better scholars and teachers than some professors who did possess earned doctorates."[59]

To what extent do ratings and rankings cause abuse of information and effect on policy? Polocano (2001) outlined ten easy steps to a top twenty-five MBA program. The recommended steps include hiring a top public relations firm; to increasing services to recruiters including valet parking, free meals, and gift baskets; and providing a wide variety of student services for MBA students such as free parking and a fitness center. His ninth recommendation is to "Adjust your admissions policies and make up your own rules so that you can report both admissions and placement data in a more favorable light. Hire staff members to collect and massage the data and respond to media surveys in the manner you prescribe. (*U.S. News* collects self-reported data that up to this point is not audited.)."[60] Obviously one of the least expensive ways to increase a program's ranking is to fudge the data. This author was not advocating these steps, merely reporting his experiences—and cautions that these suggestions may seem tongue in cheek, but are only a small portion of what deans have described to him over the years. He indicates that "rankings have damaged the business school industry by causing serious misallocation of resources."[61]

Unfortunately, buildings are built, admissions policies set, and services rendered in order to achieve a top twenty-five ranking with oftentimes little consideration actually given to the learning environment of a program.

THE TEST AND TESTIMONY OF REPUTATION

College ratings and rankings constitute a test of reputation. What have we learned about reputation and how it is formed? The first and most obvious point is that the formation takes time. We might not be surprised, then, that older institutions are better known and represented in many studies of reputation. Indeed, an institution that has been serving this nation for a hundred years or more has earned its way.

Second, size can combine with time to produce a larger number of graduates. When these graduates occupy positions of responsibility, one is also not surprised to find his or her alma mater well represented in reputational studies. And as the production levels of other American universities grow, we will not be surprised to note some expanding diversity in the institutions appearing in those ratings.

Third, national reputations associate more with publication than with teaching, more with article and book citations than with the knowledge and pleasure of one's graduates. We are not surprised that institutions attracting frequently published research scholars are favored, certainly in graduate reputational studies.

Finally, reputations can be built on some sense of distinction in curriculum or climate. We should also not be surprised that institutions are more easily recognized for quality if they have such a distinction: great books at St. John's, expository grades at Evergreen, work emphasis at Berea, general education competencies at Alverno.

Not appearing in reputational studies is a large range of institutions that are perhaps younger, smaller, less selective, a little more routine in climate and curriculum, but not necessarily of low quality. Those institutions and programs occupying the top positions in reputational studies have no justification to hold in disdain or arrogance those not appearing there. The halls of history are filled with the sounds of bare feet going up the stairs and golden slippers coming down. Graduates of Harvard, Chicago, Yale, Columbia, and Stanford will be working for graduates of Melrose A&M or Siwash College. And researchers from more prestigious schools may be scooped by an obscure scholar working in one of the "academic Siberia" laboratories. All of this gives life to the power of diversity in American higher education.

There is, by the same token, no justification for those not appearing in reputational studies to hold jealousy or prejudice against their colleague institutions for these accomplishments and recognitions. Not only achievement but daring and perseverance are represented in these ratings. With institutions as with individuals, there's little to gain in throwing oneself against the record or reputation of another. To be inspired by the lessons of risk, imagination, achievement, and perseverance demonstrated by those programs and institutions that have earned their way to prominence is a healthy response. To understand that recognition is to be earned by time and distinction is also a healthy response.

With these reflections in mind, we can begin to understand some of the constructive contributions made to quality in American higher education by ratings and rankings, the lifting effect of reputational studies.

Keeping the Concern for Quality Visible and Active

Certainly reputational studies serve this rather fundamental and simple purpose. Hutchins once said something to the effect that a first-class university is essentially an ongoing and lively argument. Conversations on the nature of quality open the possibility of new action and understanding.

Reflecting the Power of Innovation

A careful review of the ratings studies, particularly those of undergraduate programs and institutions, illustrates the variety of curricular and program innovations recognized in those studies. These experiments, some small and others large, can furnish both information and inspiration for other campuses. This is a worthy outcome, and reputational studies deserve a salute for that purpose alone.

Demonstrating the Power of Perseverance

A review of reputational studies helps develop a greater appreciation for the long and distinguished history of some of our national institutions. In a nation that thrives on everything "instant"—from coffee to personal gratification—important lessons are to be learned in the power of perseverance. Northeast Missouri State University has been recognized in the reputational studies and in other places for its daring approach to value-added instruction. What many folks do not recognize, however, is that Northeast has been developing this program since the early 1970s. The university earned this recognition over a long period of time.

Creating a Competitive Edge

We know both the advantages and dangers of competition in our society. An overemphasis on competition delivers a "dog-eat-dog" mentality in which overly ambitious personalities and institutions climb over the backs of colleagues to fulfill their selfish desires. On the other hand, the absence of the competitive edge can cause both personalities and organizations to lapse into a stupor of mediocrity or explode into arrogance.

These summary reflections on the strengths and weaknesses of reputational studies may leave some readers yearning for a set of one-armed authors, so that equivocation is not encouraged by the phrase "on the other hand." So let us state our conviction clearly: We are not inclined to see reputational studies as a very useful quality assurance tool.

Although scholarly exercises and media studies of ratings can serve to keep the quality argument in ferment and encourage the "culture of evidence" about which we spoke in chapter 2, there continue to be equivocal linkages between quality reputation and quality reality. We find no significant evidence that reputational studies furnish a very meaningful tool for enhancing student choice. Nor do we find that reputational studies make a demonstrable contribution to the most fundamental goal of evaluation and quality assurance—improvement. Finally, we find no obvious value of ratings to the other major quality assurance goal—establishing accountability with major higher education stakeholders.

Reputational studies concentrate on asking questions of those who are responsible for the design and delivery of higher education, but there is a more important respondent. Few Americans who purchase either products or services in our nation today escape a follow-up telephone call or questionnaire to ascertain customer and client satisfaction. As we shall see in chapter 4, higher education is not a newcomer to the use of client satisfaction indices as an instrument of quality assurance. We pay attention to our clients and customers: our students.

NOTES

1. McGuire, J., and Others. (1988). "The Efficient Production of Reputation by Prestige Research Universities in the United States." *Journal of Higher Education*, 59, July/August, 356.
2. Zemsky, R., and Massey, W. (1990). "The Rain Cometh." *AGB Reports*, 32(1), 21.
3. Graham, A., and Thompson, N. (2001). "Broken Ranks." *Washington Monthly*, September, 10.
4. News Bureau. (1997). "UI Ranked Second in the Midwest for Quality at a Low Price by Money Magazine." News Release. Available on-line: http://www.news.uiuc.edu/archives/97.08/14moneymag.num.
5. *Time*. (1988). September 12, 72–73.
6. Wilson, L. (1964). *The Academic Man*. New York: Octagon Books.
7. Hughes, R. (1925). *A Study of the Graduate Schools of America*. Oxford, OH: Miami University, 3.
8. Ibid.
9. Ibid.
10. "Report of the Committee on Graduate Instruction." (1934). *Educational Record*, April.
11. Ibid., 194.
12. Keniston, H. (1959). *Graduate Study and Research in the Arts and Sciences at the University of Pennsylvania*. Philadelphia: University of Pennsylvania Press, 115.
13. Cartter, A. (1966). *An Assessment of Quality in Graduate Education*. Washington, DC: American Council on Education, vii.
14. Ibid., 4.
15. Ibid., 3.
16. Ibid.
17. Roose, K., and Anderson, C. (1970). *A Rating of Graduate Programs*. Washington, DC: American Council on Education, 2.
18. Ibid., 24.
19. Dolan, W. (1976). *The Ranking Game: The Power of the Academic Elite*. Lincoln: University of Nebraska Press, i.
20. Clark, M., Hartnett, R., and Baird, L. (1976). *Assessing Dimensions of Quality in Doctoral Education: A Technical Report of a National Study in Three Fields*. Princeton, NJ: Educational Testing Service, 1.2.
21. Jones, L., Lindzey, G., and Coggeshall, P. (eds.). (1982). *An Assessment of Research-Doctorate Programs in the United States*. 5 vols. Washington, DC: National Academy Press, v.

22. Ibid., 24.

23. Webster, D. (1984). "America's Highest Ranked Graduate Schools, 1925–1982." *Change,* 15(4), 14.

24. Ibid., 16.

25. Webster, D. S., and Skinner, T. (1996). "Rating Ph.D. Programs: What the NRC Report Says ... and Doesn't Say." *Change,* 28(3), May/June, 26.

26. Ehrenberg, R. G., and Hurst, P. J. (1996). "The 1995 NRC Ratings of Doctoral Programs: A Hedonic Model." *Change,* 28(3), May/June, 46.

27. Webster and Skinner, "Rating Ph.D. Programs," 26.

28. Rogers, E., and Rogers, S. J. (1997). " 'High Science' vs. 'Just Selling Magazines?': How the NRC and *U.S. News* Graduate Rankings Compete." *AAHE Bulletin,* 49(9), May, 9.

29. Margulies, R., and Blau, P. (1973). "America's Leading Professional Schools." *Change,* November, 22.

30. "America's Best Graduate Schools." (1990). *U.S. News and World Report,* March 19, 46–78.

31. Ibid., 50.

32. Ibid.

33. Solmon, L., and Astin, A. (1981). "Part One: Departments Without Distinguished Graduate Programs." *Change,* 13(6).

34. Ibid., 27.

35. Solmon, L., and Astin, A. (1981). "Part Two: The Quality of Undergraduate Education: Are Reputational Ratings Needed to Measure Quality?" *Change,* 13(7), 19.

36. Ibid., 18.

37. "Rating the Colleges." (1983). *U.S. News and World Report,* November 28, 41.

38. "America's Best Colleges." (1985). *U.S. News and World Report,* November 25, 46–60.

39. "America's Best Colleges." (1987). *U.S. News and World Report,* October 26, 49–87.

40. Ibid., 70.

41. Ibid.

42. "America's Best Colleges." (1988). *U.S. News and World Report,* October 10, C3-C32.

43. "America's Best Colleges." (1996). *U.S. News and World Report,* September 16, 89–123.

44. "America's Best Colleges." (1999). *U.S. News and World Report,* August 30, 63–105.

45. Ibid.

46. Ibid.

47. "America's Best Colleges." (2000). *U.S. News and World Report,* September 11, 90–133.

48. Ibid., 104.

49. "America's Best Colleges." (2001). *U.S. News and World Report,* September 17, 88–116.

50. Gilbert, J. (1990). "Money's College Value Rankings." *Money Guide,* Fall, 72.

51. "Best College Buys." (2001). *Money,* September.

52. Willard, A. (2001). "Law School Rankings: Through the Education and Employment Looking Glass." Available on-line: http://www.nalp.org/Schools/rank1.htm.

53. Webster, D. (1984). "Who Is Jack Gourman and Why Is He Saying All Those Things About My College." *Change,* 13(7), 55.

54. Hutchins, R. (1966). "First Glimpses of a New World." In *What I Have Learned.* New York: Simon and Schuster, 178.

55. Johnson, R. (1978). "Leadership Among American Colleges." *Change,* 10(10), 50.

56. Lawrence, J., and Green, A. (1980). *A Question of Quality: The Higher Education Ratings Game.* AAHE-ERIC/Higher Education Research Report No. 5, Washington, DC: American Association for Higher Education, 10.

57. Caplow, T., and McGee, R. (1958). *The Academic Marketplace.* New York: Basic Books, 14.

58. Gardner, J. (1984). *Excellence.* New York: W. W. Norton, 102.

59. Webster, D. (1981). "Advantages and Disadvantages of Methods of Assessing Quality." *Change,* 13(7), 22.

60. Polocano, A. J. (2001). "Ten Easy Steps to a Top-25 MBA Program." *Selections,* Fall, Graduate Management Admission Council, 40.

61. Ibid.

Chapter 4

Follow-up Studies

The Test of Client Satisfaction

Years ago the Packard automobile company advertised its cars with the simple line "Ask the Man Who Owns One." Whether that was an adequate quality test for Packard may be debatable, because the company is no longer in business. However, the simple expedient of seeking feedback from customers and clients—our students, in the case of colleges and universities—remains a key element in any effective program of quality assurance.

Contact with faculty in classrooms and studios, contact with registrars and financial officers, contact with campus security officers and secretaries: Each day thousands of impressions are developed as our students attend classes, check their degree progress with the dean's secretary or advising center, order a transcript, pay a traffic ticket, register by phone or on-line, or check out equipment in the gym. A large university produces a million such contacts a week, each one conveying the spirit of the university to its students.

Although each of the quality assurance instruments explored in chapter 2 and chapter 3, accreditation reviews and reputational studies, makes contributions to a comprehensive program of quality assurance, in none of them do we find a primary focus on the perceptions and satisfactions of the student. To emphasize the importance of hearing from our students, it is not necessary either to diminish the premier role in quality assurance held by faculty from our own campuses and by peer colleagues from other campuses or to demean the contributions of media friends and other interested partners with board or state agencies.

After all, our students are the only ones who can furnish a view of what our colleges or universities look like from the receiver's perspective. What do our students think about our programs and services? How can their thoughts be used in improving educational and administrative services? These are simple questions, yet often ignored in the press of daily business. This point was highlighted in one of the early national efforts to obtain follow-up data. In their Carnegie Commission report *Recent Alumni and Higher Education,* Spaeth and Greeley (1970) offered a comprehensive national perspective on alumni assessments of their alma maters. In the foreword to the Spaeth and Greeley book, Clark Kerr supplied this view of student and alumni feedback: "Often neglected, too—at least until the next fund drive—is news of the whereabouts and progress of recent alumni. This is unfortunate since they, of all persons, are especially qualified to contribute insight into the ways in which college failed or served them and perhaps how it may best serve the future."[1]

This note reminds us of good advice in the same spirit issued by Robert Townsend in his book *Up the Organization* (1970). In a short passage entitled "Call Yourself Up," Townsend, former chairman and chief executive officer of Avis Rent-A-Car Company, suggests: "When you're off on a business trip or a vacation, pretend you're a customer. Telephone some part of your organization and ask for help. You'll run into some real horror shows. Don't blow up and ask for name, rank, and serial number—you're trying to correct, not punish. If it happens on a call to the Dubuque office, just suggest to the manager (through channels, dummy) that he make a few test calls himself. ... Then try calling yourself up and see what indignities you've built into your own defenses."[2] Townsend not only calls us to view our organizations through the eyes of our customers and clients but also affirms the improvement motive for quality assurance, a motive that we emphasize throughout these chapters.

A college president of a state university received an irate letter from a recent graduate complaining of treatment by the university registrar's office. Here is the essence of the complaint. It seems that the graduate had sent a five-dollar check to the registrar's office along with a transcript request. His letter and check were summarily returned with a form letter in which the following impersonal line had been checked: "Transcripts Are Three Dollars." Apparently an uncaring clerk had failed to see the wisdom of sending the transcript along with a two-dollar refund. Not only did the university president get a copy of the sizzling verbal missile but information copies were also distributed to the governor of the state, to area legislators, and to local newspaper editors. A little irritation goes a long way.

Within moments of receiving the letter, the president called the graduate with a personal apology and had the transcript personally delivered to the graduate, who lived just an hour away from the campus. Opportunities to see ourselves as our students and graduates see us are found not just in questionnaires and surveys but in the daily operational moments of our institutions. Accreditation reviews, assessment of student knowledge and skill, rankings, and ratings contribute useful elements to a comprehensive quality assurance program. They are powerfully complemented, however, by the simple expedient of asking our students what we are doing well and how we can improve the remainder.

The purpose of this chapter is to explore the nature of student follow-up studies at the national, state, and campus levels; to outline some of the instruments and approaches available for follow-up studies; to demonstrate how these studies can have constructive decision impact; and to explore some of the issues of both purpose and process in the conduct of follow-up studies.

PERSPECTIVES OF TIME AND METHOD

A few months ago a friend bought a new automobile after having driven a four-wheeled treasure for eleven years. The former car had performed superbly for 150,000 miles with routine maintenance. Its body style had been compatible with newer models for over a decade. The manufacturer never asked those who owned the vehicle if they were satisfied. By contrast, less than a month after the new car was acquired, its manufacturer (a different corporation) sent a questionnaire to determine owner satisfaction. The new owner's first response was to complete the survey with highly positive feelings; after all, the car was new and performing well. However, the company's quality assurance process would be better served by asking these questions later, for this owner's standards are long term after three years or five years, not one month.

Our graduates' standards are long term, too. Immediate gratification is nice: a job, a degree to hang on the wall. Promotions, advanced degrees, greater earning power, an improved quality of life happen over time, but we also need to measure our quality, in part at least, by students' standards within their time frame.

Long-term follow-up of graduates of our institutions is but one measure of client satisfaction. In actuality, all assessment is a form of follow-up. Examples are readily discerned. The final examination in a course is a follow-up measure of the instructional quality in that particular class. The number of students who continue in good standing may be an indicator of satisfaction with previous instruction. Retention rates of students from entry to graduation may be a measure of student satisfaction. Success rates of developmental students in freshman English and mathematics courses are follow-up measures of developmental education quality. Tests for licensure or professional school admission are comprehensive follow-up indications of undergraduate learning.

Quantitative measures that provide such data are easy enough to obtain. By searching our sources of information, we can obtain evidence to evaluate performance and goal achievement. How many developmental/remedial students satisfactorily complete their freshman year? How many first-time freshmen complete their freshman year? How many first-time freshmen complete their first semester in good academic standing? How many freshmen persist to graduation? How many baccalaureate graduates go on to graduate school? How many accounting majors pass the Certified Public Accountants(CPA) examination, or teacher education majors the National Teachers Examination (NTE), or nursing school graduates their licensure examination, or law school graduates the bar examinations? How many graduates get jobs? How much money do they make? In fact, constantly improving computer databases and increasingly user-friendly access to those data may lull institutions into the mistaken notion that here is all the information they need to establish proof of quality and of adequate performance.

There is no doubt that such quantitative information is valuable, but some question exists about whether numbers alone can testify to client satisfaction. Let us consider, then, what it is that we want to know: What should a higher education institution expect of its products (its graduates and the recipients of its services, including research)? What should its graduates (its clients) and other constituencies expect of a higher education institution?

The interactive nature of these expectations is nicely illustrated in two national follow-up studies. In the opening comments of this chapter, we cited the Spaeth and Greeley study *Recent Alumni and Higher Education.* The authors report that their study was "based on a sample of 40,000 graduates of 135 accredited or large colleges and universities. Data were collected in 1961, 1962, 1963, 1964, and 1965."[3] For what purposes? Spaeth and Greeley report that they were interested in alumni views on the goals and performance of their own colleges, alumni interests in literature and the arts, alumni political and social attitudes, alumni financial contribution profiles, and alumni views on the role of college in career planning and attainment.

The relationship studies possible among these questions and alumni classification variables such as age, race, sex, and field of study are endless. For example, Spaeth and Greeley developed three goal indices—personality development, career training, and intellectual accomplishment—which they then correlated with selected variables of college quality and control and with selected graduate variables such as sex and age.

Readers interested in understanding the rich potential in mining such studies for meaning are encouraged to review the original book-length report. We found one of the author's evaluative and concluding comments to be of particular interest: "If we were asked to make a single recommendation on the basis of the data presented in the present study, it would be not that education tie itself into the inner city, nor that it create more work study programs, nor that it establish marathon encounter groups on campus—though all these activities may be virtuous and praiseworthy—but rather that it concern itself more with the analysis and development of values, which is something rather different from 'changing values.' The college's perceived contribution to value formation seems to be the strongest predictor of alumni satisfaction seven years after graduation."[4] Where does this finding place us on the question of institutional and student expectations? It might suggest that reading Victor Frankl's *Man's Search for Meaning* (1959) could be as important as reading basic texts in psychology or physics.[5]

One other simple reflection can be noted here, one to which we will return in other chapters. If there is dissonance on the goals of higher education, we should not be surprised to see satisfaction indices vary with one's perspective on goals. The student who comes to college looking for personality development as a goal of primary interest, as opposed to the other two goal indices developed by Spaeth and Greeley—career/professional goals and intellectual/general education goals—will look back on his or her college experience with that goal in mind. Moreover, student perspectives on the importance of these goals change not only during the college experience but also during the years after graduates exit our doors. The very act, however, of getting a handle on these changing perceptions is one of the benefits of follow-up studies, benefits clearly evident in the extensive data from the Spaeth and Greeley study.

A personal and poignant commentary carried in the Spaeth and Greeley book clearly illustrates the importance of student goal perspectives and also illustrates the merit of open-ended options in follow-up studies. A businessman responding to the study offered these reflections on college experience: "College is supposed to teach a person how to think and how to live. A person must learn the meaning of life, and unless a person learns this he will be unhappy forever, and will probably make others unhappy. My college tried to mold my intellect, which I have since realized is not man's most important faculty. Man's spirit, his soul, is totally neglected by college, just as it is neglected by our materialistic world, and as a character in 'Karamazov' says, 'without God anything is possible.' "[6]

This graduate gave an unhappy and dissatisfied evaluation of his college education. It is clear that his evaluation was based on a keen view of college purpose. If the college from which he graduated is disappointed, it may take pleasure in at least two achievements. This graduate obviously developed continuing curiosity about life, and he has been exposed to at least one good book by Dostoevski. Finally, we have to note that some learnings—especially those about the meaning of life—are less likely to emerge during the years of college life than after our graduates have experienced the pain and pleasure of grappling with life problems where the answers cannot always be found in the back of a book.

A second nationally renowned study is the work begun by Alexander Astin in the early 1960s. In his book *Four Critical Years* (which he revisited in 1997), Astin (1977) outlines the cooperative institutional research program (CIRP), in which many institutions over the country have participated. Annual reports of this study appear in the *Chronicle of Higher Education* and profile shifts in student aspirations and values, while students are in college and after they graduate.[7]

Astin's chapter on "Satisfaction with the College Environment" contains a host of correlate findings. Two that might be easy to predict, but not always easy to take advantage of, are the fact that close faculty-student interaction promotes student satisfaction, as does involvement with the life of the institution. Astin has invested a large portion of his talent and career in this extensive longitudinal study of student perceptions, and his work is exemplary of thoughtful questions and well-conceived methodology driven by a scholarly perseverance over the years.

This work, by the way, illustrates yet another advantage of follow-up studies. By showing our students and our graduates that we are interested in their perceptions and evaluations, we model a performance curiosity and willingness to risk that we hope to nurture in their lives as well.

The value of student follow-up results in addressing issues of accountability—that is, the shared expectations of institutions and their graduates—has also been demonstrated by the work of Stevenson, Walleri, and Japely (1985) at Mt. Hood Community College. Their efforts were directed toward determining student satisfaction with educational services "especially after they have some time in which to reflect."[8] Other important insights into the way various people perceive the institution's purpose, programs, and performance are provided by surveys designed to measure the attitudes of an institution's various constituents. "These attitudinal surveys take many forms, address a range of publics, and generate a wealth of information to be ploughed back into the planning/evaluative process."[9]

We turn now to a review of survey instruments appropriate to the follow-up process, the kinds of information that may be acquired by survey, and the best use of the information generated.

FORMAL FOLLOW-UP PROCESSES

Ewell's *Information on Student Outcomes*[10] included a listing of student development and satisfaction indicators that are measurable either by use of test results and the usual demographic and scholastic records maintained by institutions, or by student self-reported attitudinal responses. In this report, Ewell has examined six data-gathering instruments, comparing his outcomes dimensions with them to identify which of the instruments measures directly or indirectly the various outcomes. Ewell's process is one that might well inform our own review. Among the instruments he uses for comparison are those by the National Center for Higher Education Management Systems Student Outcomes Information Services (NCHEMS/SOIS) and the American College Testing Program/Evaluation Survey Services (ACT/ESS). Not included in Ewell's listing is the family of survey instruments offered by Educational Testing Service (ETS) and Noel-Levitz. A description of those instruments useful in follow-up studies follows.

NCHEMS/SOIS

The National Center for Higher Education Management Systems Student Outcomes Information Services publishes a set of six questionnaires, in both two-year and four-year versions, designed for administration at various stages of students' college experiences and thereafter. The questionnaires gather demographic information and contain a set of common questions that allow for comparison of the various student survey populations. "The common set of questions include information about: background, personal goals and career aspirations, factors influencing choice of college, satisfaction with college experience, activities while in college, educational plans and accomplishments, and career choices and career successes."[11] Institutions may customize each questionnaire by adding up to fifteen additional questions that are specific to information desired. According to NCHEMS (2001) the six questionnaires and their purposes are as follows:

- Entering Students—where do students come from, where do students plan to go, what do they expect to accomplish before they leave?
- Continuing Students—what do student like and dislike, what are students' changing goals and ambitions, what progress do students feel they have made at the institution?
- Former Students—where are they now, why did they leave, do they have plans to return?
- Graduating Students—what do students think about their college experience, were students satisfied, what do students intend to do after they graduate, do students feel prepared to obtain the job of their choice, do students have plans to attend graduate school?
- Recent Alumni—what are students doing their first year after graduation, have students located the right job or graduate school, do students feel they were prepared?
- Long-Term Alumni—where are students three to five years down the road, do they perceive that their education was worth it, what are their present activities, commitments, and accomplishments?

Data processing and questionnaire analyses are available, as well as annual summaries of information from participant institutions.

American College Testing Program

The American College Testing Program Evaluation Survey Service (ACT/ESS) now offers sixteen survey instruments for use by colleges and universities. Each is an optical-scan instrument containing two or four pages of questions designed to permit a general evaluation of an institution's programs and services. Institutions have the option of designing up to thirty additional questions for inclusion in each survey. The American College Testing Program also offers a catalog of additional items from which institutions may select in lieu of writing their own questions. Since 1979, over six million ACT/ESS instruments have been administered at more than 1,000 institutions. This extensive use of these materials has made possible normative data for comparative studies as well as an opportunity for longitudinal studies within institutions. Among the surveys available from American College Testing Program, those of particular benefit for our purposes are reviewed below.[12]

The Alumni Survey. The Alumni Survey is useful in ascertaining the impact of the institution on its graduates, particularly after graduates have had some time away from the institution. Four-page surveys are available for two-year and four-year institutions and provide information in the following sections: background information—tailored to the two-year or four-year graduate; continuing education—providing extensive information on formal education since graduation or departure; college experiences—gauging the graduate's perception of the value and impact of his or her education in areas such as skills development and independent living; employment history—providing valuable information for alumni and placement offices, as well as for various academic programs planners; and additional questions, mailing addresses, and comments and suggestions—providing additional information that may be useful locally.

The Student Opinion Survey. With two-year and four-year forms, the Student Opinion Survey is used to examine the perception held by enrolled, continuing students of their college services and environment. The two-year form also includes items to explore the student's reasons for selecting the college and his or her overall impression of the school. Included are background information; use of and level of satisfaction with various campus services; level of satisfaction with the college environment in areas such as academics, admissions, rules and policies, facilities, registration, and general; and additional questions, comments, and suggestions.

The Survey of Academic Advising. The Survey of Academic Advising is used to obtain information regarding student impressions of academic advising services. The four-page form includes background information, advising information—including an evaluation of the academic advising system currently offered by the college and the period of time the student has been assigned to the current adviser; academic advising needs—in which the student identifies topics discussed with the adviser and expresses his or her level of satisfaction with the adviser's assistance; impressions of adviser—in which the student answers questions relating to the availability of the adviser and the level of the adviser's understanding and knowledge; additional advising information—frequency of meetings with adviser and the length of these meetings; and additional questions, comments, and suggestions.

The Survey of Current Activities and Plans. Designed for applicants to the institution who chose not to enroll, the Survey of Current Activities and Plans requests background information; impressions of the college; educational plans and activities; employment plans; and additional questions, comments, and suggestions.

The Withdrawing / Nonreturning Student Survey. The Withdrawing/Nonreturning Student Survey is produced in both a two-page and four-page format. In both, the student who chooses to leave college before completing a degree is asked to provide background information and to indicate reasons for leaving. These reasons are grouped in the following categories: personal (health, moving, marriage, social), academic (suspension, instructional quality, not challenged), institutional (scheduling problems, inadequate advising, programs or facilities), financial (availability of work or financial aid), and employment (conflict between work and school). Both forms also provide space for comments and suggestions. The long form, in addition, asks the student to rate his or her satisfaction with various institutional services and characteristics.

Alumni Outcomes Survey. This four-page survey assesses alumni's perceived outcomes related to programs and services offered by the college. Information requested includes background information; employment history and experiences; educational outcomes—alumni are asked to review a list of skills or abilities one might expect to develop while pursuing a postsecondary education and indicate the importance of each item and the impact their school experience has had; educational experiences—alumni are asked to indicate their satisfaction with an array of college programs and procedures; activities and organizations; and additional questions, comments, and suggestions.

College Student Needs Assessment Survey. The purpose of this survey is to help the institution identify personal and educational needs of enrolled students. Following background information, students are asked to provide information relating to career and life goals and educational and personal needs.

ACT offers a variety of flexible services, and institutions may elect to purchase one or more of the survey instruments or to contract for a full range of mailing, scoring, and reporting services.

Educational Testing Service

The Educational Testing Service (ETS) College and University Programs offer a different array of survey instruments focusing primarily on program planning and evaluation. Several elements of ETS offerings are pertinent to our topic and are described below.[13]

The Program Self-Assessment Service (PSAS). The PSAS consists of a set of questionnaires that addresses areas such as curriculum, program purposes, departmental procedures, faculty activity, student accomplishment, and the general environment for work and learning. The PSAS assumes that the perceptions and assessments of those most directly involved with any department or program can contribute to an improved quality and functioning of the area surveyed. Thus, the service offers three assessment questionnaires: for faculty, for students who major in the department or program, and for recent graduates of the program. Responses provide a profile of the targeted program or department and can assist in the program review process by identifying areas of strength and those that need attention.

The Graduate Program Self-Assessment Service (GPSAS). The GPSAS is the parent of the PSAS. GPSAS is cosponsored by the Graduate Record Examination Board and the Council of Graduate Schools in the United States. Instruments have been developed for both master's and doctoral-level programs and address the parallel constituent groups identified in the PSAS discussion, that is, students enrolled in the program, faculty, and recent graduates. Survey questions provide information on sixteen areas of program characteristics, including environment for learning, scholarly excellence, teaching quality, faculty concern for students, curriculum, departmental procedures, resources (such as library and laboratories), faculty work environment, student accomplishments, and others.

The Student Instructional Report (SIR). The SIR, a brief, objective questionnaire, helps instructors gain information about students' reactions to their courses and instruction, offering students the opportunity to comment anonymously. It covers six factors: course organization and planning, faculty-student interaction, communication, course difficulty and workload, textbooks and readings, and tests and/or examinations.

The SIR is not intended to replace regular student-faculty communication. It does, however, provide an additional means by which instructors may examine their teaching performance. Extensive comparative data are available through ETS based on SIR administration in the United States and Canada. The questionnaire can be obtained in Spanish and in a Canadian version in both French and English.

All of the ETS instruments offer space for optional local items, and, as with the ACT and NCHEMS, the services of basic data processing and reporting are available. Special services and professional assistance may be negotiated as well.

Noel-Levitz

With a vision to lead the charge for total enrollment effectiveness in higher education for two-year and four-year colleges and universities, Noel-Levitz was established in 1992. The company has consulted with over 1,600 colleges and universities throughout the United States and Canada and offers several products pertinent to our discussion. These are briefly outlined below.[14]

Student Satisfaction Inventory. From the data generated through this inventory, colleges and universities learn how satisfied their students are and what's important to them. This two-part instrument reveals what items should be considered most important on retention agendas and also what items are least important to students, therefore eliminating the mistake of directing funds to unimportant places. Data generated from this instrument may also be compared to national data.

Institutional Priorities Survey. This survey is to be used in conjunction with the Student Satisfaction Survey and is administered by institutions to faculty, administration, and staff members. The data generated allows institutions to confirm the correlation of students' perceptions with those of employees of the institution. The data may reveal common areas of interest and satisfaction.

Adult Learners Priorities Survey. This survey is specifically designed to determine educationally-related items most important to adult learners—twenty-five years of age or older. The satisfaction level of these learners is also determined and may be compared to national benchmark data.

Priorities Survey for On-Line Learners. The first commercially available survey to focus specifically on the needs and satisfaction levels of on-line learners, this survey instrument is currently being piloted.

Some selective combination of this wealth of instruments for measuring values, attitudes, and programmatic strengths and weaknesses can yield insightful data for the institution's efforts to ensure quality. The key word is "selective," for too much, too often, to the same people can be counterproductive and yield inaccurate or severely biased data. A careful selection of instruments includes those that will examine the various dimensions and standards established as important to the particular institution and its clients.

Inventories of Good Practice in Undergraduate Education

The Johnson Foundation[15] has published two documents designed to help institutions discern whether their undergraduate policies and practices match seven principles for good practice in undergraduate education. The two surveys include an institutional inventory and a faculty inventory. Built on the work of higher education scholars Arthur W. Chickering, Zerda F. Garrison, and Louis M. Barsi, seven good practices are advocated:

1. Good practice encourages student-faculty contact.
2. Good practice encourages cooperation among students.
3. Good practice encourages active learning.
4. Good practice gives prompt feedback.
5. Good practice emphasizes time on task.
6. Good practice communicates high expectations.
7. Good practice respects diverse talents and ways of learning.

Utilization of these introspective surveys on any campus will certainly demonstrate the "discovery" potential of a quest for quality. Having faculty complete the inventory is certain to generate a lively conversation on teaching responsibility and practice, and having students share their perspectives concerning the presence or absence of these good practices on our campuses should also furnish adequate stimulus to lead off a faculty development workshop.

Center for Postsecondary Research and Planning

Two other instruments that may prove useful for institutions interested in obtaining student feedback are the College Student Experiences Questionnaire (CSEQ) and the College Student Expectations Questionnaire (CSXQ). The CSEQ was authored by C. Robert Pace in 1990 at the Center for the Study of Evaluation at the University of California, Los Angeles, and the CSXQ was developed at the Center for Postsecondary Research and Planning at Indiana University. The CSXQ was adapted from the CSEQ.

The CSXQ website[16] states that the instrument is to be administered to new students upon their arrival to the campus. Administration time is approximately ten minutes. Results from the survey provide information to institutions on the following:

1. Estimates of nature and frequency with which students think they will interact with faculty members and peers
2. Estimates of how students expect to use facilities and other resources that institutions provide for their learning
3. Predicted satisfaction with college
4. Expected nature of college learning environments
5. Perceptions of students' views of classmates, diversity, and current world issues
6. Student background information
7. An assessment of the quality of the first year of college

The CSEQ[17] is an eight-page questionnaire that asks students information relating to their current school year—both inside and outside the classroom. Topics this questionnaire deals with include:

1. Background information about students and their status in college
2. An estimate of student engagement in reading, writing, and other learning activities
3. Student ratings of characteristics of the college environment associated with their learning
4. Estimates of student gains or progress toward important learning goals
5. An index of student satisfaction with college

CSEQ users include Florida State University, Pennsylvania State University, Stanford University, University of Chicago, Virginia Polytechnic Institute and

State University, Washington University, Indiana State University, and Middle Tennessee State University.

We have reviewed a number of commercially available instruments, many with analytical support and normative reference group data, features that make them particularly useful where personnel and support services are in short supply on campus. Providing the opportunity to include locally developed optional questions, these instruments may be tailored to the local environment.

Other Survey Options

Obviously, where special needs cannot be met through instruments such as those described above, two other options exist: contracted survey services or campus-developed surveys.

Contracted Services. Most management consultant services and marketing consultants are capable of developing and conducting surveys to determine perceptions about an institution's reputation, purposes, and programs. A number of agencies now market themselves primarily to the higher education community. There are several advantages in contracting for survey services. One is that the contract is usually for a turnkey process (that is, it includes tailoring the survey to the specific needs of the client, gathering and processing the data, and presenting and interpreting the results to the appropriate groups). Another advantage is that those surveyed may regard the contractual process more favorably because it is individualized and carries the identity of the contracting institution. Providing on-site consultants who may lend added credibility to the process and the findings through discussion with others is a third advantage.

We cite three disadvantages of contracted services. First, an institution can expect the contract cost to be significantly higher than that for commercial instruments that have already been developed for generalized use. Second, the resultant data will not have the benefits of comparability to normative or summary data from other institutions of the same level or type. And third, the time required for the full development of such services may be counterproductive.

These disadvantages can be negated, however, when the institution's needs are determined to be met best by a specially designed survey. Frequently, for example, institutions are interested in gleaning community perceptions of institutional performance, through telephone sampling or similar marketing techniques. Such services contracted by local sampling and marketing agencies can be quite successful and not unduly expensive. This approach should, in fact, be selected if (1) available commercial instruments do not meet the institution's identified need, (2) the expertise or labor force is not available in-house, or (3) the contracted arrangement can provide the data required in a cost-effective and timely manner.[18]

Campus-Developed Surveys. Locally developed survey instruments take time and expertise. However, many campuses will have individuals in their social science or education departments or in their offices of institutional research who have knowledge of the methodology necessary to develop these surveys. And, of course, their services are likely to be less expensive. H. R. Kells, in *Self-Study Processes,* reminds us that "a poorly designed instrument, used at the wrong moment with an unreceptive audience, will yield little or no useful information and it may damage the sense of community and morale at the institution involved."[19] On the other hand, recognizing and using local expertise to produce a well-developed survey and to provide prompt analysis and dissemination of results may be the most effective way to gain a sense of ownership for the entire assessment/evaluation process. For those who determine that locally developed surveys will serve them best, a look at the content of commercial surveys reviewed earlier in this section may give the developer a head start on the general areas to include.

Earlier in this chapter we pointed out other sources of follow-up information, using assessment tools and quantitative data generated primarily for other purposes. Thus, surveys are recommended to serve purposes that cannot be met by other existing data sources. There are obvious limitations and potential biases in survey data. Oversurveying a population is one way to guarantee biases and unreliability of responses. For example, surveying students at entry, as continuing students, and at exit would result in their responding to very similar questions in a one-to-two-year time span between surveys. Disregarding the "irritant factor" (the resentment at being asked repeatedly to respond), the purpose of this kind of follow-up is by nature longitudinal. Our most efficient measures of enrolled student growth and outcomes are within the classroom, through performance assessment, and by observation of various student interactions. In fact, if we must limit our activity, there is no more valuable measure of our institutions' successes over time than the views held by alumni.[20] If an institution must make a choice of commercial instruments, the alumni survey is probably the one to select.

An interesting quasi-commercial/locally developed alumni survey development approach was taken by the Tennessee Higher Education Commission,[21] when a group of survey specialists developed a survey and distributed it to all 1986 baccalaureate and associate graduates from Tennessee public institutions. This approach obviously had the advantage for the Commission of enabling comparisons among state institutions concerning alumni perceptions of institutional quality and program strengths and weaknesses. The Commission has continued this practice with its last survey going to over 1,600 graduates in the state.

Coordination of survey activity should be encouraged. The surveying institution should prevent the possibility of a graduate's receiving a request from the placement office, from the alumni office, from his or her academic department, and from institutional research all within a three- to five-year time period. These offices can send one survey at three- to five-year intervals and gain valuable information, which of course does not preclude other kinds of communication to maintain close touch with alumni. The more in touch we are, the better will be the response rate when alumni are surveyed.

The Decision Focus. Let us examine the experience of one campus in using the ACT alumni survey as but one example of the kind of information available, the limitations on its interpretation, and the applications to the planning and evaluation process. Louisiana State University in Shreveport (LSUS) graduated its first baccalaureate students in 1975. Ten years later, each graduate of its first five classes was surveyed using the ACT services for all mailing and contact. A response rate of about 42 percent yielded a sample of students from each class and all program areas.

The resulting data compilation provided information on job history, satisfaction with the degree, continuing education, and salary levels. A secondary benefit was the updating of alumni files with current employers and addresses. In addition, the survey asked alumni to rate the contribution of the institution to a number of needs, such as the development of writing skills, personal financial management, personal health maintenance, independent work habits, and use of the library. These ratings were compared to user norms to provide a picture of the rating of the university's programs and services by its alumni. This survey procedure has since been conducted additional times.

LSUS is a commuter campus serving both students in the eighteen to twenty age range and a somewhat older and more mature student population. Many of the students attending the university are already managing independent households. The low rating given to the goal of personal finance can be better understood in this context. While the university faculty had, at least until these results were reviewed, not regarded skill in managing personal finances as a high-priority goal for the general education component of the curriculum, it is entirely possible that their perspective might warrant reassessment. In the spirit of our previous discussion on the relationship between student perceptions of goal and performance, this finding presented the university faculty with an interesting question of educational goal and curriculum content. Should the practical business of equipping our students with some exposure to personal financial planning become a general education goal of the university?

Other, more pressing concerns were low ratings of satisfaction with degree choice by students who completed general studies degrees and the question of personal health maintenance. Alumni rated the university low in this area. Although national trends have focused on health concerns, a nonresident environment and a nontraditional population here complicate the effort. The point is that items from the survey have been analyzed and discussed in appropriate groups and have contributed to the total pool of information for campus decision making.

The survey used at LSUS offered the opportunity for alumni to write additional comments. These anecdotal comments recognize individual instructors or courses the graduate remembers, make an explanatory statement about a response item in the survey, state feelings about the university (positive or negative), and offer suggestions for new programs or revisions to old ones. All comments are routed to the appropriate individual or office and provide yet another, more personal, dimension to the follow-up studies.

South College, a private commuter college in Knoxville, Tennessee, surveys its alumni two years following graduation in order to obtain much the same follow-up information as LSUS. A summary of the information from all returned surveys is included in the college's annual Fact Book and evaluated by the appropriate departments. In addition, all college faculty or staff members have an opportunity to provide input regarding the data at the annual planning meeting. In 2001, information received from 1999 graduates led to the college implementing additional communication and follow-up measures from the placement office. Graduates communicated that though their job searches had proven largely successful, more assistance, communication, and follow-up were desired. Since the mission of the college is directly related to graduates' employability, this information was regarded as significant.

INTERVIEWS

The discussion thus far has centered on the application of paper-and-pencil instruments for obtaining data—with a particular focus on questionnaires. Perhaps the simplest and oldest means of acquiring feedback, however, is that of the interview. Although we do not intend this book as a handbook on evaluation and research methods, a word about the use of interviews as a tool for acquiring feedback from students and constituents is appropriate at this point.

Although the immediate advantages of questionnaire follow-up include the merit of surveying larger populations at lower cost, the disadvantage is that communication meaning conveyed in more personal settings is lost and the opportunity to pursue unanticipated threads of thought is unavailable. Interviews can be structured, and thus parallel the application of questionnaires, or unstructured. Interviews can be used to take advantage of "critical incident" types of data. An institution might choose to evaluate its registration services by sampling students who completed the registration process and asking them to describe the most effective and satisfying dimension of the registration process, and then asking them to contrast the first response by describing the most dissatisfying and most in-need-of-improvement aspect.

Panel interviews in focus-group settings can take advantage of the response freedom and flexibility afforded in interview settings, the economics of having access to the ideas of several respondents at the same time, and the ideological multiplier effect when the ideas of one respondent stimulate thought in another.

However, disadvantages also exist. There is always the danger of one or more respondents dominating the session, as well as of "groupthink," as members of the group yield their reflective independence to a group mood or momentum. In addition, there are limits in the potential to explore the background of the respondents.

Nevertheless, focus-group settings can be an effective tool for acquiring evaluative feedback from our students and other constituent groups. For example, an institution interested in evaluating and renewing its general education requirements may want to conduct group interviews with different constituent groups, such as alumni, currently enrolled sophomores or seniors, and perhaps a sample of community representatives. One of the advantages of focus-group interviews is that they can also test new concepts. A college thinking of implementing a new general education requirement may choose a focus group to test the merit of the proposal, for example. A research university graduate department desiring to evaluate its doctoral program may elect to conduct group interviews with clusters of recent graduates.

Another example of a study employing focus groups is one completed by Andrew Johnston.[22] He completed a dissertation study at a religiously affiliated private college in which he sought to determine how students at the college perceived the institution's faith commitment. In catalogs and other formal institutional documents, many American private colleges will espouse their commitment to a particular religious heritage. For many American colleges that would include a Christian heritage, often with a particular denomination accent (Baptist, Methodist, Presbyterian, etc.).

But how is that faith commitment communicated to students? In this focus-group study, students indicated that they perceived evidence of faith commitment in the caring behavior of faculty, in the open and friendly disposition of the campus, and in certain campus regulations and policies. They just as clearly perceived another important challenge in a college with religious heritage. Presumably all colleges exist to search for and transmit truth. However, for any particular religious belief system, certain questions and topics might be considered "off limits," with faculty less willing to discuss them in formal classroom settings than in private conversations for fear of sanction.

In this study, focus groups proved to be a lively and informing instrument for harvesting student perceptions about an important dimension of campus life.

INFORMAL FOLLOW-UP PROCEDURES

Most of us who have been involved for many years in colleges and universities have experienced the special pleasure of hearing from students who have long since left our classrooms. Their informal anecdotes, like those in the alumni survey, provide another follow-up dimension. The anecdotes, by their nature, tend to be positive, and they often provide insight into the best that our institutions have to offer.

- A former student was working as a clerk in a local supermarket some ten years after she had sat in a professor's English classroom. As she checked the professor's groceries, she began reciting Chaucer's prologue to *The Canterbury Tales.*
- Another student who had been in a writing class was working as a mechanic. He told of the short stories he often wrote in the evenings "for the fun of it."
- An independent businessman successfully completing his first year of operation gave credit to a support service of an institution's business school—a small business development center that had provided the businessman with assistance in setting up his business following guidelines of good management practice.
- An M.Ed. program graduate had recently been appointed to a principalship when she wrote to thank several of her professors for the knowledge gained in their courses that had prepared her for her new role.
- A business program graduate gave credit to his institution for giving him the courage to begin what is now generating annual revenue of over several million dollars.

But, of course, we do occasionally hear complaints.

- A student who had graduated from an honors program at a large research university was having difficulty in her legal research and writing course as a first-year law student. She blamed her honors program. That program (not surprisingly) had bypassed the usual freshman composition courses where college students often hone the basic skills of writing and term paper techniques.
- A first-year teacher who was struggling to maintain order in her inner-city classroom discounted her "ideal" student-teaching experience in a magnet school that had selective admission criteria.
- An allied health graduate was having trouble securing permanent employment and blamed the placement service of her institution for not finding her that desired position.

When a new chancellor first came to the city, he noted that everywhere he went, ordinary citizens told him of some experience with his university: a downtown businessman who had taken a computer class to learn a new skill, the wife of a wealthy oilman who returned to college and earned a degree after many years (and then gave back to the school as she had gained), an employer who indicated he always hired graduates from that university first, and individuals who praised first one and then another member of the faculty. Such feedback leaves us with a pleasant glow about our institutions and also serves as a legitimate method of follow-up if the feedback is routed to the appropriate office—recorded, compiled, and used to effect continuation or change in programs or procedures. "While relatively less valid and reliable than objective data, subjective data do usefully portray the state of that world of people, human values, preferences, aspirations, and interpersonal dynamics that the ... decision-maker ignores at his own peril."[23]

This accent on informal and quiet approaches to the acquisition of perception and performance data prompts the recollection of beautiful dialogue from Elspeth Huxley's *The Flame Trees of Thika.* In the closing pages, Lettice remarks that "the best way to find things out is not to ask questions at all. If you fire off a question, it is like firing off a gun; bang it goes, and everything takes flight and runs for shelter. But if you sit quite still and pretend not to be looking, all the little facts will come and peck round your feet, situations will venture forth from thickets and intentions will creep out and sun themselves on a stone; and if you are very patient, you will see and understand a great deal more than a man with a gun."[24]

What a marvelous thought and what a wonderful complement to the more formal approaches described in this chapter. With questionnaire and interview guide in hand, we may indeed be poised to learn something about institutional and program performance from those who know that performance most directly and intimately. Perhaps, however, our questionnaire and interview studies may so disturb the organization that we will have the social equivalence of the Heisenberg uncertainty principle in physics. When the optical scanner is turned off and the institutional research office is closed, when we are not on collegiate safari hunting for client responses, and when we are in quieter and more relaxed repose, perhaps even in those moments we can learn about our colleges and universities if we are receptive.

FOLLOW-UP: IN UNITS OF ONE

In these concluding thoughts on the merit of follow-up studies is a timely place to remember the theme of Jan Carlzon's book *Moments of Truth.*[25] Customers and clients, Carlzon reminds us, will remember less the sophistication of our equipment, the health of our financial ratios, and the attractiveness of our annual reports than the quality of personal contact with members of our organization.

Think of the thousands of contacts between a college or university and its students: in our classrooms and laboratories, in our registrar and placement offices, in our cafeterias and residence halls, in our bookstores and our deans' offices. Each of these contacts is a "moment of truth." We have only to search our own memories to establish the validity of Carlzon's observation. Which is carved most deeply into our memory—our feelings about the equipment we used or our gratitude for those faculty and staff members who challenged our aspirations and our talent through the quality of their caring?

The qualitative impact of colleges and universities is delivered in units of one, and our students are the only ones who can see the university from the client perspective. Formal and informal approaches to follow-up studies are a quality assurance instrument of mutual benefit. Listening to our students, to our graduates, and to our community is a learning exercise that sets a good model for each of these three constituents. And the feedback we obtain from these follow-up studies can make us stretch to our intellectual and emotional heights, encouraging a college and university to continue education about itself, a discovery exercise with constructive potential.

NOTES

1. Spaeth, J., and Greeley, A. (1970). *Recent Alumni and Higher Education: A Survey of College Graduates.* New York: McGraw Hill.
2. Townsend, R. (1970). *Up the Organization.* New York: Knopf.
3. Spaeth and Greeley, *Recent Alumni and Higher Education.*
4. Ibid.
5. Frankl, V. (1959). *Man's Search for Meaning.* Boston: Beacon Press.
6. Spaeth and Greeley, *Recent Alumni and Higher Education.*
7. Astin, A. (1977). *Four Critical Years: Effects of College on Beliefs, Attitudes, and Knowledge.* San Francisco: Jossey-Bass.
8. Stevenson, M., Walleri, D., and Japely, S. (1985). "Designing Follow-up Studies of Graduates and Former Students." In Ewell, P. T. Ewell (ed.). Assessing Education Outcomes [Special issue]. *New Directions for Institutional Research,* No. 47.
9. Bridger, G. (1989). "Attitudinal Surveys in Institutional Effectiveness." In *Institutional Effectiveness and Outcomes Assessment Implementation on Campus: A Practitioner's Handbook,* ed. J. Nichols. New York: Agathon Press.
10. Ewell, P. (1983). *Information on Student Outcomes: How to Get It and How to Use It.* A National Center for Higher Education Management Systems Executive Overview. Boulder, CO: National Center for Higher Education Management Systems.
11. National Center for Higher Education Management Systems. (2001). Available on-line: http://www.nchems.org/surveys/sois.htm.
12. American College Testing. (2001). *Assessing Attitudes and Opinions of Students and Alumni. Evaluation Survey Services 2001–2002.*
13. Educational Testing Service. (2001). Available on-line: http://www.ets.org.
14. Noel-Levitz. (2001). Available on-line: http://www.noellevitz.com.
15. Johnson Foundation. (1989). *7 Principles for Good Practice in Undergraduate Education.* Racine, WI: Johnson Foundation.
16. College Student Experiences Questionnaire Research Project. (2001). Available on-line: http://www.indiana.edu/~cseq/overview.html.
17. Ibid.
18. Bridger, Attitudinal Surveys in Institutional Effectiveness.
19. Kells, H. (1980). *Self-Study Processes: A Guide for Postsecondary Institutions.* Washington, DC: American Council on Education.
20. Marcus, L, Leone, A., and Goldberg, E. (1983). *The Path to Excellence: Quality Assurance in Higher Education.* ASHE-ERIC/Higher Education Research Report No. 1, Washington, DC: Association for the Study of Higher Education.
21. Tennessee Higher Education Commission. (1987). Alumni survey. Nashville, Tennessee.

22. Johnston, A. (2002). *How Students at a Christian University Understand the Institution's Faith Commitment.* Unpublished doctoral dissertation, University of Tennessee, Knoxville.

23. Jones, D. (1982). *Data and Information for Executive Decisions in Higher Education.* National Center for Higher Education Management Systems Executive Overview. Boulder, CO: National Center for Higher Education Management Systems.

24. Huxley, E. (1959). *The Flame Trees of Thika.* London: Chatto and Windus.

25. Carlzon, J. (1987). *Moments of Truth.* Cambridge, MA: Ballinger.

Chapter 5

Licensure

The Test of Professional Standards

Licensure is a form of quality assurance that may go relatively unnoticed as a means for colleges and universities to evaluate program quality. In many professions the only route to practice is by completing a college or university preparation program. When students are assisted in this rite of passage and find that their preparation program has enabled them to attain licensure easily, they may assign their success to the "quality" of their preparation program.

Thus, institutions whose accounting, nursing, law, engineering, teacher education, and medical graduates consistently score well on licensure and certification examinations may tout these performance scores as evidence of program quality. There are some obvious dangers here, however. In one state, for example, the supply of lawyers led to a severe tightening of standards on the state bar examination. Thus, law schools that may have found their bar examination performance satisfactory in one year might discover that the same level of performance would prove unsatisfactory in a following year. What can be said, then, about the quality of professional preparation programs under conditions of shifting standards?

This chapter defines and describes licensure as an instrument of quality assurance. The chapter also relates licensure to accreditation because, as we noted in chapter 2, the two are interwoven in several fields—with the result that neither licensure nor accreditation can be employed separately as an indicator of quality. The licensure process for four professional fields is described: law, medicine, nursing, and teacher education. The accrediting process for these same four fields was outlined in chapter 2. A concluding discussion engages some of the problems and issues associated with licensure.

THE CONCEPT AND VALUE OF LICENSURE

Webster's *Ninth New Collegiate Dictionary*[1] tells us that a license is "a permission granted by competent authority to engage in a business or occupation or in an activity otherwise unlawful." Licensure is, according to the same source, the "granting of licenses especially to practice a profession." The term "licensing" is used increasingly to describe the process or procedure by which one becomes licensed and is often used interchangeably with licensure. The word "credentialing" is also often used interchangeably with licensing, but such use strains the standard definition of licensing.

Discussion about licensure is further complicated by the use of "certification" as a synonym, such as in the granting of a certificate to teach. The word "certificate" is legitimate, however; Webster's *Ninth New Collegiate Dictionary*[2] defines it as "a document certifying that one has fulfilled the requirements of and may practice in a field." Remember, however, that both "license" and "certificate" have accepted meanings not within the context or the purpose of this chapter. All certificates do not carry the right to practice. In the case of the national certificate granted by the National Board for Professional Teaching Standards, as a current example, it is not anticipated (for the foreseeable future) that the certificate will have a licensure function. Indeed, recipients will have already been licensed by their respective states, typically through a department of education acting on behalf of a state board of education.[3] A license to operate a motor vehicle or to fish or hunt, for example, is a use of the word that is not pertinent to our treatment of licensure.

Young's definition of licensure is helpful: "Licensure is a process by which an agency of government grants permission (1) to persons meeting predetermined qualifications to engage in a given occupation and/or use a particular title and (2) to institutions to perform a specified function."[4] But his definition of certification as "a process by which a non-governmental organization grants recognition to a person who has met certain predetermined qualifications specified by that organization"[5] fails to take into account that state governments (specifically state boards of education) grant certificates to teachers.[6]

In any event, in this chapter we use "license" to describe the authority one is granted to practice a profession, and "licensure" describes the process or procedure one goes through to attain the authority. "Certification" will have two meanings: (1) a process by which one is granted the right to practice, just as in licensure, and (2) a process by which a person has met prescribed requirements to hold a position or title or to engage in a specified practice after licensure has been attained.

Licensure has several purposes that serve the public interest. Chief among them is reasonable assurance that a licensee has fulfilled requirements set forth by experts in a particular field, usually functioning in behalf of the state, that are considered essential for safe entry into that field. The process, therefore, is designed to prevent incompetents and charlatans from practicing.

A second useful purpose of licensure is the identification and publication of the knowledge and skills deemed by expert practitioners and teachers to be necessary for good performance. This enables schools and colleges to prepare students for the profession more effectively and efficiently. Admission requirements, instructional programs, and exit requirements can be established and maintained with greater confidence and effectiveness than would be the case if licensure was not involved.

A third benefit is the opportunity provided licensed professionals to use their own training and experience in devising requirements for initial licensure, and to revise and upgrade the curriculum as the profession grows in knowledge and maturity and as new discoveries and inventions place new responsibilities on the professional. The knowledge base underlying licensure in medicine, for example, is very different today from what it was at the turn of the century or, for that matter, just a decade ago.

Assisting in regulating, policing, and promoting professions is a fourth way that licensure serves the public interest. In addition to controlling entry, licensure is almost always accompanied by stated conditions that will result in revocation of the license and, thus, the right to practice. Several professions require additional study beyond initial preparation and licensure, as well as other ways of maintaining proficiency. Maintaining a license requires approval by both internal and external publics. A doctor's associates or patients, for example, may submit charges that, if proven, can result in license revocation. Similarly, malpractice complaints and suits may produce sufficient evidence to cause the appropriate body or agency to move for the accused's license to be revoked.

Several professions are not sufficiently well developed in terms of "accepted best practice" to permit the litigation of malpractice complaints. But several are. Medicine and law are considered so well developed that even the lay public (jurors in malpractice suits) is permitted to render judgments—albeit after expert opinion has been given.

A fifth benefit to society, and the one most germane to this chapter, is the use of licensure as a form of quality assurance. This benefit has at least two dimensions. First, prescribed licensure requirements virtually require colleges and universities to keep their respective curricula closely attuned to the requisite knowledge and competencies. Preparation programs can exceed but not fall below licensure prescriptions. To do otherwise would be institutional suicide, for no institution can long survive without a reasonably high proportion of its graduates meeting professional licensure requirements and, thus, becoming licensed to practice. The public rightfully expects institutions they support to ensure that students aspiring to practice in a profession are able to do so; and the public has the right to believe, with reasonable confidence, that satisfactory completion of an institution's approved program will result in the authority to practice.

With this background, we believe the reader will gain deeper insight from the following descriptions of how the concept of licensing works in four professional fields: law, medicine, nursing, and teacher education. In the case of teacher education, a somewhat fuller treatment is made of licensure for three reasons. First, teaching is the largest of all professions and one in which the public has a great stake. Second, the reform of education is a high national priority and teacher preparation and licensure are at the core of many reform efforts. Third, unlike the other three fields described, licensure for teachers is in a state of flux with several new directions and concepts emerging.

LICENSURE IN THE FIELD OF LAW

Unlike medicine, law does not issue a national license to its practitioners. Rather, lawyers are licensed to practice in one or more of the fifty states. States may, and do, require different levels of competence in their bar examinations. Licensure that results from passing a particular state's bar examination does not carry with it the right to appear in court, which requires additional licenses or "permits." Moreover, in the United States there are two judicial systems, state and federal; a separate permit is required before a lawyer can appear in either of the systems. The United States Court of Appeals and the Supreme Court also require separate permits. Thus licensure in law is jurisdiction and system specific.[7]

A license to practice law usually requires the holder to have graduated from an accredited law school and to have passed a state bar examination, as stated in chapter 2. This linkage between accreditation and licensure, in our opinion, strengthens both the accreditation principle and the legal profession. A negative consequence is that the linkage effectively removes accreditation from its voluntary status—a condition some accreditation leaders view as detrimental to accreditation, also noted in chapter 2.

According to the Legal Information Institute,[8] the general requirements for admission to the bar in the fifty states are similar. Following graduation from an accredited law school, applicants must show that they are of good moral character and that they are a resident or employee of the state. There are generally two parts of state bar examinations. The Multi-State Bar Examination, developed by the National Conference of Bar Examiners, is used in virtually all states and often takes up the first day of the state bar examination. This first part tests applicants' knowledge of basic areas of the law. The second day is usually given to tests developed by the respective state board and focuses on individual state laws. States have the right to establish their own cutoff scores, resulting in variability among the states. Some states do require a third part of the exam, the Multi-State Professional Responsibility Exam. This part tests knowledge of professional ethics.

Because of the requirement for passing the bar examination before practicing law in any state—with passing standards set by the state—one can see that law schools alone are not able to independently establish their own training curriculum and must set admission and exit requirements that choose and graduate candidates most likely to succeed in passing the bar examinations. As the unevenness of legal training received under the "reading law" tradition attracted increasing criticism, responsibility for supervising the academic education of would-be lawyers gradually became the jurisdiction of colleges and universities, most of which established law schools for that purpose. The "bench and bar" were unwilling to relinquish total jurisdiction, however, and ultimately devised the system that allows the practicing bar to retain considerable control over the education of persons who aspire to join them in the practice of law.[9] Again, this circumstance is a double-edged sword: Institutions often chafe at not having full control of their curricula, admission, retention, and exit requirements; but considerable benefits accrue when their graduates achieve approval from the profession in the form of passing the bar and being permitted to practice.

LICENSURE OF MEDICAL DOCTORS

Unlike licensure for lawyers, licensure for doctors is national in scope and function. The ability to move from one state to another and to be licensed in those states without having to be reexamined was a strongly felt motivation of medical leaders when the National Board of Medical Examiners was established in 1915. The policy of reciprocity has remained to this day, though each medical licensing authority has the right to set its own rules and regulations regarding licensure.

Until 1994, an alternative licensure route open to graduates of medical schools was the examination developed by the Federation of State Medical Boards. A substantial number of medical schools used the examination (commonly called FLEX) as an internal evaluation of students, but students electing the FLEX licensure option were not eligible to take the examination until after graduation. Most students found that taking the national board examination (the National Board of Medical Examiners) was the more functional route to licensure because it could be taken during the course of their medical education. Passing scores were set at the national level with little concern for "manpower" needs.[10]

In 1991, the United States Medical Licensing Examination was established and phased into use from 1992–94. This single uniform examination is sponsored by both the Federation of State Medical Boards of the United States and the National Board of Medical Examiners. The results of this examination are reported to state medical boards in the Unites States and its territories for use in granting the initial license to practice medicine. The examination consists of three parts and is prepared by examination committees composed of prominent medical educators and clinicians.[11]

Although national board certification (licensure) rests heavily on the examination, there are additional requirements. To be eligible for Steps 1 and 2 of the examination, candidates must be in one of the following categories at the time of the application and on the date of the test:

- A medical student officially enrolled in, or a graduate of, a U.S., Puerto Rican, or Canadian medical school program leading to the M.D. degree that is accredited by the Liaison Committee on Medical Education (LCME)
- A medical student officially enrolled in, or a graduate of, a U.S. medical school that is accredited by the American Osteopathic Association (AOA)
- A medical student officially enrolled in, or a graduate of, a medical school outside of the United States, Puerto Rico, and Canada and eligible for examination by the Educational Commission for Foreign Medical Graduates (ECFMG) for its certificate[12]

To be eligible for Step 3 of the examination, applicants must meet the following requirements prior to submitting their application:

- Meet the Step 3 requirements set by the medical licensing authority to which the application is made
- Obtain the M.D. degree (or its equivalent) or the D.O. degree
- Obtain passing scores in Step 1 and Step 2, and
- Obtain certification by the ECFMG or successfully complete a "Fifth Pathway" program if a graduate of a medical school outside the United States, Puerto Rico, and Canada[13]

The United States Medical Licensing Examination recommends to licensing authorities that Step 3 eligibility not be granted until the completion, or near completion, of at least one postgraduate training year in a program of graduate medical education accredited by the Accreditation Council for Graduate Medical Education (ACGME) or the AOA.[14]

The licensure mechanism for medical doctors is long standing, intricately designed, and powerful. The control of licensure by the profession and the close linkage between accreditation and licensure is unequaled by other professions; the states have effectively delegated their licensing powers to the several medical boards vis-à-vis accreditation and licensure. Medical schools whose graduates attain licensure, as most of them do,[15] have little problem convincing their constituencies that their programs are of high quality, especially since quality is both defined and measured by the medical profession itself.

LICENSURE OF NURSES

In nursing, licensure and certification are not used synonymously. In this field, a license is required to practice. Certification is not a precondition for practice and is, in fact, usually granted only after several years of practice. Certification is given in several levels and types—such as nurse generalist, nurse practitioner, and clinical specialist.

Licensure in nursing is the responsibility of the National Council of State Boards of Nursing (NCSBN), a national standards board comprised of executives of the respective state boards. This council recommends standards for licensure and sets standards for the national licensure examination, although licensure itself is awarded by the state agencies.[16]

As with doctors and lawyers, testing plays an important role in the licensure of nurses. A national examination for licensure is required by each state; the results then are used by each state board. The examination is prepared by NCSBN, which also sets cutoff scores. There is no separate or additional licensure examination beyond the national examination. Applicants for a nursing license must have completed an accredited preparation program. It is noted that licensure may be received after the completion of a variety of program levels—diploma, associate's degree, bachelor's degree, and so on. Accreditation procedures were described in chapter 2.

As noted above, nursing utilizes the concept of certification as an extension of licensure, not unlike the way in which doctors can become certified in certain specialty areas in addition to their generic license. The structure for certification is more decentralized and fragmented; in addition to the American Nursing Association, several other nursing organizations certify nurses in one or more specialty areas. No national standards board exists for certification examinations. Thus, in nursing, certification is used not as a license but, rather, as a professional recognition tool and as a factor in hiring and promotion decisions, often enhancing job mobility.[17]

LICENSURE OF TEACHERS

In education, the distinctions between certification and licensure are blurred. Concerning the authority to practice, the terms were virtually synonymous until recently, but distinctions are developing; certificates as extensions of licenses are beginning to appear on the scene. The National Board of Professional Teacher Standards, mentioned earlier, has developed a national certificate for persons already licensed.

Historically, most states have used the term "certificate" to mean license, or, at least, persons have been authorized to teach on the basis of a state-awarded certificate. Use of the term "license" has increased in recent years, however, both formally and informally. Tennessee, for example, systematically changed its certification procedures and requirements in 1988 as a result of the career ladder program. "This program was a state-wide effort to recognize excellent teaching, create incentives for teacher growth, create career stages, and to utilize excellent teachers in new roles such as staff development leaders and new teacher mentor."[18] In the process, the word "license" was used where the word "certificate" was formerly used; a certification system was created for teachers electing the career ladder certificate option and meeting its requirements.[19] In this section, we use both terms interchangeably except when noted, since both mean the process by which a person is granted the authority to teach or otherwise serve an educational role in schools K–12 for which a certificate or license is required.

No national licensure mechanism exists for teachers; consequently, there is no national standards board for licensure. National accreditation exists through the National Council for Accreditation of Teacher Education (NCATE), but accreditation of a program by NCATE is not a prerequisite and does not lead to national licensure for graduates of an accredited program. Moreover, only about one-half of the country's schools, colleges, or departments of education have NCATE approval. Only three states, Arkansas, West Virginia, and North Carolina, require graduation from an NCATE-accredited program as a precondition for state certification. Thus, licensure in teacher education is altogether a function of the states. Indeed, in earlier years several large systems—Chicago, for example—trained and certified their own teachers. That practice continued until quite recently but is now extinct.[20]

The typical state mechanism for handling teacher licensure is for control to be vested in the state board of education; the state department of education is assigned responsibility for implementing policies, rules, and regulations previously developed or approved by the board. Certification advisory committees have become commonplace as a means for teacher educators, school leaders, and school practitioners to have a voice in recommending policies, rules, and regulations, as well as curriculum content. National teacher education organizations have also been established.[21]

The education reform movement of the 1980s edged states a little closer to a national testing system for teachers—a licensure device currently used in medicine, law, and nursing. Rampant criticism of teachers and of schools of education provoked several legislatures to mandate testing programs for teachers. In 1980, only ten states required some form of standardized, norm-referenced testing as a condition of certification. Currently, forty-four states require some kind of standardized, norm-referenced test as a condition of certification. States not requiring testing include Idaho, Iowa, North Dakota, South Dakota, Utah, Vermont, and Washington. The National Teacher Examination was the most commonly used. The successor to this exam is the Praxis Series Tests. These tests were "developed to provide a system of thorough, fair, and carefully validated tests and assessment for states to use as part of this teacher licensure process."[22] These tests are designed to measure general and specific academic skills, knowledge in the subject or discipline planned to teach, and pedagogical knowledge.[23] Only twenty-nine states also require testing in the subject area in which teachers plan to teach.[24] Cutoff scores vary greatly among states, however, and unlike the situation alluded to earlier in medicine, cutoff scores and personnel needs do seem to be positively correlated.

A promising movement in the certificate/licensure arena in teacher education is the work of the National Board of Professional Teaching Standards, alluded to earlier. The efforts of this board, sponsored and initially funded by the Carnegie Corporation, could potentially be the forerunner of a national standards board that influences and possibly controls licensure. We say this could be possible because the board is currently focusing on the voluntary certification of experienced teachers in accordance with "high and rigorous standards ... calibrated to an advanced level of teaching proficiency, contrasting again with minimal, entry level state licensing standards."[25] However, this organization's plan to develop "high and rigorous standards for what teachers should know and be able to do" and to establish "an assessment system to determine when candidates meet these standards"[26] looks very similar to the work of national standards boards in legal and medical education early in this century.

Support for this eventuality can be inferred from comments made by Jordan[27] on the emergence of voluntary national certification: "Even though voluntary national certification standards may appear to be nonthreatening, how long can credible and well-publicized 'voluntary' standards remain voluntary?" Although Jordan was pondering the impact on state and local school boards, the possibility also exists relative to national standards being developed along the lines found in medicine and nursing.

The growing belief among state legislators and other policymakers that teachers should be licensed only after passing a standardized, norm-referenced test, as mentioned above, is yet another movement that could propel teaching and teacher education toward a more tightly controlled and more prescriptive licensure and program approval system. Several states that require teacher candidates to pass a standardized examination (in pedagogy, teaching field content, and basic skills) have legislated ways to hold schools of education accountable for their students' failure rates. The typical arrangement is to put schools of education on notice when less than 70 to 75 percent of their graduates in a given year attain a designated cutoff score. Failure to correct the condition in a specified number of years, usually three or four, results in disapproval of a school's program by the state and thus in their graduates' ineligibility for state licensure. The movement has been vigorously opposed by many teacher educators, among others, who cite the movement as being unfair, racially motivated, and without precedent in other fields of professional licensure.

It is not our intention to argue the merits or demerits of the movement but, rather, to cite it as yet another "straw in the wind" that seems to be blowing toward a more rigorous and demanding system of preparation, accreditation, and licensure. The reader may know that when the medical profession used the famous Flexner report and subsequent grants from Carnegie and Rockefeller to upgrade medical education, three openly avowed intentions were the use of the medical school at Johns Hopkins as a prototype, the replication of that model throughout the country, and the elimination of inadequate schools of medicine.

Summarizing the situation in teacher licensure, the authority to license practitioners remains largely in the hands of state authorities. There has been increasing input from the teaching profession but only modest relegation of authority to professional bodies. Indeed, during the reform decade of the 1980s state agencies tended to increase their authority, elevating standards and requirements for licensure in accordance with their own conceptions of needed corrective action. Many of the state initiatives have been met with strong opposition from the profession, an anomalous circumstance when one remembers that the stronger professions themselves elevated standards for both preparation and licensure. Once the standards were visibly and credibly high, states were willing to relegate much of their licensing authority to the respective professions. Both teacher educators and the broader profession might profit from an objective reading of the professionalization of legal education, medical education, nursing education—and others—vis-à-vis the development of standards for both accreditation and licensure.

PROBLEMS AND ISSUES

As with accreditation, and as noted in chapter 2, licensure is not without its problems or its critics. Even the several ways licensure was described as serving the public interest are not without dispute. What follows are several of the criticisms frequently voiced, along with some of the problems and issues being addressed.

Licensure is Self-Serving

This liability was also mentioned as a liability of accreditation in chapter 2, and the rationale is similar: Professional groups use the process of licensure to promote their own interests. In the case of medicine, for example, there is widespread belief that licensure is used purely and simply to control the number of persons entering the profession, that this is done to maintain a shortage of doctors, and that both the number of patients and the fees charged are intended functions of that controlled entry.

Other charges of self-service have been made, such as the one that teacher certification is essentially a monopolistic control mechanism by schools of education that prevents many qualified persons (such as graduates of arts and sciences colleges) from being professionally licensed. The degree to which colleges and universities influence, if not dictate, the requirements of licensure in several fields and the requirement of having to complete an institutional program as a precondition of licensure are often cited as additional evidence that it is self-serving.

In making this criticism, critics put the professions in a difficult position. The public is protected when licensure requirements have an expert professional opinion base, and when respected and successful practitioners have a strong voice in helping assure that both preparation programs and licensure requirements are closely attuned to competencies and skills needed for effective performance. Yet professionals exercising these judgments are sometimes suspect, viewed as pursuing selfish interests rather than protecting the public. Without the contributions from the organized professionals, however, licensure would be much more precarious and less likely to achieve its purpose.

Licensure Does Not Prevent Incompetents from Practicing

Friedman[28] contended almost four decades ago that there is no persuasive evidence that licensure does in fact sort out the competent from the incompetent. Similar allegations of more recent origins are seen from time to time.

Frequently, the evidence cited to support this criticism lacks credibility; like beauty, competence often is in the eye of the beholder. Some are quick to judge doctors, lawyers, nurses, and teachers as incompetent and unworthy of the license bestowed upon them. Sometimes our bases for the accusations are valid and provable; more often they are not. Although every profession has some prescribed way for revoking licenses, it is still rather rare for a professional license to be revoked.

Malpractice suits, especially those in medicine, attract a great deal of attention, particularly when the size of the award is great. The publicity and notoriety surrounding these cases tend to mislead the general public into believing that malpractice suits are commonplace, but, despite their increase in recent years, only a very small percentage of patient-professional relationships reach litigation, and the situation is similar in other professions.

Licensure Excludes Many Competent and Deserving Persons

This criticism is related to the accusation of being self-serving but includes also the belief that licensure requirements are not always wise and just. As noted above, many persons believe that the pedagogical requirement built into teacher licensure is unnecessary, even harmful, in the sense that it precludes the entry into teaching by arts and science graduates who have adequate preparation. For a contrasting view of the knowledge base of teaching, see Bogue's comments in "A Need to Know."[29] Bar examinations and those in the several subfields of medicine and health care are not immune from this type of criticism, despite their having been developed by knowledgeable and highly experienced professionals.

The accusation that licensure requirements are not always job related is a relatively new dimension of this criticism and one with a strong social implication. This criticism asserts that (1) blacks and other minorities are disadvantaged in their efforts to pass licensure examinations because of unequal education backgrounds and differences in their cultural backgrounds, and (2) portions of the examination that pose difficulty for these groups are not job related, that is, not essential for effective performance. Considerable litigation has taken place in this arena, the watershed case being *Griggs* v. *Duke Power Company* in 1971,[30] which directed that examination and other entry-level requirements must be job related.

Licensure Mitigates the Voluntary Nature of Accreditation

In several professions, strong linkage exists between accreditation and licensure, as noted in chapter 2. We cited some advantages of the linkage and suggested that it is a necessary condition for a strong, mature profession. Teaching, for example, was described as not fully developed as a profession, in part because of the absence of a linkage between national accreditation and state licensure (certification).

But that is one edge of the proverbial double-edged sword. The other edge is that from the perspective of institutions, accreditation loses its voluntary nature when certain of their graduates cannot be licensed without having first completed an accredited preparation program. Simply put, institutions cannot afford for their professional programs to be unaccredited and, consequently, must sometimes abide by terms and conditions imposed by others that they would not agree to otherwise.[31] In this country, accreditation was conceived as voluntary and some of its leaders contend that its great benefits will cease if it does not remain so. There is mixed opinion on whether accreditation's voluntary status is threatened by the federal government's requirement that accreditation be a condition of eligibility for federal funds.

Disturbing Contradictions between Licensure and the Actions of Policymakers

Sykes[32] contends that the "three functions of licensure systems—creating supply, constructing categories of competence, and inventing conceptions of quality—are difficult to reconcile." Using teaching to make his point, Sykes notes that several actions by policymakers in the various states appear "simultaneously to tighten and loosen the connection between qualifications and assignments in teaching, and to raise and lower entry standards."[33] Among the actions cited by Sykes are (1) administration of both entry tests and performance evaluation during the initial year of teaching, (2) enactment of alternative certification programs that usually relax professional education and other requirements, (3) issuance of substandard certificates permitting unqualified individuals to teach, and (4) assignment of teachers to classes outside areas of competence (to affect the number of available practitioners).

LICENSURE: SERVING PUBLIC AND ACADEMIC INTERESTS

Licensure systems have become rather commonplace in American society, with a large number of occupations and professions regulated and/or controlled by state agencies, and there are no signs of reduction. Indeed, the concept of licensure as a means of protecting the general public seems to be more firmly entrenched than ever, a continuing stream of criticism and dissatisfaction notwithstanding. Institutions of higher learning are inextricably involved in licensure, whether they like it or not and whether or not their best interests are always served.

This chapter has been concerned with the licensure of professionals, the method by which persons aspiring to practice in a certain field of endeavor become authorized to do so. Professional licensure was treated first in a general way and then with more specificity in law, medicine, nursing, and teaching. Professional licensure was shown to serve the public interest in several ways, such as the assurance that a licensee has fulfilled requirements believed by experts to be essential for effective performance in a particular field. Two other benefits cited were the preventing of incompetents and charlatans from practicing and the setting forth of program and curricular guidelines for institutions to follow in their preparation programs. A benefit of licensure especially pertinent to the theme of this book is the opportunity provided colleges and universities to use licensure as a quality assurance. Maintaining preparation programs that are closely attuned to what credible experts say is necessary for effective performance and successfully preparing aspirants for the prescribed entry requirements constitute a justifiable basis for institutions' claiming that they have programs of high quality.

NOTES

1. *Webster's New College Dictionary* (1983). Springfield, MA: Merriam-Webster.
2. Ibid.
3. National Board for Professional Teaching Standards. (2001). Available on-line: http://www.nbpts.org/about/news_center/facts/quick_facts.html.
4. Young, K., Chambers, C., Kells, H, and Associates. (1983). *Understanding Accreditation: Contemporary Perspectives on Issues and Practices in Evaluating Educational Quality.* San Francisco: Jossey-Bass, 457–458.
5. Ibid., p. 457.
6. Ibid.
7. Rudd, M. (1985). *Candidate Certification in Law.* Paper presented at the Conference on Enhancing the Teaching Profession: Lessons from Other Publications, Racine, WI, Johnson Foundation, October 21.
8. Legal Information Institute. (2001). Available on-line: http://www.cornell.edu/topics/bar_admissions.html.
9. Davis, F. (1987). Memorandum to Faculty, Staff, Concerned University Officials and Students, Memphis, TN: Cecil C. Humphreys School of Law, Memphis State University, October 7.
10. Jewett, R. (1985). *Interview with Task Force on Teacher Certification.* Washington, D.C.: American Association of Colleges for Teacher Education.

11. United States Medical Licensing Examination. (2001). Available on-line: http://www.usmle.org.

12. Ibid.

13. Ibid.

14. Ibid.

15. Jewett, *Interview with Task Force on Teacher Certification.*

16. Fabrey, L., and Rupp, R. (1985). *Interview with Task Force on Teacher Certification.* Washington, DC: American Association of Colleges for Teacher Education.

17. Ibid.

18. The Story of the State-Mandated Mentoring & Induction Program in Tennessee. (1998), Available on-line: http://www.teachermentors.com.

19. Tennessee General Assembly. (1987). *Public Chapter 308 of the Acts of the 94th General Assembly of the State of Tennessee.* Nashville: Tennessee General Assembly.

20. Leviton, B (ed.). (1976). *Licensing and Accreditation in Education: The Law and the State Interest.* Lincoln: Commission on Undergraduate Education and the Education of Teachers, University of Nebraska.

21. Jordan, K. (1988). *State Professional Standards/Practices Boards: A Policy Analysis Paper.* Washington, DC: American Association of Colleges for Teacher Education.

22. Educational Testing Service. (2001). *Principles of Learning and Teaching: Your Quick Guide to Understanding the Praxis Series Tests,* 4.

23. Ibid., 5.

24. School Board News. (1999). Available on-line: http://www.nsba.org/shn/1999/060899–6.htm.

25. National Board for Professional Teaching Standards. (1989). *President's 1987/88 Annual Report.* Washington, DC: National Board for Professional Teaching Standards.

26. Ibid.

27. Jordan, *State Professional Standards/Practices Boards,* 33.

28. Friedman, M. (1962). *Capitalism and Freedom.* Chicago: University of Chicago Press.

29. Bogue, E. (1991). *A Journey of the Heart: The Call to Teaching.* Bloomington, IN: Phi Delta Kappa.

30. Rebell, M. (1976). *Licensing and Accreditation: The Law and the State Interest.* Lincoln: Commission on Undergraduate Education, University of Nebraska.

31. Young, Chambers, Kells, and Associates, *Understanding Accreditation.*

32. Sykes, G. (1989). "Examining the Contradiction of Licensure." *Education Week,* March 29, 32.

33. Ibid.

Chapter 6

Academic Program Reviews and Audits

The Test of Peer Review

As with many of the other quality assurance policy systems described in these chapters, the evolution of academic program review as an instrument for quality assurance may be seen primarily as a movement of the last twenty-five to thirty years in higher education. American scholar Fred Harcleroad has suggested, however, that "academic program evaluation in the United States of America began on September 23, 1642," the day that Massachusetts Bay Company governor John Winthrop went to preside over examinations for nine seniors graduating from Harvard College.[1]

The historic roots of program evaluation may go back to that early day in Harvard's history, but both the literature and the activity in this field clearly point to the emergence of academic program reviews as a quality assurance development of more recent origin. For example, a survey of almost 900 institutions by Barak[2] showed that more than three-fourths, 76 percent, of the institutions' current policies and procedures were initiated since 1970. This more recent emergence of program reviews as an instrument of quality assurance was affirmed by Conrad and Wilson (1985), who noted that "it was not until the 1970's that forces largely outside the academy were to make program review (internal as well as external) a central feature of academic program planning in the majority of institutions and states."[3]

Our goal in this chapter is to outline the distinctive features of academic program review as an instrument of quality assurance, to identify some of the educational and political factors that led to its emergence, to reveal the variety of stakeholders involved, and to examine some of the strengths and limitations of this approach to quality assurance. At the conclusion of the chapter, we will explore briefly the concept of academic audit, a relatively new quality assurance instrument having close alliance to program reviews.

ACADEMIC PROGRAM REVIEW—A DEFINITION

What exactly is meant by "academic program review" and how do the features of this approach to quality assurance differ from other quality assurance policy systems described in this book? Essentially, an academic program review is a comprehensive evaluation of a curriculum leading to a degree. This review will ordinarily involve the acquisition of historic, current, and projective data on program purpose, resources used and needed, and an evaluation of performance. The evaluation of performance may involve elements of previously described quality assurance approaches—peer judgments and student outcome measurements, for example. Academic program reviews may be initiated and conducted within a college or university, within a system of institutions, by a state-level governing or coordinating agency, or by some element of state government, such as a legislative audit agency. The reasons for such reviews may be financial, educational, political, or ethical:

- Financial: to ascertain whether there is a need for additional support, whether resources can support existing programs, whether current resources are being applied with effectiveness and efficiency
- Educational: to ascertain whether a program should be implemented, revised, improved, or terminated; to determine quality of program performance
- Political: to ascertain whether a program is being operated within state guidelines or whether students are being protected from programs of questionable value/quality
- Ethical: to ascertain whether the program is being operated according to ethical standards set forth by the institution and/or the governing body, whether the purposes of the program are commensurate with the purposes of the institution as a whole, or whether the operations of the institution or a particular program are characterized by good management practices, efficiency, and integrity

This may be a useful time to spend a moment on the meaning of terms, because program review, program evaluation, and program audit can be found in similar contexts. In a 1979 monograph, *Developing a Process Model for Institutional and State Level Review and Evaluation of Academic Programs,* the Ohio Board of Regents offered these distinctions: The word "review" signaled a state agency role, the word "evaluation" an institutional or faculty initiative, and the word "audit" a legislative or executive initiative.[4] Although the association of these three terms with the actors cited may have some validity, all center on the evaluation of program performance and potential and suggest these questions:

1. Is the program achieving those goals for which it was designed, and are the goals still relevant to the mission of the unit or institutions in which the program is located?
2. Are the resources required to operate the program being applied in the most effective and efficient way possible?
3. Are there ways in which the impact and the efficiency of the program can be enhanced or improved?

Our previous outline of decision purposes, however, suggests other reasons for program review. Reviews can be conducted, for example, to determine whether a new program should be started, whether an existing program should be terminated, or whether institutional operations are in conformity with stated guidelines and regulations—programmatic, financial, and ethical. These purposes clearly speak to evaluation intents that go beyond the conventional purposes of program improvement. Moreover, they suggest possible evaluation roles beyond faculty and campus. Thus, one of the distinctive features of academic program reviews is the potential involvement of organizations and agencies external to the campus.

An earlier book-length treatment on *The Profession and Practice of Program Evaluation*[5] offers several reasons for program review that embrace those we have cited but also contain other purposes, among them (1) to contribute to decisions about program installation; (2) to contribute to decisions about program continuation, expansion, or "certification"; (3) to contribute to decisions about program modification; (4) to obtain evidence to rally support for a program; (5) to obtain evidence to rally opposition to a program; and (6) to contribute to the understanding of basic psychological, social, and other processes. We draw the reader's attention to the last three decision purposes, as they suggest both political and educational rationales.

An illustration here will indicate how and why agencies external to the campus may become involved in campus evaluation. In the late 1970s, one of the authors was serving with the Tennessee Higher Education Commission (THEC), a coordinating agency with responsibilities in master planning, new program review and approval, budget review and recommendations, facility review and recommendations, and review of existing programs (but with no power to terminate academic programs). A routine legislative audit conducted on a state college campus revealed that the campus had failed to implement its retention policy for two years. As a result, the auditors found that approximately 600 students were still enrolled who were academically ineligible to be enrolled—at least according to the probation policies defined in the institution's catalog. This, of course, meant that the institution had been drawing state formula funding (based on size and level of enrollments) beyond what it should have been awarded.

The Tennessee legislature passed a resolution requiring that the THEC conduct an enrollment audit on each of the twenty-one public campuses in the state (to draw random samples of enrolled students' names from the state's student information system and dispatch teams to each campus to review the academic record of these students in the sample to see if they were eligible for enrollment). No other institution was found in violation.

Here was a classic case in which a violation by one institution brought disruption and suspicion to all institutions and caused the intrusion of legislative interest into a matter ordinarily the province of a campus faculty and administration. This illustration does not fit our definition of "program review" with preciseness, because the legislative and commission audits centered not on a degree program but on retention policy. It does reveal, however, how a breach of ethical and educational responsibility on a single campus can bring external interference to all campuses.

In the next section we examine the evolution of academic program review as an instrument of quality assurance and see how and why agencies beyond the campus have become so involved.

EVOLUTION OF ACADEMIC PROGRAM REVIEWS

While American higher education has been a growth industry for most of the past fifty years and there are now approximately fifteen million students enrolled, there can be wide variations in enrollment patterns by campus and by state, with enrollments declining in some locales and states while rising in others. Moreover, there have been serious vacillations in the patterns of both state and federal funding. For some states and public institutions these financial patterns have been more sobering than exhilarating. Adding to this social/political stew are too many instances of ethical abuse within higher education and an occasional prostitution of integrity and abandonment of standards. The result described by Harcleroad in 1980 should come as no surprise: "In such a social, political, and economic climate, central agencies, whether in business, government, or education, tend to tighten controls and to move back from previous efforts to decentralize."[6] In *AGB Reports* two contiguous 1988 articles carried titles and abstracts that capture the themes we are trying to emphasize. An article by Eisenberg[7] speaks of higher education's "crisis of confidence" and is abstracted in this sentence: "Public support of higher education has been shaken, and it will take more than a glitzy public relations campaign to restore it." In the same publication, Seymour warned: "In today's financially restrictive environment, developing and approving new academic programs can be a delicate business."[8]

The emergence of interactive roles in the approval and review of academic programs is a relatively new trend with potential discomforting dimensions, especially when viewed from the campus and faculty perspective. In earlier days, if agencies external to the campus ventured into program evaluation, they were likely to examine indicators related to funding recommendations and allocations—enrollments, class sizes, faculty salaries. Questions raised by agencies beyond the campus tended to focus on "how much" rather than "how effective."

The quality assurance efforts of both regional and professional accrediting agencies, as outlined in chapter 2, were quietly accepted by state agencies. No longer is that the case, however.

In the last quarter of the twentieth century, executive and legislative officers increased their oversight activity. In the late 1970s, for example, the governor and the legislature of Colorado proposed substantive changes in the programs of Colorado institutions, going well beyond analyses and recommendations related to size of budgets. In an accrediting visit to a southeast university campus, one of the authors observed three different legislative audit teams at work, even as the self-study visit was taking place. Apparently, the presence of these audit teams had resulted from an unfortunate combination of factors on the campus: the nonvoluntary departure of the president and a pending nonvoluntary departure of the provost, dissent among the faculty over institutional heritage and mission, and questions about financial operations. The audit teams were examining not only financial operations of the college but also a series of personnel and other policy matters.

The point here is that institutions have experienced a rising interest in program, policy, and operations review from a variety of external agencies. Why is this so? In 1985, Conrad and Wilson[9] suggested three reasons: a widespread interest in improving program quality, the need to respond creatively to severe financial constraints, and expectations, or accountability by institutions' external constituencies. Not much has changed in the intervening years.

Another reason has to be that higher education has grown bigger, more expensive, and more complex. In addition, public confidence in a number of our social institutions has declined; the "crisis of confidence" alluded to in the earlier citation by Eisenberg. Yet another factor can be traced to the size and visibility of education budgets, which in many states account for 50 percent or more of the state budget—when one combines the expenditures for elementary, secondary, and higher education. Moreover, these budgets are often the major source of discretionary spending, because many state expenditures involve required transfer payments and expenditures tied to federal appropriations.

As our previous illustration makes clear, however, there is yet another reason for the increasing number of reviews by external agencies: an emerging concern with the ethics of policy and practice at the campus level. The misuses of institutional funds, the failure to administer federal aid programs properly, the abuse of state resources such as cars and travel funds, the neglect of building and equipment maintenance, and abuses in intercollegiate athletics furnish the stimulus for increased external interest that goes well beyond quality assurance.

In 1979, the American Assembly published a paper entitled *The Integrity of Higher Education* that stated that "academic life carries for its members obligations of personal conduct (by trustees and administrators, faculty and students) that lift expectations of behavior beyond the ordinary."[10] Ethical suspicion of a social institution from which the public has the right to expect nobility of performance is particularly regrettable because, among other results, a breach of ethics often brings pressure for increased control.

We stand now more than two decades from the report by the American Assembly. Has much changed? Sadly, higher education remains high in the public eye for a range of integrity violations on the part of faculty and administrators. For each of the last twenty years or so, we have seen at least one book critical of the academy, ranging from such works as the 1988 book by Charles Sykes entitled *PROFSCAM*[11] to the 1990 book *Killing the Spirit* by the well-known historian Page Smith. Offering a devastating critique of the American university, Smith indicates that faculties at the elite universities "are in full flight from teaching,"[12] that "there is a mad reductionism at work. God is not a proper topic for discussion, but 'lesbian politics' is,"[13] that what universities "are clearly pursuing with far more dedication than the truth is big bucks."[14] Finally Smith accuses the modern university of "spiritual aridity": "By 1990 the university had cast out every area of investigation and every subject that could not be subsumed under the heading 'scientific' and had made all those that remained (like literature and philosophy) at least profess to be scientific. Excluded were such ancient and classic human concerns as love, faith, hope, courage, passion and compassion, spirituality, religion, fidelity—indeed one is tempted to say, anything that might be somewhat encouraging to young people eager to receive some direction, or, in the words of a student survey form, develop 'a philosophy of life.' If love could not be discussed, sex, of course was a lively topic."[15]

Neither civic friends nor those who labor in our colleges and universities would accept these indictments as a majority descriptor of faculty and administrators or their institutions. In their 2000 book *Exploring the Heritage of American Higher Education,* Bogue and Aper furnish a more expansive and disappointing story of ethical abuse in higher education in the closing years of the twentieth century, as carried in both professional press such as the *Chronicle of Higher Education* and in the public media such as *Wall Street Journal* and *USA Today.* They conclude that: "The difficulty is that just one departure from the path of nobility, from our responsibility to exemplify integrity is one too many; and each departure diminishes public trust in our colleges and universities."[16] And this is precisely the point Harcleroad was making over twenty years previous.

In coming chapters, we will explore issues of integrity and accountability more fully and trace the sad costs of duplicity in higher education more fully. There is no lack of clarity here, however. Wrongdoing and irresponsibility in higher education, as in any organization, have destructive costs and consequences. They include a loss of confidence and a diminution of trust, a narrowing of campus management discretion and a more controlling and active voice of external stakeholders on questions of accountability and quality. While there may be many expressions of such external interest, they certainly often include legislative and executive regulation.

Our discussion thus far suggests varying levels of initiative and responsibility for academic program review and evaluation. A 1980 monograph by Craven[17] pointed to evaluation activities by four stakeholders: institutions, multicampus systems, state agencies, and accrediting agencies. We described the role of accrediting agencies in chapter 2. In this chapter, we examine the program review initiatives at the campus level, the system/coordinating level, and the state agency level, which may include both executive and legislative involvements.

CAMPUS-LEVEL PROGRAM REVIEW

From the campus or institutional perspective, academic program review or evaluation can be one of several instruments of quality assurance. Program review can also be a useful instrument to link planning, resources, and performance. In the Craven monograph previously cited, Munitz and Wright[18] described campus-level review systems at three institutions: Michigan State University, the University of Michigan, and the University of Houston.

At Michigan State University, departmental reviews are embedded in an annual evaluation and report (AER) system. The two major components of the AER system are evaluation and report materials that contain a variety of statistical and activity profiles describing faculty activity and accomplishments, staffing patterns, enrollments, graduation trends, and work-load profiles. The department also prepares a "qualitative assessment of its own performance during the previous year in the three categories of instruction, research and professional activities, and public service. The unit is also invited to address major problems and imperative needs which were not adequately conveyed by the comparative data schedules. Both strengths and weaknesses are assessed in these evaluations. Departments are encouraged to incorporate results from external evaluations into their summary of unit performance."[19]

The planning and budgeting materials furnish an opportunity for the department to forecast future goals, their priorities, and the funding needs associated with each. Two plans are involved: a change plan and a flexibility plan. The change plan calls for a listing of prioritized department goals, with the funds necessary to support each and projected for the next five years. "The flexibility plan specifies how the department intends to reserve from long-term commitments a marginal percentage of its budget in anticipation of possible future reductions in general funds available."[20]

Planning questions and materials to be completed by each academic and administrative unit were built on a major university policy paper entitled *The Refocusing, Rebalancing, and Refining of Michigan State University.* These three processes are described as a "new concerted effort to assure that the university is "doing the right things, doing things right, at the right time in our history."[21]

This approach to planning and program review at Michigan State was intensive and extensive. The three-year planning cycle, built on the document cited above, required each unit to engage questions related to proposed new activity and proposed terminated activities. Fiscal notes are required on both. Among the more interesting planning questions: "In addition to re-balancing to a new base budget level, what will be done differently to look at innovations that either produce a *simplification of work necessary to the operation* of the major administrative unit (MAU) and the units contained within the MAU, will produce *collaborative efforts* with other units extramural to the MAU, will *enhance the academic distinction* or assure the quality of programs in both the short and long run, and will effectively use all funds available to the unit."[22]

Munitz and Wright also described review approaches used at the University of Michigan and the University of Houston, including a two-dimensional evaluation matrix for all programs at the University of Houston on the basis of (1) the extent to which the program was central to the mission of the university, and (2) judgments of the overall academic quality of the program (eminence/distinction, strength/better than average, and adequate/sound but not distinguished). In late 1989, the University of Houston was also participating in a five-year review of doctoral programs initiated by the Texas Higher Education Coordinating Board. We will have more to say on the Texas Review Plan later in this chapter.

While we are examining campus-based approaches to program review and evaluation, it may prove helpful to recall from chapter 4 that the ETS offers the Program Self-Assessment Service (PSAS) "to help colleges and universities carry out departmental or program reviews at the under-graduate level."[23] This service provides a participating campus with a series of three program assessment questionnaires to be completed by faculty, undergraduate students, and alumni, giving comparative data (means and standards deviations) on sixteen scales, incorporating students, faculty, curriculum, policies and procedures, and several other aspects of university life.

Here would be a good place to describe program review policy and practice at one other major research university and to profile the ETS self-assessment in action. The University of Tennessee has for years maintained a comprehensive and formal system of program review. The formal policy manual is entitled *Academic Program Reviews* and was last issued in 1999.[24] This manual provides a detailed account of the purpose and procedures for program reviews and a schedule for both ten-year reviews and five-year midcycle reviews to the year 2004.

In 1995–96, the program in educational leadership at the University of Tennessee participated in the university program review process, taking a year for self-study and development of the self-study report. This report engaged questions of program mission, diversity, enrollments, faculty credentials and performance, program strengths and issues, and facility adequacy. Accompanying the self-study report was a companion report built on the use of the ETS Graduate Program Self Assessment and a subsequent analysis of data on eleven scales: Environment for Learning, Scholarly Excellence, Quality of Teaching, Faculty Concern for Students, Curriculum, Departmental Procedures, Available Resources, Student Satisfaction with Program, Assistantship and Intern Experiences, Resource Accessibility, and Student Accomplishments.

One of the important findings emerging from the program review and more specifically the ETS self-assessment was the need for a stronger feeling of community and connection expressed by both master's and doctoral students. This finding, with other important contextual factors, was important in the program faculty designing and securing graduate school approval for cohort graduate study experiences at both the master's and doctoral levels and for the design and implementation of an enriched doctoral residency experience.

The subtitle of this chapter is "The Test of Peer Review." In the case of the University of Tennessee program review just cited, the report was read and reviewed by three senior faculty from other university departments and two senior professors from other research universities over the country. This five-member team spent three days on site interviewing students, faculty, and administrators and presented a report to the dean of the College of Education, the dean of the Graduate School and the university provost.

We should not leave the impression that program reviews are a quality assurance tool exclusive to institutions offering graduate programs. As a particular campus illustration, we cite the practice of El Camino College in California. The *Academic Program Review Guidelines*[25] of this college describe a six-year review cycle for all programs, a review cycle involving self-study and a three-year midcycle review. The community colleges comprising the Illinois Community College System prepare an annual *Accountability and Productivity Report* for each year, with campus-based program review being one source of data for this annual report.[26] The Indiana Vocational-Technical College two-year college system also reports the active use of academic program review at its thirteen regional campuses.[27] Additional illustration may be found in a summer 1995 issue of New Directions for Institutional Research with the theme *Using Academic Program Review*.[28]

In summarizing the basic issues concerning program review and evaluation at the campus level, we encounter the same questions as those likely to be posed for any effective educational evaluation:

Purpose: What is the purpose of the review/evaluation?

- To start or implement a new program
- To assess the quality of an existing program
- To revise or discontinue an existing program
- To ascertain resource needs

Criteria: What indicators of activity and performance will be used to judge the program?

Evaluators: Who will make the judgments of quality?

- External and/or internal peer evaluators
- Currently enrolled students
- Alumni
- Advisory panels
- Deans or other administrators

Time: When and how often will reviews be conducted? Will programs be reviewed every year, on some recurring multiyear cycle, or on the basis of some performance signal?

Costs: How much will reviews cost and who will pay?

GOVERNING AND COORDINATING BOARD PROGRAM REVIEW

As we noted earlier, governing and coordinating boards have in recent years become primary actors in reviewing and approving new program proposals. Typically, such reviews provide various assurances: to demonstrate the need for a new program that is requested or to ensure that the program will not be an unnecessary duplication. Sometimes the reviews concentrate on the institution's capability for mounting and sustaining the requested new program and the availability of funds. Reviews by governing and coordinating boards can also focus on how the requested new program relates to both institutional and system mission. Approval for new programs by agencies beyond the campus is not, however, our main concern in this chapter. Although governing and coordinating board involvement in the approval of new programs can certainly be seen as an instrument of quality assurance, our main concern is on reviews of existing programs.

Barak,[29] an important and early writer on the theme of program review, noted the extensive involvement of external agencies in program review. Bogue[30] explored the roles of three state-level agencies in reviewing existing academic programs. One of the agencies, the THEC, then as now, had authority to review and recommend but not to terminate existing programs. However, the THEC regularly conducts reviews of low-producing programs, and following these reviews, campuses and their governing boards will often voluntarily agree to terminate programs.

Here a small diversion will prove informing—but not necessarily encouraging from the standpoint of integrity and honesty. When low-enrollment–low-graduate academic programs come under public scrutiny from coordinating boards, some campuses may and do elect to engage in academic camouflage. A low-enrollment major or program, especially if it is a graduate program, may simply be collapsed in title with other programs. Where there once appeared on the coordinating board academic program inventory four majors, one or two with marginal enrollments and thus subject to review and inspection, the alert campus dean can arrange to create a single new major, albeit with four specializations or concentrations. The terminology of academic programs allows for endless game playing.

Reviews conducted by the Washington Council for Postsecondary Education (CPE) were similar to those in Tennessee, beginning with a review of programs that "evinced low chronic productivity" and centering on the goal of minimizing unnecessary duplication. As described in the paper by Bogue, the Washington CPE staff conducted extensive research on the three key principles or arguments most often used by institutions seeking new programs and attempting to retain existing ones about which there may have been questions: (1) the essentiality of a certain complement of programs for an institution to remain truly comprehensive, (2) the essentiality of graduate programs in providing for the growth and satisfaction of faculty by providing for programs in research, and (3) the essentiality of graduate programs to undergraduate program quality. Research by the CPE staff revealed the exaggeration of these three often-cited arguments.

Also reported in the paper by Bogue were the program review actions of the Louisiana Board of Regents, one of the oldest, most thorough, and most continuous state-level reviews in the nation. In the mid to late 1970s, for example, the Louisiana Board of Regents reviewed over 900 programs. These reviews involved the following steps: Affected departments or programs completed a program self-review, after which out-of-state consultants conducted on-site visits and subsequently submitted comprehensive reports. Affected institutions responded to the reports, after which the Academic Affairs Committee of the Board of Regents held public hearings. Following the hearings, the staff of the Board of Regents submitted recommendations to the Academic Affairs Committee, which then sent recommendations to the full board for its action.

The important and critical difference in the authority of the Louisiana Board of Regents and other coordinating agencies cited here is that the Louisiana Regents have the statutory power to terminate programs, and they did! Actions of the Board of Regents during this review period from 1975 to 1983 resulted in 325 program discontinuations. Over 100 of these were at the graduate level and included several doctoral programs. The Board of Regents also issued commendations for those programs that peer reviewers considered to be of exceptionally high quality. Of the 909 programs reviewed during this period, 24 were cited for excellence.[31]

Mentioned earlier was the Texas Higher Education Coordinating Board, which initiated a review of doctoral programs in October 1987. Each review involved a three-stage procedure, with each stage requiring progressively more information. Doctoral programs were grouped into categories of related programs, and a separate panel of consultants with appropriate expertise was engaged to review the programs in each category. These reviews essentially rated the programs for continuation or for further review. The final or third-stage review placed a program in one of four categories: adequate for continuation, adequate for continuation subject to specific limitations, inadequate for continuation unless specific improvements are made within a specified time, and inadequate for continuation and should be phased out.

Earlier in the discussion we stated that the purposes of program reviews were financial, educational, political, and ethical. We suggested that the essential questions centered on the relationship between purpose and performance and on the question of resource adequacy. But there is another question that often drives program reviews, especially those initiated external to the campus and involving public institutions. This question centers on whether a state is offering too many programs within a given field and level: the question of "unnecessary duplication." This term appears frequently in the lexicon of American higher education and most often within the context of academic program reviews. To pause a moment and explore its different meanings may prove helpful.

We note first that the base term "duplication"is rarely found without its modifier "unnecessary,"as though all duplication were unnecessary. That all duplication is not unnecessary is patently obvious to anyone who thinks about the matter. For example, in most urban centers in the United States, one can find a public university and community college both offering lower-level instruction in such fields as English, mathematics, science, and history. Indeed, within a single institution we often see multiple sections of English and mathematics as well as courses in descriptive and inferential statistics taught in a variety of disciplines: mathematics, psychology, quantitative business methods, agriculture, education. Is such duplication "unnecessary"? The answer may depend upon one's academic discipline and responsibility. If each class section is filled to capacity, it can be argued that the duplication is necessary. But what is an optimal class size: 25 for English and 250 for introductory psychology? Like a bad piece of taffy candy, the argument grows as it is chewed.

Historical factors are at work in our understanding of the definition of unnecessary duplication. In the early 1970s, the THEC conducted a statewide study on the need for master's of business administration (MBA) programs in the state. The conclusion at that time was that perhaps four might be the optimal number. Today, all but one of the nine senior universities in Tennessee offer the MBA degree, and each is considered basic to the programs of those schools. What has changed in the few short years since the original study was completed?

The historical unfolding of our understandings about unnecessary duplication may also have financial roots. In a word, state policy perspectives and attitudes turn more conservative when money is tight. In the last quarter of the twentieth century, almost every state in the South, and others over the nation as well, built a second medical school and a new veterinary medicine school (both highly expensive educational operations) accompanied by loud and passionate arguments that usually moved back and forth between the legislature and state-level coordinating and governing agencies. Once state resources began to shrivel, legislative and higher education officials began to scratch their heads about whether their decisions of earlier years were smart ones.

In 2002, THEC, in cooperation with the two public governing boards in the state, conducted a study in two academic fields, engineering and agriculture, for purposes of identifying possible unnecessary duplication in those fields. This study was driven by political perspectives and pressures concerning the question of whether the state was attempting to operate too many programs in those two fields, given difficult revenue conditions in the state.

Another factor that has fanned the flames of discussion over program duplication is the growing pressure to make additional programs available to major urban population centers. Certainly this generalization will not hold for every state; but in many states, the early establishment of major universities, with their comprehensive array of educational programs, tended to be away from major population centers. The idea was to keep undergraduates safe from the sins of the city. In earlier years, citizens in Memphis, Tennessee, for example, could reach St. Louis and a number of other population centers with major universities more easily and quickly than they could Knoxville, where the University of Tennessee with most of the state's doctoral programs was located. On the other hand, citizens living in Knoxville and other parts of East Tennessee found the 400- to 500-mile trip to Memphis for medical school equally discomforting, a factor that accounts for the creation of new graduate programs and professional schools. In Florida, citizens living in Miami, Orlando, and Tampa, for example, began to believe that they should have as much access to advanced graduate programs as those living closer to Tallahassee and Gainesville.

Combinations of educational and philosophical forces also appear to be at work concerning duplication. For example, Georgia has a population base of approximately 6.2 million people but operates only one public engineering program, at Georgia Tech. With a population base of 4.8 million, Tennessee operates six public engineering programs; and the state of Louisiana, with a population of 4.5 million, operates six public engineering programs. The point is that the question of unnecessary duplication is exacerbated by a variety of educational, historical, political, and financial factors.

We propose this definition: *Unnecessary duplication occurs when the number of programs available in a particular curriculum is producing more graduates than needed; the number of programs available is more than can be operated with high quality, considering the resources available; or the number of courses and/or programs is not being delivered with the most efficient application of existing resources.*

Again, program and/or course duplication is sometimes necessary. Access, availability, and course delivery schedules are also important considerations. It is reasonable for students to have access to basic, core courses in their own college, even if these same courses are offered across town. Students who are limited to evening classes have a right to a full curriculum, even if the courses they need are offered earlier in the day for day students.

Another state coordinating agency that has been active in institutional effectiveness policy and program evaluation is South Carolina's. In June 1988, "cutting-edge legislation" was passed declaring that "each institution of higher learning is responsible for maintaining a system to measure institutional effectiveness in accord with provisions, procedures, and requirements developed by the commission on higher education."[32] Among the effectiveness components endorsed by the commission were many of those discussed in several chapters in this book, including assessment of student performance on measures of general education and major field, follow-up studies and licensure, and certification examinations. A component of direct interest to this chapter is this requirement: "*Reports of Program Changes That Have Occurred as a Result of External Program Review-Evaluation* and assessment of programs is expected to produce change that enhances student achievement. Change that takes place as a result of external program evaluations should be reported to the Commission" (italics in original).

Of additional interest in the South Carolina approach is the requirement that institutions report on the number of student athletes who fail to meet regular admissions requirements and the graduation rate for students by sport, race, sex, field of study, and degree earned. This state is clearly in the vanguard of attempts to bring order and integrity to what many believe to be a troubled sector of higher education.

One of the better examples of multicampus or system-level program review efforts is found in the State University System of Florida. Policies, procedures, and philosophy for the nine universities in the State University System of Florida (SUSF) were outlined in the SUSF "Procedural Guidelines for Review of Existing Programs."[33] Program reviews in the state system are conducted on five-year rotating cycles. An outline of the program review cycles over a sixteen-year time period for each program area was promulgated, showing the year each program was to have its initial review.

The policy manual furnishes extensive outlines of responsibilities for both campus and consultant roles in the review process, guidelines for content and form of reports, special issues to be engaged in the statewide reviews, and criteria to be employed. The twelve criteria contained in the SUSF policy document are clear, concise, and comprehensive. They range from role and scope consideration to program costs, from quality indicators to characteristics of students to be served, and from the question of unnecessary duplication to the accessibility of the program via the Academic Common Market of the Southern Regional Education Board.[34]

These criteria are used by the system staff and external consultants to the board in their preparation of recommendations to the Board of Regents. In addition, the SUSF furnished consultants with a specific and detailed set of evaluative questions concerning the following elements of program activity and achievement: appropriateness of program goals, program quality, program resources, program priority, relationships with other agencies, equal access and equal opportunity, and personnel needs. Of more than passing interest in this list of review areas is "equal access and equal opportunity." Here, consultants were asked to review the sex, age, and ethnic composition of the faculty and student populations and the affirmative action activities of the program.

An excerpt on how the consultants viewed their evaluative responsibilities in a particular program area, psychology, may be instructive and is indicative of the role consultants can play in an external review: "The Committee attempted to review each program objectively and sympathetically. Committee members took the position that their task was to assess the quality of each program and to do so in a supportive and helpful fashion. The Committee further took the position that its role was to encourage and assist the programs in their efforts in improving quality and to provide suggestions and recommendations that were consistent with overall program objectives."[35]

The psychology report reveals one of the major strengths of system-level reviews, namely, the opportunity to examine general issues in a discipline or program. The state legislature considered the review initiative by the SUSF to be of sufficient importance that the program review responsibility of SUSF was enacted into law. More recently, the governance system for higher education in Florida has undergone revision, with the overall governing board being replaced by individual campus boards and with those boards, along with the community college board, coming under the purview of the state Department of Education. How program review will unfold in the new governance structure is not clear.[36]

No discussion of academic program reviews would be complete without some reference to New York. In that state, the New York Board of Regents holds a historic and strong role in program review and approval authority. It is currently the only state agency to be recognized by the U.S. Department of Education as an accreditation body. The Board of Regents approves and registers every new degree program and also conducts periodic reviews in different fields of study. This authority for program registration/approval and review also embraces programs offered by private institutions, including proprietary schools. The regulations of the commissioner of education and the guidelines published for the periodic self-studies present standards that are similar in content to those used by regional accrediting agencies reported in chapter 2. With over 300 institutions of postsecondary education in New York, more than can be found in clusters of several states, it becomes easier to understand why New York has developed this comprehensive approach.

We close this discussion on system roles in program review with an example from outside the United States, an illustration helpful in exploring some of the potential pitfalls in academic program review. A contemporary and critical reviewer of program reviews is Skolnik, who telegraphs his position with the title "How Academic Program Review Can Foster Intellectual Conformity and Stifle Diversity of Thought and Method."[37] Skolnik emphasizes how our philosophical set conditions our worldview, our view of the university, and our view of how to gauge quality: "Many of the questions posed by the humanist would be dismissed by the scientist as metaphysical or mystical, thus of dubious legitimacy, or the university. Scientists, on the other hand, are preoccupied with counting, and this explains, for example, their preoccupation with citation indices as measures of quality, reflecting what Lindsey describes as a logical positivist bias in evaluation."[38]

Skolnik examined the program review policies and procedures used by the Ontario Council on Graduate Studies, an arm of the Council of Ontario Universities. He claimed that the Ontario review process is heavily weighted in favor of the sciences, furnished evaluative data to support his claim, and concluded that "what are purported to be measures of quality are, in reality, measures of the degree of conformity to the model of graduate programs which obtains in the sciences."[39]

In what we believe to be an instructive exercise, Skolnik engages three issues that are important to any well-balanced and effective program review process, at least at the graduate level. The first issue centers on an adequate definition of research, one that goes beyond quantity of publication: "Besides stimulating a torrent of pedestrian publishing, the practice of assessing quality by counting inhibits work which has a long gestation period and penalizes those whose inclination to publish is when they have something highly significant and polished to offer."[40]

The second issue concerns the balance of faculty effort devoted to instruction, research, and service. Skolnik claimed that Ontario reviews focus almost entirely on research outputs and fail to consider the merit of the "reflective practitioner" model: "In many professions, a new paradigm of the 'reflective practitioner,' which emphasized the development of theory through personal reflection on experiences in practice, is replacing the older linear view of the relationship between theory and practice, which was rooted in logical positivism."[41]

Finally, Skolnik criticized the reviews for not looking at student-development outcomes, which he claims, with legitimacy, should be as important as measures of faculty research productivity—however that productivity might be measured. Skolnik concludes that the system of program review now in place in Ontario "works to suppress diversity, innovation, and non-conformist approaches in the search of knowledge."[42]

Suppression of diversity, innovation, and nonconformist approaches to the search for knowledge would be counted disappointing and unwelcome outcomes for any quality assurance exercise. Hence, Skolnik's concerns merit attention. We add these concerns about the appropriateness of evaluative model and evaluative criteria to those cited earlier in this chapter.

We conclude this discussion with an acknowledgment that, although external-agency involvements in program review have expanded in recent years, such involvements are not without liability. Criticisms are numerous and often have foundation. We identify six frequently voiced criticisms of reviews by external agencies.

1. Reviews are top down, furnishing little involvement at the campus level in selection of review criteria and consultants.
2. The selection of consultants ignores mission distinctions (for example, faculty from research universities reviewing programs at primarily undergraduate schools).
3. Visiting consultants show little knowledge of institutions they are visiting, leaping to large conclusions on the basis of little data and time.
4. Agency staff show little sensitivity to campus concerns, institutional nuances, and distinctions.

5. Reviews have the appearance of a punitive rather than an improvement function.
6. Agency staff exhibit personal and sometimes unfair bias in selecting and briefing consultants or in interpreting consultant reports to fit their own biases and goals.

These criticisms notwithstanding, the contributions of state agencies to quality assurance via program review are not without merit. Bogue noted that "With artistic leadership, state agency roles in academic program evaluation can complement institutional and governing board roles and enhance the renewal function of evaluation."[43]

ACADEMIC AUDITS

We include in this chapter a concluding conversation on the concept of academic audit. Academic audit as an instrument of quality assurance is a concept that has enjoyed initial dialogue and implementation more in other nations than in the United States, where there is an emerging conversation. Academic audit has enjoyed extensive application in the United Kingdom and Europe[44] and in Asia.[45] It is described as an approach that accents the improvement of student learning by an examination and evaluation of an institution's or program's processes of quality assurance.

In chapter 2 and in this chapter, we have emphasized that both accreditation and program reviews typically begin with a reflective and evaluative self-study at both the institutional level (for regional accreditation) and at the program or departmental level (for professional accreditation). According to Dill,[46] such self-studies might not be typical of an audit, though Dill does indicate that the Association of European Universities (CRE) did involve self-studies in its approach to audit. Massy and French also indicate that institutions in Hong Kong filed a twenty-page document preliminary to an audit visit.[47]

Institutions participating in audits would file a reflective report in advance of the audit visit, detailing a campus's or program's processes for assuring quality. It is not clear that there is yet a recognized common expectation for what elements should appear in such reports, nor is there uniformity on what "evidence" might be offered. The purpose of an academic audit is often cited as that of examining what some call "education quality work." That phrase—education quality work—has been operationalized in these two questions: How do you know your department's or program's quality is good, and what are you doing to improve it? These questions are not strange or new to American higher education. And indeed, they were cited in our opening chapter as fundamental to any program of quality assurance.

In writing about academic audit, Dill has suggested that the accreditation process is too "formulaic" and expensive. As a parenthetical reflection, Dill later describes some of the visits in Europe as involving the audit team in preliminary visits and on-site visits of several days. Massy describes the process in Hong Kong as involving eight months of engagement and study. Based on these reflections related to academic audit, it is not clear that the process is less expensive than accreditation.

Dill further describes the audit, as practiced in the United Kingdom and other countries, as follows: "Unlike accreditation or subject assessments, however, academic audits make no attempt to comprehensively revise an institution's or program's resources and activities, nor to directly assess the quality of teaching or learning."[48] If this is indeed the case, it might be argued that academic audit is at least a partial throwback to the earlier years of accreditation in which the focus was on conditions and processes and not on outcomes and results.

In chapter 11, we propose the concept of audit as an accountability option for American colleges and universities, but we have in mind a concept a little more embracing and different than what is now being practiced under that conceptual banner. We have in mind well-trained academic auditors who would drop into a campus and look at evidence of design, implementation, and outcome. They might examine, for example, statements on program philosophy, goals, and expected student outcomes—the work of design. They might examine course syllabi, instructional practices, course evaluations, and other artifacts such as electronic products and network products and processes—the work of implementation. They might examine data on student performance, outcomes, and perceptions. The assumption of that approach would be that if an institution or program was following "good practice" or was following accreditation standards, then it should be following those all of the time and be open to inspection at any time.

PROGRAM REVIEWS—A PARTNERSHIP PERSPECTIVE

It is clear that program reviews, as instruments of quality assurance, can have negative as well as positive potential. Both campus and external evaluations can flow from contexts with a negative tone: fiscal austerity, enrollment declines, unnecessary duplication concerns, management and academic malpractice. It is also clear that academic program reviews involve several participants with whom the potential for tension is high: the role of faculty and administrators within an institution and the role of system, coordinating, and state agencies external to the campus.

Moreover, even within formalized systems of academic program review, academic cosmetology and modest forms of academic skullduggery are possible. One of the authors participated in an academic program review in which it was discovered that the entire self-study had been written by the department chair. When, during the peer review progress, faculty were questioned about the content, findings, and recommendations of the self-study report, they acknowledged little familiarity with the report—but were quick to indicate why. The faculty of this program had just emerged from a serious and sustained two-year program accreditation exercise, where the maintenance of program accreditation was central to the continuance of graduate programs in the department. Not surprisingly, this accreditation self-study and review commanded a major investment of faculty energy and care. To turn immediately, then, to an institutional program review also requiring self-study seemed unduly and perhaps understandably burdensome. And so the chair spared the faculty this burden and wrote the report himself. Just because the institution's policy manual states that a program review will occur in year xxxx does not justify an academic administration ignoring other quality assurance efforts requiring faculty time and energy. This integration of quality assurance policy systems is an issue we will engage in our final chapter.

The previously cited work by Conrad and Wilson pointed out that we currently lack an informed basis on which to judge the merits of program review. They comment that "the stubborn fact is that not much is known about the effects of program review."[49] On this same point, Skubal[50] earlier noted that many institutions and states involved in program review did not know whether resources had been saved or how much money had been spent in conducting program reviews.

Institutional, multicampus-system, and state-agency-initiated program review may, in some cases, then, be built as much on a foundation of faith as fact when it comes to the question of whether program reviews achieve the purposes we cited earlier: the improvement of quality, the improvement of resource allocation and application, the demonstration of accountability, and the improvement of decisions related to program revision and/or termination.

Having cited just previously an example of a campus-based program review with marginal involvement of faculty and one with questionable academic benefit, it may be appropriate to balance that anecdote with another story chronicling a difficult department and program journey but a story with a long-range positive outcome. One of the authors had the opportunity to participate in a campus-based program review as one of five peer evaluators (three internal and two external faculty reviewers). A major discovery of this review, and one not apparent in the program's self-study, was that faculty relationships in the program were in shambles. Senior professors were engaged in constant and often demeaning bickering in department meetings, with graduate students being used as pawns in department power games. Civility was infrequently found in departmental interpersonal relationships. When interviewed, new and junior faculty indicated that they were so disgusted with the climate of the department that they only came to campus on the days in which they had classes. The rancor of faculty relationships had been enlivened by mixed vote on the recent appointment of the department chair and his subsequent and relatively quick resignation on an integrity issue. At the time of the review, a newly appointed department chair was making a valiant effort to restore a sense of community among faculty and students.

The program review team recommended that the department be given one year in which to get its act together or face being placed in academic receivership and possibly losing its doctoral program. This recommendation furnished a notable incentive for action. The faculty did indeed get its act together, civility was returned, and the chair has now been serving effectively for more than six years. For this particular program and department, there was no program accreditation agency. It is unlikely that the dysfunction's of the program and faculty relationships would have been caught in any other quality assurance exercise such as an assessment or an institutional accreditation.

Human interactions will inevitably have both positive and negative valences. Review and evaluation done without care and competence can damage community, demoralize personnel, and promote prejudicial and parochial views. With artistic and sensitive leadership at every level, however, academic program reviews can realize a renewing purpose. Whether the stimulus is internal or external to the campus, systematic program reviews challenge the campus—interrupting our inertia and diffidence and causing faculty and academic administrators to ask questions of purpose, of priority, of performance.

Throughout the book we have emphasized the interactions among our various approaches to quality assurance. Barak and Breier illustrate the contributions of a well-conceived system of program review to accreditation and to institutional planning. As to assessment and student outcomes, these writers comment: "A good starting point for integrating assessment data into the planning and budgeting process is to include them as a criterion for program review. Thus, student outcome data become one measure of program effectiveness, which in turn is one criterion in a program review's data set."[51] We commend this book as a useful resource for those campuses interested in developing a systematic approach to academic program review.

For those interested in enhancing their knowledge and understanding of program evaluation, we also recommend *Program Evaluation* by Worthen, Sanders, and Fitzgerald.[52] They offer a comprehensive and informing resource on different approaches to evaluation. For example, they classify contemporary models (they prefer the term "conception"to "model") of evaluation into those that are objectives oriented, management oriented, consumer oriented, expertise oriented, adversary oriented, and naturalistic and participant oriented. The diversity of the philosophical and technical bases of these evaluation conceptions makes clear that program evaluation is not a totally rational exercise that unfolds by following simple and sequential steps but rather an activity complicated by ethical and political considerations. The concepts and illustrations offered in this helpful treatment will enhance the artistry and effectiveness of those responsible for the conduct of program reviews at the collegiate level.

Achievement of the renewal potential of academic program review will be enhanced if all parties to the process—whether internal to the campus or external—build on the following principles:

1. Reviews should be built on consensus agreements concerning evaluation criteria, standards, and model.
2. Reviews should reveal appropriate sensitivity to campus and program mission in selection of consultants and/or review panels.
3. Reviews should reflect a consensus among those involved in the review as to the decision purpose of the exercise.
4. Reviews should respect diversity of models for scholarship in different fields, models that respect the many different avenues by which we search for and advance truth.
5. Reviews should furnish adequate advance preparation and on-site time for consultants and evaluators, with the realization that short visits cannot possibly bring consultants a totally adequate knowledge of the policy and personality history of a program or of the complex environment in which the program may exist.
6. Review results should be made a matter of public record and offer the programs and institutions being evaluated an opportunity for response.

NOTES

1. Harcleroad, F. (1980). "The Context of Program Evaluation." In *Academic Program Evaluation,* ed. E. Craven. San Francisco: Jossey-Bass.
2. Barak, R. (1982). *Program Review in Higher Education: Within and Without.* Boulder, CO: National Center for Higher Education Management Systems.
3. Conrad, C., and Wilson, R. (1985). *Academic Program Review: Institutional Approaches, Expectations and Controversies.* ASHE-ERIC Higher Education Report No. 5, Washington, DC: Association for the Study of Higher Education, 4.
4. Ohio Board of Regents. (1979). *Developing a Process Model for Institutional and State-Level Review and Evaluation of Academic Programs.* Columbus: Ohio Board of Regents.
5. Anderson, S., and Ball, S. (1980). *The Profession and Practice of Program Evaluation.* San Francisco: Jossey-Bass, 14–42.
6. Harcleroad, "The Context of Program Evaluation," 12.
7. Eisenberg, R. (1988). "Higher Education's Crisis of Confidence." *AGB Reports,* no. 24, November/December, 5.
8. Seymour, D. (1988). "The Changing Face of Program Approval." *AGB Reports,* no. 24, November/December, 24.
9. Conrad and Wilson, *Academic Program Review.*
10. American Assembly. (1979). *The Integrity of Higher Education: Final Report of the 56th American Assembly.* Harriman, NY: Arden House.
11. Sykes, C. (1988). *PROFSCAM.* Washington, DC: Regnery.
12. Smith, P. (1980). *Killing the Spirit.* New York: Viking, 6.
13. Ibid., 5.
14. Ibid., 13.
15. Ibid., 20.

16. Bogue, E., and Aper, J. (2000). *Exploring the Heritage of American Higher Education.* San Francisco: Jossey-Bass, 210.

17. Craven, E. (1980). *Academic Program Evaluation.* San Francisco: Jossey-Bass.

18. Munitz, B., and Wright, D. (1980). "Institutional Approaches to Program Evaluation." In *Academic Program Evaluation,* ed. E. Craven. San Francisco: Jossey-Bass

19. Ibid., 24.

20. Ibid., 25.

21. Michigan State University (1989). *The Refocusing, Rebalancing, and Refining of Michigan State University,* Internal Discussion Paper, Document Version 2.0. East Lansing: Michigan State University, i.

22. Michigan State University. (1989). *1989 Academic Program Planning and Review.* East Lansing: Michigan State University, 8.

23. Educational Testing Service. (n.d.). *Program Self-Assessment Service.* Brochure. Princeton, NJ: Educational Testing Service.

24. University of Tennessee. (1999). *Academic Program Reviews.* Office of the Provost and Senior Vice Chancellor for Academic Affairs: Knoxville: University of Tennessee.

25. El Camino College. (1999). *El Camino Academic Program Review Guidelines.* Torrance, CA: El Camino College.

26. Illinois Community College Board. (1997). *Accountability and Productivity Report for the Illinois Community College System—Fiscal Year, 1997.* Springfield: Illinois Community College Board.

27. Walters, S., and Giovannini, G. (1994). "Institutional Effectiveness for a State-Wide Technical College System." Paper presented at the Annual Meeting of the North Central Association (99th), Chicago, March 27–29.

28. Barak, R., and Mets, L. (eds.). (1995). Using Academic Program Review [Special issue]. *New Directions for Institutional Research,* No. 86, Summer.

29. Barak, *Program Review in Higher Education.*

30. Bogue, E. (1980). "State Agency Approaches to Academic Program Evaluation." In *Academic Program Evaluation,* ed. E. Craven. San Francisco: Jossey-Bass.

31. Louisiana Board of Regents. (1984). *1984 Master Plan,* Chapter 9. Baton Rouge: Louisiana Board of Regents.

32. South Carolina Coordinating Commission. (1988). *Guidelines for Institutional Effectiveness.* Columbia: South Carolina Coordinating Commission, October 28.

33. State University System of Florida. (n.d.). "Procedural Guidelines for Review of Existing Programs." *Academic Program Review in the State University System of Florida.* Tallahassee: State University System of Florida.

34. Ibid.

35. State University System of Florida. (1987). *Program Review of Psychology.* Tallahassee: State University System of Florida.

36. Schmidt, P. (2001). "Key Panel Approves Governance Overhaul for Florida's Universities." *Chronicle of Higher Education,* 47(25), A24.

37. Skolnik, M. (1989). "How Academic Program Review Can Foster Intellectual Conformity and Stifle Diversity of Thought and Method." *Journal of Higher Education,* 60(6).

38. Ibid., 624.
39. Ibid., 633.
40. Ibid., 634.
41. Ibid., 636.
42. Ibid., 638.
43. Bogue, "State Agency Approaches to Academic Program Evaluation," 69.
44. Dill, D. (2000). "Designing Academic Audit: Lessons Learned in Europe and Asia." *Quality in Higher Education*, 6(3), 187–207.
45. Massy, W., and French, N. (2001), "Teaching and Learning Quality Process Review: What the Programme Has Achieved in Hong Kong." *Quality in Higher Education*, 7(1), 33–45.
46. Dill, op. cit.
47. Massy and French, op. cit.
48. Dill, op. cit., 188
49. Conrad and Wilson, *Academic Program Review*, 65.
50. Skubal, J. (1979). "State-Level Review of Existing Programs: Have Resources Been Saved?" *Research in Higher Education*, 2, 231.
51. Barak, R., and Breier, B. (1990). *Successful Program Review: A Practical Guide to Evaluating Programs in an Academic Setting.* San Francisco: Jossey-Bass, 123.
52. Worthen, B., Sanders, J., and Fitzgerald, J. (1996). *Program Evaluation: Alternative Approaches and Practical Guidelines.* New York: Addison-Wesley.

Chapter 7

College Outcomes

The Test of Results

Resources, reputation, results—our discussion of quality assurance approaches in American higher education has unfolded within a primary emphasis as suggested in these three words, though the simplicity there is overdrawn. The early standards of accrediting agencies, as outlined in chapter 2, centered primarily on resources—faculty, library, financial, and so forth—though that chapter also pointed to the shift in emphasis to institutional effectiveness and student outcomes. And in chapter 3, we noted that college reputations have not yet been fully linked to hard evidence on student growth.

This chapter explores college outcomes as primary indicators of both program and institutional quality. We will examine the history of outcomes assessment, take a look at several outcomes models, and then examine the decision issues that associate with this quality assurance approach.

THE EMERGENCE OF OUTCOMES ASSESSMENT

The current emphasis on outcomes and questions of educational and managerial effectiveness in American higher education was predicted almost thirty years ago by Kenneth Mortimer (1972), who wrote in his monograph *Accountability in Higher Education* that "there will be more concern about the management of higher education and attempts to relate managerial efficiency to educational effectiveness."[1] He also predicted the focus on results: "Accountability accentuates results—it aims squarely at what comes out of an educational system rather than what goes into it."[2]

What exactly do we mean by the term "college outcomes"?Put simply and directly, college outcomes, at least in terms of student outcomes, center on student growth—on changes in knowledge, in skill, in attitudes, and in values. The question is whether there are differences in knowledge, skill, attitudes, and values from college entry to college exit. This is the "value-added" question of quality assurance.

Why the emphasis on outcomes? The Dartmouth College Case in 1819 provided early colonial colleges with "effective barriers against advancing democratic forces pressing for control of higher education and alteration of conventional curriculum policies,"[3] but the latter quarter of the twentieth century saw various stakeholders, concerned with clear and sustained quality in higher education, begin to more vigorously demand increased evidences of the thoughtful use of monetary allocations given to institutions. Students and parents began to seek greater levels of comfort that completion of a college degree would provide assurance of a bright future. State and federal agencies began requiring increased evidences that colleges and universities were meeting their mission and utilizing increasingly limited state and federal funds appropriately. Corporate enterprises, plagued with increasing international competition, demanded graduates possessing the skills necessary for these enterprises to "keep up." To reaffirm, we have this note from Stephen Spangehl (1987): "In industry after industry, we've discovered that we are not competitive, that other countries can make higher quality products more quickly and cheaply than we can. It should surprise no one that these concerns have spread to academe, where, for nearly a thousand years, we have organized ourselves on a precapitalist, pre-technological, pre-management science model."[4]

Banta and Fisher (1984) discussed the emergence of accountability issues in the following passage:

> with the eighties have come reduced confidence in the entire system of publicly assisted education in America and a critical need to make well-informed decisions concerning the appropriate allocation of scarce resources among a variety of social services. These forces have counteracted any immunity from public scrutiny that colleges and universities enjoyed in the past, and today there is increasing recognition of the need for comprehensive program evaluation in institutions of higher education.[5]

Gaither, Nedwek, and Neal (1994) wrote that: "The belief that faculty and administrators were those best suited to determine institutional effectiveness and appropriate student outcomes was replaced by a rising societal skepticism about higher education's effectiveness in an era when all large organizations were coming under close scrutiny including corporations, religious organizations, and government agencies."[6] Jones and Ewell (1987) stated that being accountable not only means "effectively discharging an obligation" but also being answerable for the results.[7] The focus of higher education's obligation in terms of accountability evolved from one primarily focused on the means of education to one focused on the ends of education.[8]

Five of the most influential reports written that raised serious questions regarding the accountability of higher education are *A Nation at Risk* (National Commission on Excellence in Education, 1983), *To Reclaim a Legacy* (National Endowment for the Humanities, 1984), *Involvement in Learning* (National Institute for Education, 1984), *Integrity in the College Curriculum* (Association of American Colleges, 1985), and *Time for Results* (National Governors Association, 1986). The first report, *A Nation at Risk,* was a catalyst for undergraduate reform, assessment of higher education performance, improved efforts for quality, and increased accountability. The reports emphasized the need for higher education to assess knowledge, skills, attitudes, and the basic design of academic and student services programs. They raised a concern that American higher education was not showing evidence of its coherence, purpose, or success.[9]

In a 1987 article appearing in *Change* magazine, New Jersey governor Thomas Kean wrote: "You are understandably attentive to your critics. What do they say? They say that higher education promises much and delivers too little. They say you are too expensive and inefficient. They say your graduates can't write clearly or think straight. And they say you dare not assess your work, evaluate your product, or validate your claims. The public wants you to prove the critics wrong. You can."[10]

In a thoughtful article appearing in the November/December 1989 issue of the *Journal of Higher Education,* Patrick Terenzini offered these reasons for the emergence of outcomes assessment: "Now that the costs of a college education are identifiable and measurable, important people (for example, legislators, parents, students) now want to know what the return is on their investments. What does one get out of a college education? The question forces a fundamental introspection on the part of both individual faculty members and institutions."[11]

There can be little doubt that campuses have become more involved in assessment. Due to many of the accreditation criteria changes discussed in chapter 2, most accredited colleges and universities are required to engage in some form of assessment. At the end of 2000, seventeen states were participating in some sort of performance funding initiatives,[12] which require assessment in various forms.

Not everyone is convinced, obviously, that this goal of focusing on outcomes is the right prescription or that we have a correct diagnosis. In an article appearing in the October 19, 1988, issue of the *Chronicle of Higher Education,* Jon Westling posed this question: "In short, assessment is based on a fundamental misdiagnosis of the malaise of American higher education. Does anyone really believe that the failure of colleges and universities to produce adequately educated young people is the consequence of our failure to develop precise instruments to measure what we are doing? Or that true education requires elaborate technical writers to evaluate its effectiveness?"[13]

Another dissenting voice is Ernst Benjamin in the March/April 1989 issue of *AGB Reports.* Benjamin accuses campus administrators of acquiescing to the current demand for accountability through assessment and suggests that this is one of the major reasons why faculties are often unhappy with campus administrators. Benjamin also holds the opinion that "measurement of student performance will not itself improve learning. In fact, it may inherently interfere with learning if standardized or intrusive measures shape teaching and curriculum."[14] Thus, Benjamin highlights the limiting effects of "teaching to the test."

In the preface to his 1991 book *Assessment for Excellence,* Alexander Astin, one of the more thoughtful and thorough contributing scholars in this field, concludes that "although a great deal of assessment activity goes on in America's colleges and universities, much of it is of very little benefit to either students, faculty, administrators, or institutions. On the contrary, some of our assessment activities seem to conflict with our most basic education mission."[15]

Benjamin's comments can also perpetuate the perspective that faculty and academic administrators are adversaries rather than partners in the learning enterprise. We make no argument that the values and behaviors of some academic administrators offer unhappy evidence of the former rather than the latter. We emphasize, however, the power of partnership throughout this book.

What of trend and momentum? One of the better-known national authorities on college outcomes and assessment, Peter Ewell, points out that assessment in higher education is not new. He cites early examples where assessment was directly tied to instruction and learning at the University of Chicago and in General College at the University of Minnesota; the early uses of the Graduate Record Examination (GRE), ACT, and SAT; and attempts such as the Pennsylvania General College Test Program in the late 1920s and early 1930s. Ewell suggests, however, that these assessments were intended primarily "to serve as an additional mechanism for gauging an individual student's mastery of a particular body of knowledge in order to provide guidance for future development."[16] Early efforts, then, centered on the student as the unit of primary evaluative interest; contemporary efforts may center on curriculum, program, and institution.

What can we say about what is happening over the country in outcomes? By the early 1990s, more that two-thirds of the states required some assessment initiative in their colleges and universities. As indicated earlier, at the end of 2000, seventeen states were participating in some form of performance funding. Several states have mandated statewide testing programs, including Florida's College Level Academic Skills Test (CLAST), Tennessee's general education outcomes testing, Georgia Regents' Rising Junior Examination, South Dakota's Higher Education Assessment Program, and New Jersey and Texas programs for basic skill assessment. There is little doubt that institutional management boards, state-level coordinating agencies, and legislatures have become more active partners in assessment and outcomes measurement and thus in quality assurance.

Campus administrators and faculties are understandably anxious about and disquieted by this external interest. The fear is that the mandated testing dampens the rich diversity of American higher education and encourages the fiction that colleges are another form of American factory whose product is a competent student. The important concern is whether outcomes assessment constitutes just another exercise in busywork that will cause a momentary ripple on the surface of higher education and then pass on, leaving the depths undisturbed. Also of concern is whether campuses discover instructional, learning, and renewal value in outcomes assessment—as claimed by some writers and scholars. D. W. Farmer (1988) places the issue nicely in these notes: "If faculty approach assessment as being divorced from learning and as simply being a bureaucratic hurdle for students to overcome, assessment will lose its credibility and be treated by faculty and students as busy work."[17] The jury is still out on this question.

There are, however, encouraging models where institutions and their faculties have discovered that effective outcomes assessment exactly parallels good teaching, where the effectiveness of impact on student knowledge, skill, and attitudes and values can be enhanced by intervention in the instructional process. At South College, a four-year, private, proprietary institution in Tennessee, outcomes assessment and evaluation are a systematic part of each department's annual planning process. Applicable measures (survey results, standardized testing results, institutionally designed testing results, focus group findings, peer consultant reports, etc.) are identified by each department, taking into consideration the mission of the department and that of the institution. Minimum expectations are established for each of these measures and the results are reported and evaluated annually for possible changes in the educational process that will improve effectiveness. In a recent study completed by a colleague at Walters State Community College in Tennessee, a somewhat similar environment was reported.[18]

There are also institutions on the other side of the fence, whose posture is described by Spangehl as follows: "Pitted against this rush to assess are a host of universities that have traditionally viewed their missions as more complex than simply turning out students who can outperform other schools' graduates on tests. Their philosophies, funding and budgetary structures, and organizational folkways are ill suited to assessment; they will be hostile to any attempt by a state board or accrediting agency to measure their worth on a simple minded, one dimensional scale."[19]

And then there are those who have good intentions, but whose focus has waned as time has passed. In a recent study completed by one author, the University of Tennessee in Knoxville provides an example of how outcomes assessment, even those mandated by state legislatures, has led to uneven impacts on the educational activities of an institution. When a new policy is implemented, many times a great deal of focus is centered on that policy. It is new, and whether interesting or cumbersome, those affected by it must expend much time and attention in determining the best way to address the policy. In studying the awareness and impact of the Tennessee Performance Funding Policy on the University of Tennessee over the past twenty years, this scenario appears to describe the university's initial response to the policy. Though not greeted with open arms by all, the university focused time and money on developing assessment and evaluation procedures sufficient to meet the requirements of the policy. Committees and task forces worked diligently to create meaningful processes. Information was communicated to all involved on a regular basis.

In doing so, the university received nationwide attention through publications by administrators involved in overseeing the process and by department heads and deans. An award for measurement methods was even earned. At a time when accountability issues in higher education were escalating in the 1980s and most institutions were struggling with assessment and evaluation, the University of Tennessee, Knoxville, appeared to lead the way.

However, as many times occurs with policies that are implemented and as their associated requirements become familiar, a policy may become routinized. The processes involved become rote and less meaningful than when they were new. Other internal and external factors may become more pressing. The University of Tennessee, Knoxville, seems to have also fallen into this scenario as well. Many factors seem to have affected this routinization—turnover in personnel administering the program, lack of emphasis placed on the policy by the administration, faculty's lack of confidence in the value of many required outcomes measures, and the increasingly scarce financial resources available to state institutions. The administrators, deans, and department chairs have been forced to focus on meeting student course needs with fewer faculty and fewer resources. As a result, less attention has been given to assessment and planning.

Except for the academic program reviews that remain departmentally focused, the awareness and impact of the assessment and evaluation practices required by the performance funding program have gone from a somewhat focused and organized attempt to establish an institutional assessment program, to a situation where few understand the policy and the necessary data is only gathered to obtain the monetary rewards associated with the policy or to meet the requirements of regional and programmatic accrediting agencies.

OPERATIONAL DEFINITIONS OF COLLEGE OUTCOMES

The term "assessment" historically implies more than one measurement or approach to evaluation. An assessment of college outcomes, then, requires that we acquire multiple evidences of those outcomes. First, however, we may need some common understanding of just what we mean by the term "outcomes." Given the diversity of some 4,000 campuses over the United States—their missions, histories, and environments—we would be surprised to find a single model of college outcomes to fit all of these colleges. It is appropriate, however, to ask whether there are fundamental knowledge, skills, and attitudes/values that might associate with completion of the bachelor's degree, whether one is graduating from West Point, Oberlin, or the University of California, Los Angeles.

Writing in a 1985 paper, assessment and evaluation scholar Ewell outlined a four-element model for college outcomes:

- Cognitive development: an assessment of general education and major field knowledge expected of the college graduate
- Skills development: an assessment of basic skills such as communication, critical thinking, and analytical skills

- Attitudinal development: an assessment of students' values and changes in those values
- Behavior after college: an assessment of student performance in work or further study after the first degree is received[20]

Ewell emphasizes the potential for enhancing the learning and instructional process via assessment of these four elements. Asking questions of ends inevitably forces us to focus on questions of beginnings. Questions of performance call us to questions of purpose.

For a more extensive model of college outcomes, we turn to Howard Bowen's earlier book-length treatise *Investment in Learning*. Bowen opens his book with two comments that place us in an immediate tension: "Higher education has a clear responsibility to operate efficiently and to report its costs and results to the American people in ways that transcend the tired rhetoric of commencement speeches and slick brochures."[21] This is an argument in favor of outcomes assessment. But then, Bowen reminds us that "Learning—like liberty, equality, love, friendship, charity, and spirituality—carries qualitative connotations that defy numerical measurement."[22]

Bowen suggests a two-factor model or catalog of college goals. Individual goals include these: cognitive learning, emotional and moral development, practical competence, direct satisfactions, and avoidance of negative outcomes. Societal goals embrace advancement of knowledge, discovery and encouragement, advancement of social welfare, and avoidance of negative outcomes.[23]

Because avoidance of negative outcomes is a concept not found in most other outcomes models, a brief word on Bowen's ideas may prove useful. He suggests that higher learning may produce men and women who are more informed, but who may apply their talents for both integrity and duplicity. Some outcomes of higher education may produce dissent rather than conformity, controversy rather than community. Whether a specific outcome is considered positive or negative may well depend on the values of those sitting in judgment, or on the timing or the circumstances involved. Bowen's cautions remind us of the arguments on the ethics of means and ends found in Saul Alinsky's volume *Rules for Radicals* (1971). Alinsky concludes, for example, that if America had dropped the atomic bomb on Japan immediately after Pearl Harbor, there would have been little ethical argument over that decision.[24]

In *Assessment for Excellence* (1993), Astin presents a double-entry table for college outcomes classified by two types of outcomes and two types of data.[25] Table 7.1 is taken from that presentation. Again, we are made to realize the complexity of collegiate outcomes. A further complexity may be added, as suggested by Astin, if we consider a third dimension of time. For example, we may want to assess student satisfaction with college during enrollment and immediately after graduation. Satisfaction with job and career is a longer interval measurement, which may or may not correlate with the earlier satisfaction variable.

One of the more comprehensive institutional models of college outcomes is the one developed at Alverno College. A small, private, liberal arts college,

Table 7.1
A Taxonomy of Student Outcomes

	Types of Outcomes	
Type of Data	*Cognitive*	*Affective*
Psychological	Subject-matter knowledge Academic ability Critical thinking ability Basic learning skills Special aptitudes Academic achievement	Values Interests Self-concept Attitudes Beliefs Satisfaction with college
Behavioral	Degree attainment Vocational achievement Awards or special recognition	Leadership Citizenship Interpersonal relations Hobbies and avocations

Source: Reprinted with permission of Oryx Publishing from p. 45, *Assessment for Excellence,* by Alexander W. Astin. Copyright 1993 by the American Council on Education and Oryx Publishing Company, a division of Greenwood Publishing Group, Inc.

Alverno decided in the early 1970s to develop a competency-based liberal arts degree program. Faculty were involved in the definition of general goals, the identification of assessment techniques, and the development of validation methods for each of eight outcomes finally adopted: communication skill, analytical skill, problem-solving skill, facility in value judgment, facility in social interaction, understanding individual and environmental interactions, understanding world events, and responsiveness to arts and esthetic awareness.[26]

Each of these eight outcomes or competencies is further segmented into attainment levels. For example, outcome seven, understanding world events, begins with the simple expectation of awareness of world events, moves to a knowledge of their historical and cultural antecedents, and then goes on to the expectation that the student will take a personal position on the issue.

It is obvious that these speak to more than cognitive outcomes. The strengths of the model are that it is specific to the educational goals of the institution, that it involves the allegiance of the faculty in development and implementation, and that it is directly linked to the curriculum and instructional processes of the institution.

An earlier developmental model for collegiate outcomes is one furnished by Arthur Chickering in his award-winning volume *Education and Identity* (1969). Chickering lists seven major "developmental vectors" for the intended outcomes of a college education:

- Achieving competence: intellectual, physical, social
- Managing emotions: increased awareness of emotions—aggressive and sexual impulses—and learning effective modes of expression
- Becoming autonomous: achievement of independence and recognition of our interdependence

- Establishing identity: discovery of those experiences that resonate with our personality, development of purpose, and personal integrity
- Freeing interpersonal relationships: less anxiety and defensiveness and more tolerance and trust; development of friendships and love that transcend time, separation, and disagreement
- Clarifying purposes: development of direction for life and discovery of activity that furnishes a foundation of meaning
- Developing integrity: moving from rigid to the discovery of ethical choice, bringing behavior into consistency with values. Any collegiate educator looking at these potential outcomes quickly realizes the poverty of our measurement and assessment approaches if we are to be serious about determining whether we are successful in producing these outcomes in our students[27]

One of the earliest and most comprehensive approaches to the study of college outcomes was the work completed at the National Center for Higher Education Management Systems (NCHEMS), reported by Lenning and others (1977). A descriptive profile of the NCHEMS outcomes can be found in Exhibit 7.1[28]

An earlier report by NCHEMS researchers Sidney Micek and Robert Walhaus (1973) suggested a three-dimensional model concerned with college impact on students, college impact on graduates, and college impact on society.[29] The time dimension is incorporated into the Micek and Walhaus work, which served as a predecessor to the more extensive model reported by Lenning, Lee, Micek, and Service.

Though most of these early scholars have long since departed NCHEMS, their research was a pioneering effort in the United States, one that had a stimulus effect on both thought and action. The concern for outcomes remains active at NCHEMS today through the work of Ewell, which is referenced throughout this and other chapters.

Their work encourages the observation that, with any good idea or practice, effective quality assurance does not happen overnight. We are now over two decades beyond this conceptual trailblazing at NCHEMS. We are sure that many of these scholars must take pleasure in seeing the range of assessment and outcomes activity currently under way, as they reflect on their stimulus roles in producing the early points of this trend line. However, they were without that reinforcement in their early work; those who sow are not necessarily those who reap. Many of the more active and visible scholars cited in this chapter and others stand on the shoulders of those who built this pioneering foundation at NCHEMS.

Predating all of these outcome models are the taxonomies of educational objectives developed by Benjamin Bloom (1956). Three monographs outline taxonomies for cognitive, affective, and psychomotor objectives—knowing, valuing, and acting, matters of head, heart, and hand. To illustrate the nature of these, we briefly explore the taxonomy of cognitive objectives here. In this domain, Bloom and colleagues suggested a hierarchy of intellectual skills: knowledge, comprehension, application, analysis, synthesis, and evaluation.[30]

Exhibit 7.1
The Major "Type-of-Outcome" Category Names and Definitions

Economic Outcomes—Maintenance or change in economic characteristics and conditions of individuals, groups, organizations, and communities, such as in economic access, in economic mobility and independence, in economic security, and in income and standard of living.

Human Characteristic Outcomes—Maintenance or change in human makeup and characteristics (other than knowledge and understanding) of individuals, groups, organizations, and communities, such as aspirations, competence and skills, affective characteristics, perceptual characteristics, physical and physiological characteristics, personality and personal coping characteristics, recognition and certification, and social roles.

Knowledge, Technology, and Art Form Outcomes—Maintenance or change in the knowledge and understanding, technology, or the art forms and works possessed or mastered by individuals, groups, organizations, and communities, such as discoveries and inventions, technical developments, syntheses and reformulations of knowledge, new schools of thought in art and work created in those new traditions, renovations of art works.

Resource and Service Provision Outcomes—Maintenance or change in the direct resources and services (other than those included above) provided to individuals, groups, organizations, and communities, such as providing facilities, events, advisory assistance, analytic assistance, teaching, health care, and leadership.

Other Maintenance and Change Outcomes—Examples would be: maintenance or change in the format, arrangement, activity, or administrative operation of an organization or institution; maintenance or change in the asthetic/cultural level of the local community; maintenance or change in family or community activities, practices, and traditions.

Source: Lenning, Lee, Micek, and Service, 1977, p. 23.

Here is where knowledge enlivens the art form of instruction. For the amateur teacher, and for many who would not be classified as amateurs, teaching is simply a business of spooning out facts and figures; testing amounts to the regurgitation of those facts and figures; and this exchange defines the teaching-learning process. This, however, works on the most elementary level of educational practice.

Knowledge is defined as those activities that emphasize recall; the storing of information; and the later presentation of facts, terminology, trends, classification, or principles. For example, we may expect the student to learn the parts of speech, which is a primary level of educational objective.

Comprehension involves the understanding of what has been presented and encompasses the skills of interpretation, translation, and extrapolation. Here we may expect the student to take these parts of speech, his or her knowledge of their relationships, and the principles of good grammar and not only recall these definitions and relations but also construct sentences that reveal understanding.

Application emphasizes the ability to show understanding and application by putting ideas and concepts to work in solving problems. At this point, we ask students to write a basic business letter, a resume, a short essay, and a book review.

Analysis emphasizes the ability to break problems and materials into constituent parts and relationships, for example, to distinguish fact from opinion. Given a newspaper advertisement for a new product or a political advertisement, we want the student to write an analysis of the appeal or argument used in these materials.

Synthesis recognizes the abilities needed to take the parts of knowledge and put them together into a whole. One may know, for example, the parts of speech and be able to write and diagram a sentence. Synthesis involves putting together words, thoughts, and sentences into paragraphs and essays.

Evaluation is the ability to make judgments of merit or worth, to discriminate. Here we will have students evaluate an essay using these criteria: grammatical correctness; effective use of supporting materials such as illustration, quotes, statistics, and logic or argument; and effectiveness of transition.

The Bloom taxonomy is a useful instrument. It not only makes us think about the levels and types of instructional goals and outcomes but also gives us a useful instrument for doing so. Finally, it furnishes an instrumental link to the final and perhaps most critical part of the teaching process—that of evaluating learning.

Since we have used the Bloom taxonomy to focus on the nature of teaching and learning, let us note in passing an informing and provocative book entitled *Open to Question*.[31] Bateman urges teachers to move past the "empty bucket" theory of dishing out content to the art of teaching by inquiry. His book is rich in conception and illustration. If, for example, we add to the ideas furnished by the Bloom taxonomy the developmental stages of learning advanced by Perry (1970) and illustrated by Bateman, we can begin to understand college teaching as something more than an amateur's occupation. Bateman's book is more than informing; it is fun. It also reveals the "discovery" pleasure enjoyed by those willing and equipped to ask good questions. Curiosity about purpose and performance thus can lead us to curiosity about the activities that link the two—the nature of teaching and learning.

We close this section on outcomes models with a citation not directly related to college outcomes per se but containing concepts worthy of our reflection. We have noted that the work of Bloom enlarges our understanding of the nature of human abilities and levels of performance within each of the three major taxonomies that Bloom developed: cognitive, affective, and psychomotor.

An equally provocative work is the model of multiple intelligences developed by Howard Gardner and reported in *Frames of Mind* (1983).This paragraph in the early pages opens us to the limitations of single-factor views of intelligence:

> But what if one were to let one's imagination wander freely, to consider the wider range of performances that are valued throughout the world. Consider, for example, the twelve year old male puluwat in the Caroline Islands, who has been selected by his elders to learn how to be a master sailor. Under the tutelage of master navigators, he will learn to combine knowledge of sailing, stars, and geography so as to find his way around hundreds of islands. Consider the fifteen year old Iranian youth who has committed to heart the entire Koran and mastered the Arabic language. Now he is being sent to a holy city, to work closely for the next several years with an ayatollah, who will prepare him to be a teacher and a religious leader. Or, consider the fourteen year old adolescent in Paris, who has learned to program a computer and is beginning to compose works of music with the aid of a synthesizer.
>
> ... It should be equally clear that current methods of assessing intellect are not sufficiently well honed to allow assessment of an individual's potentials for achievements in navigating by the stars, mastering a foreign tongue, or composing with a computer.[32]

The remainder of Gardner's book then centers on the empirical and experiential basis for the identification of six intelligences: linguistic, musical, logical-mathematical, spatial, bodily-kinesthetic, and personal intelligence.

A second contemporary work that opens up our curiosity on the nature of talent diversity and intelligence definition is Robert J. Sternberg's book *The Triarchic Mind* (1988). Sternberg offers a critique of Gardner's work, suggesting that intelligence be defined as the capacity for selecting new environments, adapting to new environments, and shaping our environments. On the basis of that definition, Sternberg argues that musical ability should not be considered an "intelligence," that a person can function quite adequately in most environments without musical ability. Sternberg also demolishes some of the more conventional and narrow notions of intelligence: to be quick is to be smart, to have a large vocabulary is to be smart, and to solve problems with a fixed strategy is to be smart. As an example, we take the case of the person who operates on the assumption about vocabulary and intelligence, who spends time memorizing from the dictionary—a person who knows many big words with little comprehension of their meaning or their application.

In summary, Sternberg offers the theory that there are three forms of intelligence: analytical skill, synthetic skill, and practical or applied skill. His work is helpful in distinguishing between problem solving that may occur in structured climates such as schools and colleges and the more complex climates of applied and practical settings.[33]

In school and college, there is a tendency to compartmentalize problems so that they fit the framework of our academic field or discipline. There is also a tendency to suggest that every problem has a solution, which can be found at the back of the book. Finally, there is a tendency to teach about methods of inquiry independent of the personal, cultural, and ethical factors that often attend the pursuit of truth.

In the world of practice, problems often involve elements from many different fields of thought and impose agonizing choices that defy the black and white neatness of computer solutions. The pursuit of what is right—intellectually and ethically—may pit us against the power of popularity and the inertia of the status quo. The history of ideas makes clear that new ideas often make a bloody entrance, that they require a level of character and perseverance not always reflected in the simplicity of a grade point average.

As we engage questions related to the definition and measurement of student learning and development outcomes, we are led on unexpected and serendipitous learning journeys. When we ask questions of results, we are eventually moved to consider questions of beginnings (of intent) and style (of method). Thus, our efforts to assure quality in collegiate settings will be a journey in learning and discovery. In any field of inquiry, there will be found interesting and illuminating interactions between knowledge and technology, and we believe this learning bridge exists for our ventures in quality assurance as well.

What can we learn from the variety of these models for student outcomes? Among the primary fears of faculty is that governmental policymakers will impose a unitary model on higher education, or that accrediting agencies might do so. As shown in chapter 2, the regional accrediting agencies have not thus far insisted on common measures. They have, instead, held institutions to a standard of effectiveness of their own election—but insisting that the standard and the evidence be both public and measured against the goals of the institution.

What of governmental decision makers? There are, of course, some states that have insisted on common measures, for example, the rising junior examination in Georgia and the CLAST program in Florida. In a study of five states, however, Ewell and Boyer (1988) reported: "Contrary to wide belief, we found state leaders more than willing to listen to a range of local options in assessment—if intelligently sold. Harder for state leaders and policymakers to accept was institutional silence on the issue."[34] To return to an earlier theme, the absence of an offensive agenda concerning educational effectiveness often leaves higher education on the defensive.

ASSESSMENT ISSUES

We will not attempt in this chapter to furnish an inventory of current instruments available for assessing college outcomes. There is a wide diversity of such institutional and commercial instruments such as the ETS Academic Profile, the ETS Major Field Tests available for fourteen disciplines, the California Test of Critical Thinking, the ACT Collegiate Assessment of Academic Proficiency (CAAP), and the College Base. Readers interested in more information on designing assessment plans and instruments are referred to the helpful book by Erwin (1991), *Assessing Student Learning and Development,* which offers specific guidance in such areas as identifying student learning objectives, selecting assessment methods, collecting information, analyzing and evaluating information, and reporting and using assessment results.[35] Those interested particularly in the design and assessment of courses and curricula are referred to Robert M. Diamond's (1998) *Designing and Assessing Courses and Curricula: A Practical Guide;*[36] *Involving Colleges: Successful Approaches to Fostering Student Learning and Development Outside the Classroom* (1991) provides insight as to the design and assessment of the out-of-classroom experiences of students.[37] A 1999 publication by NCHEMS, edited by Trudy Banta, offers an update of assessment during the first ten years of the assessment movement and describes assessment efforts by many states and several individual institutions.[38]

What we want to accomplish in this section is to place before the reader some of the decision issues related to the design and development of a college outcomes assessment process.

Matching Assessment to Outcomes Definition

The most obvious question is whether a given assessment instrument or approach matches the outcomes desired and defined by the faculty of an institution. Given the diversity of outcomes models previously outlined, it is obvious that the transport of an instrument from one institution, such as Alverno College, to another, such as the University of Michigan, may be neither feasible nor desirable.

Because the involvement of faculty in the definition of outcomes is a tedious process, there is an unhappy tendency to let the instrument define the outcomes. This approach is like that of the neophyte graduate student who has found a useful questionnaire and goes in search of a research problem to which he or she can affix the questionnaire, rather than vice versa. Here is a commercial instrument: It purports to assess writing skills, mathematical skill, and critical thinking skill; its cost is modest. Let us adopt it for the assessment of general education outcomes that will satisfy the board or the regional accrediting body, and so forth. Besides, it saves us the pain of having to think about what outcomes we really want in our students.

McMillan (1988) cautions us to remember the trade-offs that may be necessary if an institution decides to use a commercially published instrument: "Consequently, if an institution decides to use general measures like the GRE or National Teacher Examinations, there should be a recognized trade-off between the advantages of psychometric quality and institutional comparisons with the disadvantage of a possibly weak correspondence between the test content and content objectives of a curriculum. Without a sound judgment about content-related evidence, however, it may be easy to overlook this disadvantage and make invalid inferences about the results."[39]

Ensuring Validity and Reliability

Measurement theorists tell us that a good measurement instrument will have high validity and high reliability. There are technical definitions for both terms, but the basic idea is that a high-validity instrument measures what it purports to measure, and it does so consistently and with low error (reliability). As noted, locally developed instruments have the advantage of responding more directly to institutionally defined outcomes and decision needs, but this possible absence of validity and reliability information is a liability of locally developed instruments.

Selecting Score Options

Another decision concerns score options. An institution interested in a comparative standard of performance beyond the institution might be more effectively served by a nationally developed assessment instrument that offers comparative score profiles from other institutions.

Other issues here turn on whether decision makers need data for individual or group decisions. If an assessment instrument is being used to make decisions about a program, a sampling of students and total scores may prove adequate. If, however, the decision affects the counseling, placement, or certification of a particular student, then item and scale scores are necessary. Criterion scores reflecting levels of proficiency and not just comparison with other students may be needed.

If, for example, an institution wants each of its students reaching the junior year to have mastered a certain level of mathematical proficiency before the student is admitted to a major field or upper-division study, then normative or comparative scores will be of less utility than criterion or proficiency scores. Many national companies are starting to recognize this decision need. The Academic Profile developed by ETS offers both a normative and a proficiency or criterion score.

Evaluating Time and Money Costs

Institutionally developed assessments will generally take large investments of time and money for design, field test, scoring, and administration. Only the institution can evaluate the trade-offs involved in local development vis-à-vis the selection of an "off-the-shelf" instrument whose costs are relatively modest and whose development already includes the extensive field tests necessary to produce an instrument of proven reliability and validity.

Another question of cost centers on who will pay for the assessment. Some institutions are sufficiently well funded that the institution or the state recognizes costs through the general fund budget. In other institutions, individual students will be asked to pay the cost, just as they are asked to pay breakage, laboratory, or graduation fees to help defer selected costs beyond basic instruction.

A part of the cost question turns on the amount of time needed for test administration. Assessments whose primary decision needs are for the evaluation of programs may allow testing strategies of greater simplicity and brevity than those whose decision purposes relate to individual students.

Terenzini (1989) examines the cost issue from a different perspective. He suggests that the costs of not assessing outcomes must be considered: "Important opportunities may be missed, including, for example, the chance to clarify institutional goals, to review and revise (or reconfirm the value of) existing curricular purposes and structures, and to examine the successes and failures of current policies and practices. The costs of rejecting or deferring assessment may be substantial, if difficult to calculate."[40] The associated beneficial outcomes cited by Terenzini affirm the discovery potential of quality assurance, a point we emphasized earlier.

Isolating Sources of Bias

One of the major criticisms heard of standardized and commercial assessments in the United States is that they are insensitive to differences in experience, language, culture, and gender. Normative data, it is asserted, tend to encourage labeling and the maintenance of cultural prejudice. In a word, we are told that tests and assessments are often biased and discriminatory.

A complication on this issue turns on whether the bias is in the test, in the culture, or in the use of the test. Often, there are confounding effects. Flaugher (1974) defines these sources of test bias.[41]

- Test content: Is the assessment insensitive to differences in experience or language?
- Test administration: Is the atmosphere of the assessment (the time, the place, the sex or race of the test administrator) or the attitude of the test taker (an expectation of confidence vis-à-vis an expectation of prejudice) a source of bias?
- Test use: Is one group systematically favored in selection, classification, or benefit?

Although the existence of bias on all these points can be demonstrated, curious and equally unfortunate scenarios are played out by those hoping to avoid bias. One of the authors knows of a state in which the validity of a state assessment used to make decisions about licensure of teachers was decided by whether the assessment yielded equal pass rates by race and sex.

As Diamond (1976) suggests, the options are to declare a moratorium on all tests until any and all biases can be rooted out, or to use assessments with discretion as we attempt to control for the three sources of bias identified. Diamond then indicates that "to declare a moratorium on the use of tests requires a corresponding but unlikely moratorium on decisions—employment decisions, selection decisions by colleges and universities, and decisions based on the evaluations of various educational and social programs."[42]

Diamond also observes that "if tests are guilty of reflecting middle class values, will the judgments of the middle class teachers, counselors, administrators, and employers necessarily be less so?"[43] Diamond's conclusion centers on the need for multiple sources of data on an individual, a principle whose importance is celebrated throughout each of these chapters. Finally, Diamond offers a series of steps designed to remove or alleviate sources of bias. They include a number of statistical and technical devices, the use of representative groups (to include minorities) in reviewing test content, and the application of advances in computer capabilities.

Examining Levels of Difficulty

Clifford Adelman (n.d.) suggests that it may be possible for an assessment instrument to be valid (a technical criterion we explored earlier) and still leave some question as to difficulty level. He uses in illustration an example taken from Northeast Missouri State University (now Truman State University).

Northeast Missouri State University used the mathematics subtest of the National Teacher Examination (NTE) to test the mathematics knowledge of seniors graduating in teacher education. This subtest is a twenty-five-item test. Adelman reports that in the twenty-five items "virtually identical questions are asked of college seniors (on the NTE) and high school juniors (on the CEEB)."[44] Adelman concludes: "The NTE! Math may be very valid—hence appropriate—for NMSU though one would hope that prospective high school math teachers also know trigonometry, intermediate algebra, solid geometry, elementary functions and analytic geometry, set theory, elementary statistics and probability."[45]

Adelman proceeds to explore several schemes for evaluating the difficulty level of assessments. For example, the Foreign Service Institute uses a scale comprising four criteria to rate language proficiency in terms of speaking, listening, reading, and writing. There are levels of performance on each of these four language skills in eleven intervals from "0" to "5." Adelman also suggests the Bloom taxonomy, previously discussed, as a means of judging difficulty level in intellectual tasks.

A correlate problem of assessment difficulty levels is described by Jacobi, Astin, and Ayala (1987) as "the likelihood that students will bottom out on a pretest or top out on the posttest."[46] If a test is too difficult, scores may show little variance, and there is a concomitant danger that students may begin academic careers with anxiety and frustration in trying to deal with an assessment that is well beyond their capacity. And, as the authors suggest, "these negative effects may be particularly acute when such tests are administered to incoming freshmen, many of whom are already uncertain about their ability to succeed in the new more demanding college environment."[47]

Reconciling Value-Added Issues

In knowing whether its instructional program has made a difference in student knowledge, skill, or attitude/value, an institution is interested in the "value-added" question. There are, however, lively debates on the difficulties in developing adequate value-added assessments.

Among these issues are those that reveal that changes in student performance can often be assigned to variables outside the instructional process. Here are examples.

- *Maturation:* Did the improvement in performance occur simply by virtue of student maturation rather than the instructional intervention?
- *Other experience:* Can improvement on a particular set of questions or assessment experiences be more properly assigned to an extracurricular experience (for example, foreign travel, summer camp, computer gaming, and so on) rather than instruction?
- *Pygmalion effect:* Do the expectations of those making judgments bias the actual performance or perception and evaluation of performance?
- *Regression effect:* Does the statistical tendency for low scores to increase and high scores to regress affect the observed change in scores in value-added exercises?

Readers interested in one of the more lively debates centered on value-added assessment can refer to two articles appearing in the bulletin of the American Association for Higher Education. Jonathan Warren (1984) fires the first shot in an article entitled "The Blind Alley of Value-Added," opening with these notes: "In the abstract, the logic of value-added gives it great appeal. In practice, I'll argue, it seldom leads anywhere. Its results are often trivial, difficult to make sense of, and peripheral to most instructional purposes."[48] Warren refers to value-added as the reigning gospel of contemporary higher education assessment. In a follow-up article entitled "The Value-Added Debate ... Continued," Astin (1985) responds to Warren with these criticisms: "Value-added assessment, as Warren suggests, is not a panacea to be applied mechanistically or insensitively in every situation. But my experience has been that institutions are smarter than Warren gives them credit for. A far greater danger is that which Warren's position itself exemplifies: of trivializing a powerful concept to the point that institutions are unwilling to experiment with developmental outcomes assessments of anykind."[49]

Finally, Leonard Baird (n.d.) warns us about the limitations of value added. After touching on some of the issues already outlined in this discussion, Baird concludes that "perhaps the greatest practical problem with assessing gain on a common criterion is that the method allows (and in some cases may encourage) invidious comparisons."[50] He is concerned with comparison of average gain scores across disciplines, colleges, and institutions.

These concerns bring us back to questions of financial support levels and ultimately, as Baird suggests, "lead an institution to lose sight of its educational purpose."[51] On that point, let us now examine an assessment issue that may prove fundamental to all others.

DECISION PURPOSES OF OUTCOMES ASSESSMENT

How exactly do we intend to use assessment data? Essentially, we face two decision domains—that of the individual student and that of the program or institution—and in each of these two domains are two additional decision applications:

Student Decisions	Program Decisions
Counsel or place	Accept or improve
Certify	Retain or terminate

Readers are referred to Millman's (n.d.) informing discussion on decision purposes.[52] Millman clusters the assessment decision purposes, for example, under the following: placement decisions, certification decisions, course and program evaluation decisions, and institutional evaluation decisions. Two other reports that will prove useful to those interested in identifying and improving campus decision utility of outcome results are those prepared by Ewell and published by NCHEMS (1985). In both volumes, entitled *Using Student Outcomes Information in Program Planning and Decision Making,* Ewell outlines five lessons.[53]

- "Lesson One: Information about student outcomes is generally available on campus if you look for it—but rarely in the form you want it."
- "Lesson Two: Address your data utilization effort to a particular commonly recognized issue or problem."
- "Lesson Three: Involve as many kinds of people from as many parts of the campus as possible."
- "Lesson Four: Efforts to utilize outcome information are often positively influenced by external forces and individuals."
- "Lesson Five: When raising questions about student outcomes, be prepared for discussions to turn eventually to broad issues of institutional mission and effectiveness."

In a further work (1988), Ewell furnishes an informing and thorough treatment of three themes: the identification and assessment of college outcomes; the attribution of outcomes, or linking outcomes to educational experiences; and valuation, or deciding what the results mean and to whom they apply. In a concluding section of this excellent paper, Ewell engages the decision question of "getting there: using outcomes information as a change agent."[54] His analysis of institutional attempts to make more effective decision use of outcomes and assessment information provides a sobering but useful counterpoint to Astin's note, cited earlier, that much of the current assessment is having little impact. Ewell's paper makes clear that many institutions are struggling with the decision application issues. Ewell closes his paper with a comment on what he calls the classic academic dilemma: the requirement to know everything before attempting anything. He then emphasizes a point that we salute throughout this book: the call to act on what we already know.

Let us cite a really simple example of how quality assurance ventures can begin to have an impact on institutional policy. A large research university opened an inquiry on how it could more effectively measure the results of its required general education curriculum. The question of how to assess the outcomes of the general education sequence eventually led the faculty and staff task force back to the university catalog to see what educational goals and rationale had been offered to support the forty-eight-semester-hour requirement in English; mathematics; and discipline clusters in the humanities, social sciences, sciences, and health and physical education. Did they find there an educational rationale that made sense to students—such as developing skill in written and oral communication, facility in numerical analysis, and acquaintance with modes of thought by which we advance on truth? No. What they did find was a single lead sentence indicating that the purpose of the general education curriculum was to "facilitate transfer" of credits among institutions in the system. The task force concluded that this was an empty and inadequate rationale for the university faculty to offer its students, and they set about fashioning a more meaningful educational preamble.

One might argue that this result is of small moment. It is, however, an improvement that might not have been made had the university been about business as usual. We certainly encourage the kinds of conceptual and action research outlined by Ewell in his 1988 paper, but we are impatient with those who want to stand around wringing their conceptual hands. Improved impact for our students and our institutions is possible with the knowledge we have at hand now.

Evaluating Other Assessment Options

An inclination obvious in previous commentary on assessment issues is that some of these concerns relate to more conventional assessment approaches—predominantly those of the paper-and-pencil variety. However, many institutions have been and are trying more imaginative models, among them senior capstone courses, portfolio assessment, assessment centers, external examiners, connoisseurship, and disguised observers.

For example, in the latter portion of the 1980s, King's College began requiring that each student participate in a senior seminar (capstone course) designed to strengthen and ultimately assess a student's transfer of liberal arts skills to his or her major field.[55] In 1990, Miami University in Oxford, Ohio, began evaluating student portfolios, which may consist of research papers, exams, self-evaluations, personal essays, journals, mathematical analysis exercises, photographs or projects, computer programs, and case studies. This assessment procedure was developed to ascertain the effectiveness of descriptive assessment.[56] Alverno College, which uses portfolio as part of it student assessment-as-learning process, has created a diagnostic digital portfolio.

> This first-of-its-kind, web-based system enables each Alverno student—anyplace, anytime—to follow her learning process throughout her years of study. It helps the student process the feedback she receives from faculty, external assessors, and peers. It also enables her to look for patterns in her academic work so she can take more control of her own development and become a more autonomous learner.[57]

Winthrop University attempts to conduct one-year postgraduation telephone surveys with graduates.[58]

Some campuses are using "assessment center" approaches. An example is the teacher education program at the Indiana University of Pennsylvania, where a series of simulations and other activities test student teaching mastery and simultaneously develop additional competence. Activities in the teacher education assessment center call for students to analyze and evaluate short videotapes of classroom episodes, to prepare a short lesson plan and present the lesson, to organize a districtwide education, and to plan an educational museum exhibit.[59] In 1990, Ohio State University published information regarding its Center for Teaching Excellence that provides assistance to instructors by providing "workshops, individual consultation, and written materials in the construction and interpretation of objective tests, essays, performance measures, and other means used to assess students' learning in courses and larger programs."[60] Other colleges are using the "external examiner" approach. Berea College uses external faculty examiners to assess learning in the students' major fields, via written and oral examinations given by these external faculty.[61]

One of the more creative concepts being applied to assessment of academic programs is that of Eisner's connoisseurship model at the University of Nebraska, Lincoln, where program review involves a team that includes students and faculty—both external to the department and to the university. This process remains very active for this university today. Indeed, Eisner's book (1985) *The Act of Educational Evaluation* furnishes an excellent reason for the utilization of multiple approaches to evaluation: "To fish for trout in a stream using bait designed to catch salmon and to conclude from our failed efforts that no trout are there, is to draw what might very well be an erroneous conclusion. Our nets define what we shall catch. If there is one message I would like to convey in this book it is the desirability of weaving many types of nets."[62]

Now, finally, we mention one other approach to program evaluation, just to illustrate that the assessment of collegiate outcomes furnishes a splendid opportunity to utilize our imagination. Several years ago, one of the authors was involved with pilot assessment projects in a variety of colleges in Tennessee.[63] The College of Pharmacy at the University of Tennessee Center for Health Sciences decided to evaluate some of their recent graduates with a "disguised observer" approach in which graduate pharmacy students posed as customers. The purposes of the evaluation were to ascertain whether practicing pharmacists could recognize customer description of symptoms that needed referral to physicians, to ascertain the accuracy of prescription fillings, and to ascertain pharmacists' ability to spot fraudulent prescriptions.

DEFINING THE OUTCOME

Earlier we noted that any attempt to evaluate performance inevitably brings up questions of purpose. Asking "how good a job are we doing?" certainly requires that we have some notion of "what did we hope to achieve?" The decision challenge for American higher education is nicely placed by L. J. Benezet as follows: "What is to be learned in college is judged differently according to whether one sees college as a place to absorb man's heritage of knowledge and culture, or to sharpen already superior intellectual talents, or to prepare for a graduate profession, or to become a discoverer of new knowledge or creator of new arts forms, or to mature as a thinking, feeling, and rationally acting person, or to relate better to other human beings, or to start on any of a hundred different careers requiring skills beyond the high school, or to learn what needs to be learned in order to attack the most urgent problems of mankind."[64] Obviously, some choice is necessary, because most colleges and universities will not find it possible or even desirable to assess all possible outcomes—especially the longer-range and social/economic outcomes suggested by some of the models outlined.

If, for example, we elect to restrict our focus to student outcomes, we are still left with a formidable set of questions. Let us for the moment say that we want to elect the apparent simplicity of the first three elements of Ewell's model and center our assessment on student knowledge, skills, and values/attitudes. Let us look at the questions that might follow.

Knowledge

Perhaps we might decide early that we should assess student knowledge in both general education and the major field. But exactly what model of "general education" do we select? Most general education curricular requirements are implicit in what we might call a "mode-of-thought" model. That is, asking our students to sample courses in a variety of disciplines—humanities, science, and so on—we apparently are asking that they know something about how humans advance in their search for the truth. Certainly, it is a highly legitimate general education goal for our students to take an epistemological journey—to know that truth may emerge from the objectivity of science, the heat of adversarial arguments, the rationality of analysis, the interpretative and passionate moments of art and music, the revelatory moments of literature and religion, and the quiet moments of history.

There are other models to choose from, however. Instead of a "mode-of-thought" model for general education, we might select one with a cultural/historical bent. The historian Will Durant (1954), for example, says that if we hope to understand the flow of history and culture, we must examine the ways in which society deals with economics, education, religion, art forms, and political/governance issues.[65] One might also choose, for example, to build a general education model on the multiple intelligences outlined by Gardner or Sternberg. This question leads to yet another decision challenge. How might we elect to distinguish between knowledge and skill?

Skill

Presumably, we move here from cognitive acquisition to acting, from knowing to doing. But precisely what skills do we wish our students to acquire? Which of the following skills might fit within our outcomes model: communication—oral and written, analytic/problem solving, judgment/evaluative, interpersonal, creative/artistic, psychomotor/physical? There are some who say that contemporary education neglects the education of the intuition. See, for example, Robert Ornstein's (1972) important work *The Psychology of Consciousness.*[66]Western intellectual traditions tend to be verbal/intellectual in their emphasis. The reflective and contemplative traditions of the Orient offer realities that are often disturbing to the Western mind, yet provoking to our curiosity as well. Might the education of what is described as intuition find its way into our general education skill considerations? Here we find ourselves moving into the realm of philosophy and religion, which bridges nicely to our third element, that of values.

Values and Attitudes

Nothing is plainer in its truth than that many college graduates place themselves, their customers and clients, and their organizations and institutions in harm's way, not because of technical incompetence but because graduates abandon their integrity. No college or university would subscribe to the notion that they sought to nurture no values in the education of their graduates. Well, then, what are the values we wish to impart to our graduates and what role do assessment and outcomes play in the ethical makeup of our students? And how many colleges are explicit about the values they hope to impart and the methods used to develop these values?

There are surely some fundamental values we can salute: dignity, courage, responsibility, and so forth. In one of the more impressive displays of commitment, the Board of Regents for the State University System of Florida adopted a set of fifteen values in their master plan for 1988–89 through 1992–93. We take the liberty of reproducing them here in their entirety:

- Personal integrity that is rooted in respect for truth and love of learning
- A sense of duty of self, family, and the larger community
- Self-esteem rooted in the quest for the achievement of one's potential
- Respect for the rights of all persons regardless of their race, religion, nationality, sex and age, physical condition, or mental state
- The courage to express one's convictions, and recognition of the rights of others to hold and express differing views
- The capacity to make discriminating judgments among competing opinions
- A sense of, and commitment to, justice, rectitude, and fair play
- Understanding, sympathy, concern, and compassion for others

- A sense of discipline and pride in one's work; respect for the achievements of others
- Respect for one's property and the property of others, including public property
- An understanding of, and appreciation for, other cultures and traditions
- A willingness to perform the obligations of citizenship, including the right to vote and the obligation to cast an informed ballot, jury service, participation in government and the rule of law
- Civility, including congenial relations between men and women
- A commitment to academic freedom as a safeguard essential to the purposes of the university and to the welfare of those who work within it
- The courage to oppose the use of substances which impair one's judgment or one's health[67]

Addressing the question of what outcomes to assess, then, can be an exercise of formidable challenge. The quest for quality offers a journey of philosophical and technical complexity. It is, however, a journey with significant learning potential as well.

Linking Knowledge and Practice

Before we issue a concluding note about the renewing impact of outcomes assessment, we provide this reflection about promoting public confidence in higher education. Collegiate educators need not believe that quality assurance for colleges is more complex than that for corporations. Both are multifactor enterprises where the evidence can and should be varied. The nature of a performance guarantee in our colleges and universities also is no more complex than in many other professional fields. Indeed, there are few clinical professions whose history will not reveal imperfect and inadequate links between knowledge and practice—and equally serious questions about links between expenditures and outcomes. We think of medicine and law as two examples.

It has been scarcely a hundred years since the largest medical issue facing the nation of France was how to import several million leeches when the domestic supply was exhausted. Quinine was used in the treatment of malaria, successfully so, long before we understood the causal relations involved. There is some question as to whether future perspective might make some of today's surgeries—tonsillectomies, radical mastectomies, and heart bypasses—look rather barbaric.

As physician-researcher-author Lewis Thomas recounts in *The Youngest Science: Notes of a Medicine Watcher* (1983),the medical literature of the turn of the century makes horrifying reading today: "Paper after learned paper recounts the benefits of bleeding, cupping, violent purging, the raising of blisters by vesicant ointments, the immersion of the body in either ice water or intolerably hot water, endless lists of botanical abstracts cooked up and mixed together under the influence of nothing more than pure whim and all these things were drilled into the heads of medical students."[68]Thomas reports that as late as the middle of 1930 "we didn't know much that was really useful, that we could do nothing to change the course of the great majority of the diseases we were so busy analyzing, that medicine, for all its facade as a learned profession, was in real life a profoundly ignorant occupation."[69] The scientific base of the art of medicine is for the most part a development of the past fifty years.

Even now, with all the scientific and technical advances of modern medicine, the philosophy and values of the contemporary practitioner continue to have a powerful impact on the health and well-being of patients. Consider the practice of medicine represented in the following illustrations shared recently by a physician friend. An elderly man had been operated on by an orthopedic surgeon for a fractured hip. Following the surgery, the patient failed to regain consciousness and remained in a comatose state. Given the patient's age, the surgeon and one other attending physician were not optimistic about his recovery. However, friends of the patient asked a family physician friend to come by and look in on him. His diagnosis was that the man had contracted pneumonia with attendant high fever causing the comatose state, apparently not an unusual matter in older patients. Treatment for the high fever brought the patient back to consciousness in short order, producing what appeared to be a miracle in the eyes of the patient's family. In the first diagnosis, the narrowness of the surgeon's interest prevented him from seeing other options, whereas science and art were both at work in the second, more constructive, one.

As for the profession of law, we were well into the latter half of this century before the poor of this nation stood before the bar with a court-appointed attorney to represent them. It took a prisoner in a Florida penitentiary—see *Gideon's Trumpet* (Lewis, 1964)—to bring about that change.[70] If we are to break the logjam in today's courts or lighten the weight of frivolous and unnecessary lawsuits, the probabilities are that someone other than a lawyer will be the author of ideas to achieve those changes.

It took farmers twenty-five years to accept hybrid corn and equally as long to accept other empirical and scientific principles concerning the raising of other crops. The distance between the activities of yesterday and recent advances in catfish and crayfish farming, for example, is long indeed. Developing an educated human being is far more complex than developing a better breed of corn or catfish.

In his informing book entitled *Knowing and Acting: An Invitation to Philosophy,* Stephen Toulmin (1976) concludes with this note: "Rather than prolong this survey any further, therefore, let me simply invite you to put this book aside, face the philosophical problems that you find most perplexing in your own mind and begin tackling them for yourself, and in your own ways."[71] Those collegiate educators interested only in armchair philosophy, in a wringing of hands over the liabilities and limitations of collegiate outcomes assessment, will surely have a more restricted and less advantageous journey of learning than those who are willing to act on the possible while awaiting perfection.

In a word, our potential for understanding and improving our impact on our students is not enhanced by passive and argumentative modes of thought *alone.* We develop no muscles as spectators; the harnessing of action and reflection is the beginning of discovery and adventure in learning. We will languish in both intellectual and emotional poverty, as will our students, if we are unwilling to pose and answer the question: "What has been our impact on our students and how do we know?"

NOTES

1. Mortimer, K. (1972). *Accountability in Higher Education.* Washington, DC: American Association for Higher Education, 48.

2. Ibid., 6.

3. Brubacher, J. S., and Rudy, W. (1997). *Higher Education in Transition: A History of American Colleges and Universities* (4th ed.). New Brunswick, NJ: Transaction Publishers, 35.

4. Spangehl, S. (1987). "The Push to Assess: Why It's Feared and How to Respond." *Change,* 19(1), January/February, 35–36.

5. Banta, T. W., and Fisher, H. S. (1984a). "Performance Funding: Tennessee's Experiment." *New Directions for Higher Education,* 12(4), 29.

6. Gaither, G., Nedwek, B. P., and Neal, J. E. (1994). *Measuring Up: The Promises of Performance Indicators in Higher Education.* ASHE-ERIC/Higher Education Research Report No. 5, Washington, DC: Association for the Study of Higher Education.

7. Jones, D. P., and Ewell, P. T. (1987). *Accountability in Higher Education: Meaning and Methods.* Boulder, CO: National Center for Higher Education Management Systems (ERIC Document Reproduction Service No. ED 282 511), v.

8. Ibid.

9. Astin, A. W. (1993). *Assessment for Excellence: The Philosophy and Practice of Assessment and Evaluation in Higher Education.* Phoenix, AZ: Oryx. Morrell, L. C. (1996). Acting on the Possible while Awaiting Perfection: The Effect of General Education Assessment at Public Two-Year Institutions of Higher Education in Tennessee (Ed.D. dissertation, University of Tennessee, Knoxville). *Dissertation Abstracts International, 58–06A,* 1–192.

10. Kean, T. (1987). "Time to Deliver: Before We Forgot the Promises We Made." *Change,* 19(5), 11.

11. Terenzini, P. (1989). "Assessment with Open Eyes: Pitfalls in Studying Student Outcomes." *Journal of Higher Education,* 60(6), 645.

12. Burke, J. C. (2000). *Performance Funding: Easier to Start than Sustain.* Unpublished manuscript.

13. Westling, J. (1988). "The Assessment Movement is Based on a Misdiagnosis of the Malaise Afflicting American Higher Education." *Chronicle of Higher Education,* 35(8), B1.

14. Benjamin, E. (1989). "Administrative Acquiescence in Assessment." *AGB Reports,* 31(2), 14.

15. Astin, *Assessment for Excellence,* ix.

16. Ewell, P. (1985). "Assessment: What's It All About?" *Change,* November/December, 32.

17. Farmer, D. (1988). *Enhancing Student Learning: Emphasizing Essential Competencies in Academic Programs.* Wilkes-Barre, PA: King's College Press, 151.

18. Shaw, T. (2000). *An Evaluation of Tennessee's Performance Funding Policy at Walters State Community College.* Unpublished dissertation, University of Tennessee.

19. Spangehl, S. (1987). "The Push to Assess: Why It's Feared and How to Respond." *Change,* 19(1), January/February, 35.

20. Ewell, "Assessment: What's It All About?" 32–36.

21. Bowen, H. (1978). *Investment in Learning: The Individual and Social Value of American Higher Education.* San Francisco: Jossey-Bass, 22.

22. Ibid., 24.

23. Ibid., 31–59.

24. Alinsky, S. (1971). *Rules for Radicals.* New York: Vintage Books.

25. Astin, *Assessment for Excellence,* 45

26. Mentkowski, M., and Doherty, A. (1984). "Abilities That Last a Lifetime: Outcomes of the Alverno Experience." *AAHE Bulletin,* February, 514.

27. Chickering, A. (1969). *Education and Identity.* San Francisco: Jossey-Bass.

28. Lenning, O., Lee, Y., Micek, S., and Service, A. (1977). *A Structure for the Outcomes of Postsecondary Education.* Denver, CO: National Center for Higher Education Management.

29. Micek, S., and Walhaus, R. (1973). *An Introduction to the Identification and Uses of Higher Education Outcomes Information.* Technical Report No. 40. Boulder, CO: National Center for Higher Education Management Systems.

30. Bloom, B., and Others. (1956). *Taxonomy of Educational Objectives: The Classification of Educational Goals Handbook I.* New York: McKay.

31. Bateman, W. (1990). *Open to Question: The Art of Teaching and Learning by Inquiry.* San Francisco: Jossey-Bass.

32. Gardner, H. (1983). *Frames of Mind: The Theory of Multiple Intelligence.* New York: Basic Books, 4.

33. Sternberg, R. (1988). *The Triarchic Mind: A New Theory of Human Intelligence.* New York: Viking.

34. Ewell, P., and Boyer, C. (1988). "Acting Out State Mandated Assessment: Evidence from Five States." *Change,* 20(4), 47.

35. Erwin, T. (1991). *Assessing Student Learning and Development.* San Francisco: Jossey-Bass.

36. Diamond, R. M. (1998). *Designing and Assessing Courses and Curricula.* San Francisco: Jossey-Bass.

37. Kuh, G., Schuh, J., Whitt, E., and Associates. (1991). *Involving Colleges: Successful Approaches to Fostering Student Learning and Development Outside the Classroom.* San Francisco: Jossey-Bass.

38. Banta, Trudy (ed.). (1999). *Assessment Update: The First Ten Years.* Boulder, CO: National Center for Higher Education Management Systems.

39. McMillan, J. (1988). "Beyond Value-Added Education: Improvement Alone Is Enough." *Journal of Higher Education,* 59(5), 567.

40. Terenzini, "Assessment with Open Eyes: Pitfalls in Studying Student Outcomes," 654.

41. Flaugher, R. (1974). Bias in Testing: A Review and Discussion. TM Report No. 36, Educational Resources Information Center Clearinghouse on Tests, Measurement and Evaluation. Princeton, NJ: Educational Testing Service.

42. Diamond, E. (1976). "Testing: The Baby and the Bath Water are Still with Us." *Testing and the Public Interest: Proceedings of the 1976 Educational Testing Service Invitational Conference.* Princeton, NJ: Educational Testing Service.

43. Ibid.

44. Adelman, C. (ed.). (n.d.). "Difficulty Levels and the Selection of 'General Education' Subject to Examinations." In *Performance and Judgment: Essays on Principles and Practice in the Assessment of College Student Learning.* Washington, DC: Office of Educational Research and Improvement, U.S. Department of Education, 188.

45. Ibid.

46. Jacobi, M., Astin, A., and Ayala, A. Jr. (1987). *College Student Outcomes Assessment: A Talent Development Perspective.* ASHE-ERIC/Higher Education Report No. 7, Washington, DC: Association for the Study of Higher Education, 35.

47. Ibid.

48. Warren, J. (1984). "The Blind Alley of Value-Added." *AAHE Bulletin,* 37(1), 10.

49. Astin, A. (1985). "The Value-Added Debate ... Continued." *American Association of Higher Education Bulletin,* 37(8), 11–13.

50. Baird, L. (n.d.). "Value-Added: Using Student Gains as Yardsticks of Learning," In *Performance and Judgment: Essays on Principles and Practice in the Assessment of College Student Learning,* ed. C. Adelman. Washington, DC: Office of Educational Research and Improvement, U.S. Department of Education, 213.

51. Ibid., 214.

52. Millman, J. (n.d.). "Designing a College Assessment." In *Performance and Judgment: Essays on Principles and Practice in the Assessment of College Student Learning,* ed. C. Adelman. Washington, DC: Office of Educational Research and Improvement, U.S. Office of Education.

53. Ewell, P. (1985). *Using Student Outcomes Information in Program Planning and Decision Making.* 2 vols. Denver, CO: National Center for Higher Education Management Systems.

54. Ewell, P. (1988). "Outcomes, Assessment, and Academic Improvement: In Search of Usable Knowledge." In *Higher Education: Handbook of Theory and Research,* Vol. 4, ed. J. Smart. New York: Agathon Press, 85.

55. Paskow, J. (ed.). (1988). *Assessment of Programs and Projects: A Directory.* Washington, DC: American Association for Higher Education Assessment Forum.

56. Assessment Update. (1994). September-October, 6(5). In Banta, Trudy (ed.). (1999). *Assessment Update: The First Ten Years.* Boulder, CO: National Center for Higher Education Management Systems, 372–375.

57. Alverno College. (2002). Available on-line: http://www.alverno.edu.

58. Assessment Update. (1996). November-December, 8(6). In Banta, Trudy (ed.). (1999). *Assessment Update: The First Ten Years.* Boulder, CO: National Center for Higher Education Management Systems, 397–400.

59. Paskow, *Assessment of Programs and Projects.*

60. Assessment Update. (1990). Summer, 2(2). In Banta, Trudy (ed.). (1999). *Assessment Update: The First Ten Years.* Boulder, CO: National Center for Higher Education Management Systems, 488–490.

61. Paskow, *Assessment of Programs and Projects.*

62. Eisner, E. (1985). *The Art of Educational Evaluation.* Philadelphia: Falmer Press, 7.

63. Bogue, E., and Brown, W. (1982). "Performance Incentives for State Colleges." *Harvard Business Review,* 60(6).

64. Benezet, L. (1989). "Learning What?" In *Evaluating Learning and Teaching,* ed. C. R. Pace. San Francisco: Jossey-Bass, 11.

65. Durant, W. (1954). *The Story of Civilization: Vol. 1. Our Oriental Heritage.* New York: Simon and Schuster.

66. Ornstein, R. (1972). *The Psychology of Consciousness.* New York: W. H. Freeman.

67. State University System of Florida. (1988). "Procedural Guidelines for Review of Existing Programs." *Academic Program Review in State University System of Florida.* Unpublished manuscript. Tallahassee: State University System of Florida.

68. Thomas, L. (1983). *The Youngest Science: Notes of a Medicine Watcher.* New York: Viking, 19.

69. Ibid., 29.

70. Lewis, A. (1964). *Gideon's Trumpet.* New York: Random House.

71. Toulmin, S. (1976). *Knowing and Acting: An Invitation to Philosophy.* New York: Macmillan.

Chapter 8

Total Quality Management

The Test of Continuous Improvement

While the quality assurance systems of previous chapters have enjoyed birthrights primarily within academic circles, total quality management (TQM) is a quality assurance system having origins in corporate organizations and profit sector enterprise, principally in the manufacturing industry. Accreditation (chapter 2) is a concept employed in other sectors of our national life, such as hospital accreditation, but its heritage resides primarily in higher education. Acquiring customer feedback and client satisfaction (chapter 4) is certainly not exclusive to higher education organizations, as anyone who has purchased a product or service will attest. The practice of surveying enrolled students and alumni in higher education has a long history in higher education.

What we find in TQM, however, is a philosophy and a technique that emerged primarily in manufacturing organizations and then was transferred to colleges and universities. The movement of TQM into higher education quality assurance is a fascinating story, with much fanfare and euphoria in the beginning and uncertain times following, as higher education faculty and administrators await the question of whether this practice adapted from the corporate sector will experience a quiet departure as have other management techniques adapted from other organizational settings. In this chapter, we first explore the philosophical heritage of TQM, the ideas and concepts undergirding TQM. We will then examine some of the technical tools associated with the application of TQM. We can then probe applications of the concept in colleges and universities and conclude with an assessment of its benefits and liabilities.

THE FANFARE FOR TQM

Two books on the application of TQM in higher education celebrate the contributions of the concept in colleges and universities. An informing and integrating work, one offering a favorable treatment of TQM as applied to higher education, is Daniel Seymour's 1992 book *On Q: Causing Quality in Higher Education.*[1] Seymour offers the conviction that "accrediting agencies, program reviews, standing committees, control-minded governing boards, and the occasional well-intentioned task force will not be instruments for causing quality in higher education."[2] He offers TQM as an answer to the question: "Is there a better way to manage higher education?" Those who have been on the giving and receiving end of accreditation and program reviews will know the limitations of these quality assurance systems; and, indeed, we have pointed to the strengths and limitations of those in previous chapters. As we shall soon see, however, TQM was hardly on its way into higher education applications when management scholars in the corporate sector were offering significant critiques of TQM even there.

In the preface to their 1994 book *Total Quality in Higher Education,* Lewis and Smith offer this favorable reflection in their preface:[3]

> Question: Why total quality in higher education? Answer: Because it is right. We believe that it is right because:
>
> - It builds on the tradition of concern for quality that has characterized higher education in the United States and throughout the world.
> - It recognizes the need for continuous development of the people who are part of the higher education system, whether students, faculty, or administrators.
> - It involves principles applicable to institutional administration and classroom teaching, thus providing a bridge between traditionally separated parts of the system.
> - It will help us meet the challenges of the 1990s and build effective universities and colleges of the twenty-first century.

Whether these strident and affirming views on the value of TQM in higher education will withstand the test of time and the evidence is a question for our engagement in this chapter. Let us move, therefore, to an exploration of TQM systems. What are the principles, the ideas, and the concepts on which this approach to quality assurance is built?

THE PHILOSOPHICAL AND CONCEPTUAL HERITAGE OF TQM

W. Edwards Deming, an American Ph.D. in physics, expert on statistical quality control and management pioneer, is widely cited as the principal conceptual father of TQM. Deming was a consultant to Japanese industry following World War II and his ideas were central not only to the recovery of Japanese manufacturing industry but to its eventual highly competitive ascendancy in automobile and electronics manufacturing. In essence, an American took his ideas, which were initially not well or widely received in this country, to Japan. The success of industry in Japan and the Japanese challenge to American industry brought visibility to the importance of TQM ideas, so that in large measure American industry imported ideas to this country that had originated in an American mind but that had been exported to Japan. An informing and concise biographical sketch of Deming's life can be found in Mary Walton's book *The Deming Management Method.*[4]

To gain some understanding of the philosophic foundation of TQM, we can turn to the writings of Deming himself, to commentators who have enlarged upon his writings, and to writers who have translated TQM concepts to higher education. We should say here that a number of other terms and acronyms have emerged that carry the same general meaning as TQM. Among these are Strategic Quality Management (SQM), Continuous Quality Improvement (CQI), and Quality Improvement Program (QIP).

The management philosophy that undergirds TQM is captured in Deming's "14 Points for Management," and he sets forth these fourteen points in his 1986 book *Out of the Crisis*:[5]

1. Create constancy of purpose toward improvement of product and service, with the aim to become competitive and to stay in business, and to provide jobs.
2. Adopt the new philosophy. We are in a new economic age. Western management must awaken to the challenge, must learn their responsibilities, and take on leadership for change.
3. Cease dependence on inspection to achieve quality. Eliminate the need for inspection on a mass basis by building quality into the product in the first place.
4. End the practice of awarding business on the basis of price tag. Instead, minimize total cost. Move toward a single supplier for any one item, on a long-term relationship of loyalty and trust.
5. Improve constantly and forever the system of production and service, to improve quality and productivity, and thus constantly decrease costs.
6. Institute training on the job.
7. Institute leadership. The aim of supervision should be to help people and machines and gadgets to do a better job. Supervision of management is in need of overhaul, as well as supervision of production workers.
8. Drive out fear, so that everyone may work effectively for the company.
9. Break down barriers between departments. People in research, design, sales, and production must work as a team, to foresee problems of production and in use that may be encountered with the product or service.
10. Eliminate slogans, exhortations, and targets for the work force asking for zero defects and new levels of productivity.
11. a. Eliminate work standards on the factory floor. Substitute leadership.
    b. Eliminate management by objective. Eliminate management by numbers, numerical goals. Substitute leadership.

12. a. Remove barriers that rob the hourly worker of his right to pride of workmanship.
    b. Remove barriers that rob people in management and in engineering of their right to pride of workmanship.
13. Institute a vigorous program of education and self-improvement.
14. Put everybody in the company to work to accomplish the transformation.

Deming also identifies several "deadly diseases" that work against quality improvement and management effectiveness. The original five deadly diseases were as follows:

1. Lack of constancy of purpose
2. Emphasis on short term profits
3. Evaluation of performance, merit rating, or annual review
4. Mobility of management
5. Running a company on visible figures alone

To these were added two others pertinent to the United States, which were excessive medical costs and costs of warranty.

Let's pause just a moment for reflection. First there are in this management philosophy ideas that should resonate with anyone who has been in a work setting of any kind. That a focus on short-term results impedes and inhibits a longer-term vision has long been a criticism of American management. And this criticism is directly tied to the disease of management by the numbers. Indeed, years ago, American scholar and college president Robert Hutchins once observed that Americans were timid philosophers. If we could not put a number or a dollar mark on something, we did not know what to do with it. The concern with "management mobility" speaks to the leadership concept that persistence and dogged determination are highly underrated but essential qualities for organizational effectiveness in any setting, and certainly no less so in college and university settings, whose missions embrace the call to conserve heritage, criticize the present, and construct the future.

And who among us wants to live with a supervisor breathing down our neck, depriving us of independence and responsibility. Writing over eighty years ago, Mary Parker Follett was prescient in her comment on management responsibility in saying that "What the leader's job is is to show every man what he needs to do to be responsible."[6] Deming's work is filled with quick examples of how performance variation in any system can occur independent of worker performance, and that such variation is imbedded in the system itself. Consequently, one job of quality assurance is to identify sources of variations, or mistakes or errors, and to eliminate and/or minimize those.

We cited Seymour and Lewis/Smith as writers who have championed the transfer of TQM concepts into higher education settings. Seymour translates the Deming principles as follows:[7]

1. Quality is meeting or exceeding customer needs.
2. Quality is everyone's job.
3. Quality is continuous improvement.
4. Quality is leadership.
5. Quality is human resource development.
6. Quality is in the system.
7. Quality is fear reduction.
8. Quality is recognition and reward.
9. Quality is teamwork.
10. Quality is measurement.
11. Quality is systematic problem solving.

Lewis and Smith offer this conceptual distillation of the management pillars of TQM: customer satisfaction, continuous improvement, speaking with facts, and respect for people.[8] And centering on what are widely cited as the bedrock concepts of TQM, Seymour offers this definition of strategic quality management: "The leadership of an organization must, by word and deed, convey the message that customer satisfaction through a process of continually improving quality is the responsibility of every member of the organization."[9]

Here it may prove informative to indicate that the concept of total or strategic quality management flows from an evolution of thought in how we view the purpose of quality control in industrial and manufacturing settings. Writing in *Managing Quality*, a work cited in our opening chapter, David Garvin suggests that early years of the twentieth century centered on detection of defective parts and products and this "inspection" approach was designed to eliminate delivery of defective products, but did not focus on what led to the defective products in the beginning. The "statistical quality control" approach, often associated with Walter Shewhart and a contemporary of Deming, emphasized product uniformity and the reduction of variance. The "quality assurance" movement of the 1950s through 1980s featured a proactive and coordinated approach throughout the production process. TQM broadened the concern for quality to the entire organization from shop floor to boardroom.

A major organizational incubator for both the ideas and the personalities associated with the heart of the quality movement, especially the statistical and sampling approaches, resided heavily with Bell laboratories where Shewhart worked, as did Joseph Juran, who pioneered the concept of "fitness for use" and "conformance to standards," concepts described in chapter 1. Deming and Juran both worked at the Western Electric Hawthorne plants,, where the pioneering work of Elton Mayo and the now famous Hawthorne studies revealed that if American management was truly interested in quality, it must be concerned not only with physical variables related to efficiency but with human relations factors. With an experience base also in electronics production, Philip Crosby popularized the concept of "zero defects" as an important quality assurance concept, one in which expectations flow into standards of performance. Bio sketches on these and other quality forerunners such as Kaoaru Ishikawa and Armand Feigenbaum may be found in the previously cited books by Seymour and Lewis/Smith.

Here we may take a brief diversion to note a certain paradox in higher education's approach to quality assurance where TQM does furnish a useful spotlight. The concepts of accreditation and program review, briefed in chapters 2 and 6, certainly accent the concept of improvement in educational services. Seymour is correct, we think, in that these important quality assurance instruments can give rise to a "good enough" and "minimal standard" mentality. We dutifully go through the exercise, the discipline of accreditation and program review self-studies. Thoughtfully orchestrated and aggressively prosecuted, such activities should indeed lead to the identification of improvement options in both educational and administrative services. However, with less thought and diligence, they may also lead simply to the goal of surviving the exercise, so that an institution or a program is "safe" for another five or ten years. And all thought of the need for "continued improvement" evaporates once the review team has departed. Such a mindset is especially probable in academic life, where it is easier for both faculty and administrators to talk about grand purpose and activity than about hard evidence on performance.

THE CONCEPTUAL ACCENTS OF TQM

The previous discussion makes clear that we have several different organizational options as we attempt to understand TQM and its application in higher education settings. We propose four summary themes or accents whose meaning we engage in the following discussion; and we will weave illustration in with the conceptual discussion so that the principle is illuminated. Whether the metaphors are those of "pillars," "cornerstones," "foundations," or "accents," the aspiration here is to assist the reader in understanding what it means to translate the philosophy of TQM as a quality assurance system into colleges and universities. We propose these accents:

- An accent on the needs, aspirations, and satisfactions of those to be served.
- An accent on the will to continuously improve educational and administrative services.
- An accent on process analysis and performance measurement.
- An accent on civility, candor, and responsibility in human relationships.

Before we proceed, however, it will prove useful to present TQM as a system, which is what Lewis and Smith do in their book *Total Quality in Higher Education.* This view emphasizes leadership responsibility to focus on the workings and integration of the social and technical systems in which we do our work, whether in an academic department or in an enrollment management office. In another writing, one of the authors has suggested that leadership is more a matter of our passion than our position and that a leader without caring is no leader at all.[10] The leader has a responsibility to care for the soul, the standard, and the system. Caring for the soul calls for us to attend the needs, the dreams and aspirations, and the talent of those whose promise is entrusted to our care. Caring for the standard calls for the leader to honor principles of excellence and integrity in all that we do. Caring for the system calls for the leader to examine the design and effectiveness of the social and technical systems in which we do our work. It is possible for talented and well-intentioned men and women to practice within systems that are flawed and ineffective in design.

Taking a position as a young registrar at the University of Memphis in the mid-1960s, one of the authors inherited a registration system in which student "customers" were being badly mistreated and ill served. A registration system designed to serve 2,000 students, with registrar and business staff hiding behind their counters, was not working with an institution that had grown to 10,000 students and was enrolling 2,000 to 3,000 additional students each fall. A comprehensive reworking of the entire system from start to finish produced a registration process that reduced registration time from several hours to less than one hour. Today's phone and Internet systems take even less time. Now this management attention to system and to students took place some twenty years before the concept of TQM became a favorite acronym of higher education. It nevertheless illustrates an important idea behind TQM, which is the leader's responsibility to care for both social and technical systems, the way in which we organize human talents and integrate those with technology. And it leads us to the first and perhaps premier accent of TQM, which centers on the interests and welfare of those to be served. We are deliberately avoiding the use of the phrase "customer" for reasons that will become apparent in our next discussion.

AN ACCENT ON WELFARE, NEEDS, AND SATISFACTION OF THOSE TO BE SERVED

One of the most important and also one of the most debated propositions and concepts that travels under the banner of TQM is that of serving the customer or client. This is a concept whose translation in manufacturing and service industries is well enough understood. No matter how careful our production processes, no matter whether we build to standard or specifications, if the customer does not like or purchase the product, all else is moot. "Conformance to specification" as an indicator or measure of quality becomes less salient than customer satisfaction with "fitness for use" as an indicator or measure of quality. When I get a follow-up phone call or customer satisfaction questionnaire from my car dealer, retailer, or hospital, clearly the intent is to discern whether the customer has been well served.

Who can argue with wanting to know how our students perceive our record in furnishing educational and administrative services? After all, they are often the only ones, beyond the professor, who know what is going on in the classroom, laboratory, or studio. Few would argue that we listen enough to our students. Why, then, are faculty often so resistant to the use of the term "customer" for students? Writing in his book *Stewardship,*[11] management scholar Peter Block suggests that one can be a customer only when there is a choice. Students have a choice when they select a particular institution; but there is only one registration, financial aid, and business office—no choice. And they may have limited choices of courses and professors. So are they customers or not? Is "client" a more accurate term? Well, students are customers in the sense that they are recipients of educational and administrative services for which they pay. But there are important and critical differences. Bogue and Aper offer the following reflection:

> There are important and critical differences between corporate and collegiate settings in the application of this principle and the concept of the student as customer. Any faculty member who has found his or her caring for students in tension with caring for standards knows the limitation of this quality test for colleges and universities.[12]

In other words, colleges and universities can be caught in a tension as they attempt to exemplify a qualitative caring for both student promise and educational standard. Moreover, unlike production processes where metal, plastic, and wood yield passively to the shaping forces of the production process, students are active and critical contributors to the quality of a learning experience. A professor may be filled with caring and high expectations for his or her students, gifted in the orchestration and delivery of learning experiences, artistic in the construction of evaluations; but a student without care or motivation can bring all this to a shallow and sad ending.

Writing in the book previously cited, *On Q,* Seymour suggests that students vote with their feet. On those sad occasions when they vote for options of questionable merit—with shallow, mediocre, or even duplicitous investments—the ideal of quality should not be exchanged for the notion of satisfaction. Education is one work where the customer may be at once satisfied and ignorant. Graduates of diploma mills may be perfectly satisfied customers, having made easy intellectual passage with little value added.

In this endeavor, both science and phenomenology have a role to play. There is a place for questionnaires and statistical analysis in probing the satisfactions of students and graduates, the work of chapter 4; and there is a place for listening to and exploring the experience of a single student whose dreams have been mangled by uncaring faculty, dysfunctional policy, or distorted management systems.

If TQM has caused colleges and universities to listen more attentively to the needs and hopes of our students, then it will have made an important contribution. If TQM suggests that the student as customer is purchasing a service or product in the same sense as a customer buying a car or a dress or a phone and that the concept of quality resides only in the student's satisfaction, then TQM has done higher education a major disservice, because it will have ignored or dismissed the student's responsibility for reflection and discipline, for imagination and initiative in the educational process. The debate over this "idea" or "pillar" of TQM can be seen in the titles of two pieces appearing several years ago. The January 25, 1994, issue of the *Roanoke Times and World News* featured an article by James Mingle, Executive Director of the State Higher Education Executive Officers (SHEEO); the title of the piece was "Colleges Must Think of the Customers."[13] In a 1989 publication, *At BG*—a house publication of Bowling Green State University—Alumni Honored Teacher-of-the-Year M. Neil Browne authored an article with the title "Students Are Too Important to be Treated as Customers" and offered this note: "As teachers, we are entrusted with the necessity of making certain choices our customers will not like at the time but will benefit from later on."[14] Students are not just shoppers in the windows of higher education but partners in the educational process and beneficiaries who may not come to appreciate that benefit until the passage of some time. We may not enjoy the discipline of our teachers' judgments at the moment, but if we attend carefully, we may come to be grateful in the future.

Of course, students are not the only "customers" of higher education. One can make a decent argument that employers of our graduates are in some sense a customer and that various administrative offices have "internal customers" in those who are recipients of such services as accounting, motor pool, investment, maintenance services, and so on.

In an organization where it is easy for faculty in particular to shift from an accent on serving student interests to serving their own self-interests, the call for thinking about the students as customer is not a misplaced call. We agree with Seymour that higher education is not a service enterprise exempt from the call of qualitative curiosity nor from the call to think of the welfare of our students. It is a call, however, that must be interpreted with a clear understanding of the nature of the enterprise. We have made clear the limits of a student as a customer. Within the more global mission of searching for truth, the more specific mission expectations of higher education—conserving our heritage, criticizing the present, and constructing the future—destine our colleges and universities to live always in the crucible of public criticism and to experience the reality of always having some unhappy customers. Faculty and students should also have a relationship more complex and constructive than viewing one as a seller and another as a buyer.

AN ACCENT ON CONTINUOUS IMPROVEMENT IN ADMINISTRATIVE AND EDUCATIONAL SERVICES

While we may reasonably advance the idea that higher education faculty and staff have had a long interest in improvement and that the longest-standing system of quality assurance, accreditation (chapter 2), features improvement as a cornerstone concept, we should recognize that the concern for improvement may not meet the "continuous" test suggested by TQM philosophy. Accreditation visits typically occur at five or ten year intervals, as currently practiced, and this tends to create spurts of energy and activity designed to meet the minimal expectations of accreditation standards/criteria, as outlined in chapter 2. This satisfaction with the minimal standard is what Seymour calls the "good enough" mindset.

The conditions of alert and commitment that associate with the will to seek continuous improvement are described by the Japanese term *kaizen,* presented in a book by that same name by Masaaki Imai.[15] The model for continuous improvement first advanced by Shewhart and then by Deming is captured in a Plan, Do, Check, and Act diagram as shown in Figure 8.1.

Upon first consideration, then, the concept of continuous improvement appears reasonably worthy, reasonably simple, and reasonably clear. We improve or we go out of business. In the competitive world of automobile and electronics manufacturing and in such major services as transportation, the failure to remain competitive can bring loss of profits or corporate death. Who will want to argue, then, with the idea of wanting to work more effectively and efficiently?

The idea of continuous improvement implies a desire to continuously learn, a compulsive and continuing curiosity about our work. With TQM philosophy, we would have not only individuals who were interested in learning more about their work and how to improve, we would have organizations that in their corporate culture would exemplify corporate curiosity. They would be what Peter Senge termed in his book *The Fifth Discipline* "learning organizations": "organizations where people continually expand their capacity to create the results they truly desire, where new and expansive patterns of thinking are nurtured, where collective aspiration is set free, and where people are continually learning how to learn together."[16] While the term "learning organization" was popularized by Peter Senge and many writers have seized the term, peppered their discourse liberally with this new phrase, and made it so obviously fashionable to those who are "really in the know," the extent to which folks in the corporate or collegiate sector remember and understand the substance of the concept as they remember and understand the term itself might be interesting. Learning organizations would be those continuously engaged with questions of purpose and performance: what's our mission, goal, and objective; and how good a job are we doing and how do we know.

Higher education faculty are more naturally attracted to the design of new programs and services than we are to the evaluation of existing programs and services. We would rather be engaged in the grand work of designing something new than the sober work of evaluating what is already in place. Moreover, colleges are built for solitary and reflective work as faculty labor often in isolation in our classrooms and laboratories. Nor do classical appointment conditions such as tenure always furnish an imperative for improving our learning processes.

Figure 8.1
Plan, Do, Check, Act

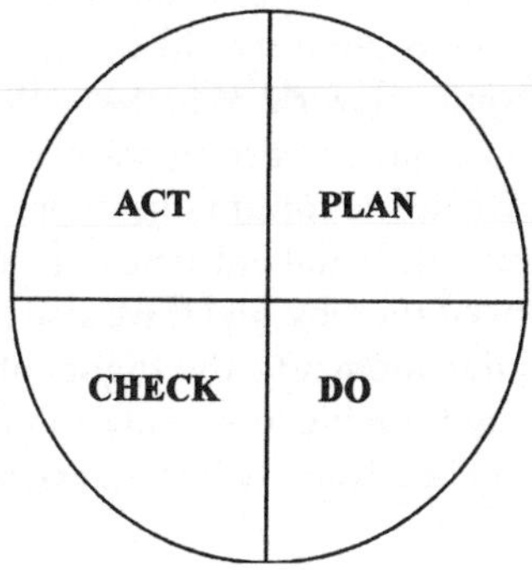

It is not that faculty are inherently lazy or uninterested in improvement. It is that they just don't think of their work as a manufacturing process, turning out so many human widgets, nor do they think of themselves as being in competition with English or economics professors in neighboring institutions. Moreover, as we noted earlier, many academics will argue that the "buzz phrase" of continuous improvement is old wine in new bottles, that the concept of improvement has been central to historic processes of accreditation. In addition they may ask whether a scientist or engineer, driven by continuous improvement slogans/philosophy and working to improve the internal combustion engine, will be inclined to the reflective flight of imagination that could lead to a replacement for this powerful but pollution-breeding instrument and thus make the hegemony of petroleum obsolete and land, water, and air safer for our future?

While TQM centers our vision on continuous improvement, not an unworthy goal, and on reduction of error and variance, we need places where new ideas and understandings can take root in the soil and debris of our mistakes and our errors. As Lewis Thomas writes in *The Medusa and the Snail:* "Mistakes are at the very base of human thought. . . . A good laboratory, like a good bank or a corporation or government, has to run like a computer. Almost everything is done flawlessly, by the book, and all the numbers add up to the predicted sum. The days go by. And then, if it is a lucky day, and a lucky laboratory, somebody makes a mistake. . . . The capacity to leap lightly across mountains of information to land lightly on the wrong side represents the highest of human endowments."[17] TQM philosophy is constructed to minimize and even eliminate error. But will it eliminate the possibility of our seeing opportunity for learning in error and mistake?

Both competition and imagination/reflection are central to innovation, innovation furnishing the seeds of not only improvement in existing products and services but also the creation of the genius for new products and services. This is an idea not lost on American management expert Peter Drucker, who interestingly describes the modern American university as a model of innovation and entrepreneurship.[18] Whether the Internet is going to prove as powerful an innovation in the education world as did the lowly textbook is a story waiting to be told. Surely FedEx must be counted a notable example of imagination and innovation in the corporate world, but so might the American community college in the educational world. Whether either of these ideas emerged primarily from attempts to improve existing postal or higher education service is debatable. If, however, we define continuous improvement as more than the urge to enhance the effectiveness and efficiency of existing processes, and the products and services derived thereby, and if we also include under the banner of that concept the reflective moments, the flights of imagination, the call of curiosity, and the disciplined intelligence ready to take advantage of mistake and error, then there should be a friendly hospitality for the concept in our colleges and universities.

AN ACCENT ON PROCESS ANALYSIS AND PERFORMANCE EVIDENCE

One of the more important contributions of TQM in both collegiate and corporate settings has been its call to process analysis and measurement. In *The Improvement Process,*[19] H. J. Harrington wrote that "If you can't measure something, you can't understand it; if you can't understand it, you can't control it; if you can't control it, you can't improve it." Whether understanding requires numbers we will leave to another philosophical forum; but we might take issue with the sweep of this generalization. An absence of measurement is not an absence of reality. The point, however, is that there are processes in both manufacturing and educational settings in which analysis and measurement can assist us in understanding, control, and then improvement.

Shewhart and Deming showed that in any process or system of production there are important variations having nothing to do with worker skill or commitment. And regardless of talent/commitment, some workers would always be below average and some above. No form of management direction and close supervision can change random or chance variation. There are two important and relatively simple illustrations of the role of chance variation in production processes and in systems operations. The reader will find the famous "Red Bead" experiment popularized by Deming and reported in his book *Out of the Crisis*[20] and the "Beer Game" detailed by Senge in his book *The Fifth Discipline*[21] easy-to-follow illustrations of how individual variation in performance can be traced to system function rather than individual effort or talent. If TQM does nothing more than alert higher education administrators that, as stated earlier, they must love the system as well as people and standards of integrity and excellence, TQM will have made an important contribution to our thinking at every position of leadership in our colleges and universities. In the earlier cited and relatively simple illustration of the flawed university registration system, good people who mow their yards and pay their taxes were doing their best to serve students. It was the system of registration that was in need of work, not the efforts of those working within the system.

Among the other analytic tools that are often associated with TQM process analysis are these: flow charts, cause and effect of fishbone diagrams, Pareto charts, histograms, run charts, scatter diagrams, and control charts. Readers who have an elementary exposure to computer programming and/or basic descriptive statistics will already have some familiarity with these tools and other readers will not find them difficult to understand. Here we explore four of these analytical tools.

Flow Charts. Whether we are charting the processes for admissions, for registration, for payroll, or for promotion/tenure, the act of visually depicting the sequence and flow of events, the decision options and responsibilities, and the offices and actors involved is a useful device for eliminating redundancy and inefficiency ... and potential bottlenecks. In a management text masquerading as a novel entitled *The Goal,*[22] author Eliyahu Goldratt takes his readers through a delightful exercise involving the difficulty of getting a group of Boy Scouts on a hike to a designated camping site on time. Discovering that a troop of boys was beginning to spread out over a long distance and that the time of the hike was such that they would fail to reach their camping site by dusk, fictional manufacturing executive and Boy Scout leader Al Rogo began a simple process of analysis and discovered that the "bottleneck" was a chubby fellow who could not keep up with the other boys and thus the entire team of scouts could move no faster than the slower hiking speed of "Chubby." Solution: Relieve "Chubby" of a major portion of his backpack load by distributing the load among the other scouts. Rogo then takes this lesson back to his manufacturing plants and begins looking for bottlenecks in his manufacturing process. In essence, then, flow diagrams allow us to look for "bottlenecks" that constrict or slow the process ... whether in unnecessary checking, four-part signatures, foolish routing, or other inefficiencies built into the system.

Cause and Effect / Fishbone Diagrams. Traced primarily to the work of Japanese writer Kaoru Ishikawa, the fishbone diagram is an analytical tool that permits us to look at potential causes of an "effect." Seymour details an application at the University of California, Berkeley, in which graduate officers were concerned that the average time to completion of a doctorate in history was close to ten years. We have the effect, but what was causing this relatively long time line? If history professors might have an active career of forty years, does it make sense to spend one-fourth of this time getting ready? If we depicted for analysis some of the variables that might associate with this effect we could have something like the following:

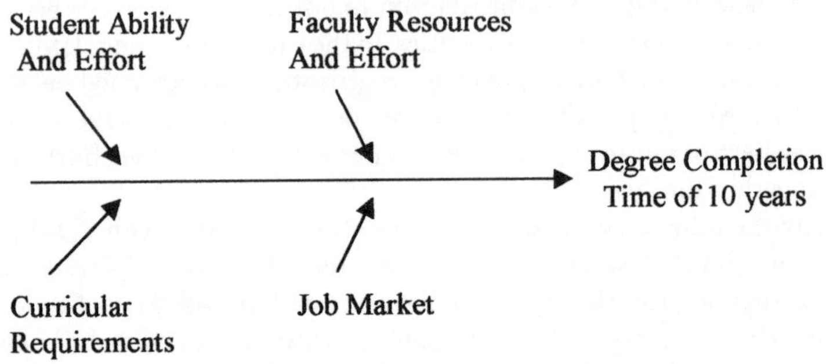

Here are some elementary notes about this analysis. Even on this program and curricular analysis, we have measurement (average completion time of ten years). And we have a qualitative approach to inquiry that involved interviews with faculty and students. And what the graduate officers found was that students were in no big hurry to graduate because they would "rather be an advanced graduate student at Berkeley, enjoying the weather, drinking good coffee, having a great library at their disposal, than being an unemployed Ph.D. in History."[23]

Pareto Analysis. A Pareto analysis is a means of visually and numerically depicting the rank order of causes related to an effect. Suppose, for example, an institution finds that its retention rate from freshman to sophomore year is only 50 percent and that this seems unreasonably high when "benchmarked" against institutions of similar mission, setting, and student aptitude. Questionnaire and/or interview follow-up with nonreturning students might reveal a diagram such as that of Figure 8.2.

We pause here to recall a term inserted into this discussion, "benchmarking." Students of educational program evaluation and measurement will recognize this as another way to talk about measurement and evaluation standard. A temperature of 102 degrees has no meaning without some standard or "benchmark." An ACT score of 24 has little meaning without some referent point or "benchmark." Benchmarks may be derived from a criterion expectation established by a panel of experts or from performance records set by similar units or institutions.

Histograms. A histogram is a simple visual device known to all who have completed elementary statistics and one allowed visual image of events. Suppose, for example, we wanted to plot the average time from submission of an admission application to admissions decision for institutions similar in mission. A "disguised observer" approach could be taken in which admission applications could be submitted to ten institutions on the same date and the process time till receipt of decision plotted on a bar chart or histogram depicting the process time for each of the institutions. One presidential aspirant known to the authors engaged in a qualitative venture in which he traveled incognito to the

Figure 8.2
Pareto Diagram for Studying Retention

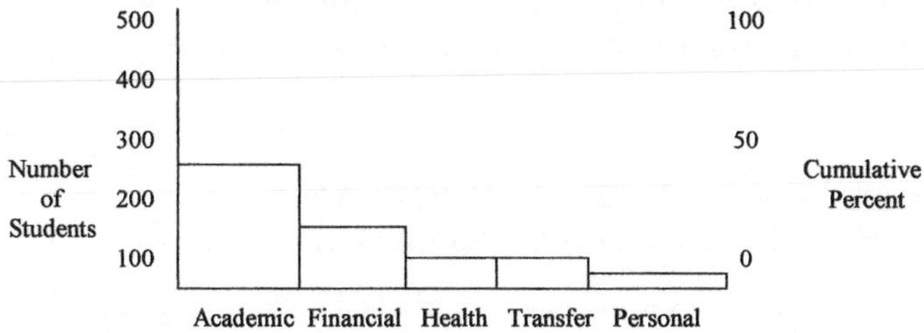

campus where he was soon to be a presidential candidate and visited the admissions and financial aid offices to see what kind of treatment was extended to potential students and parents. And he also subscribed to the local newspaper and campus student newspaper for four months prior to his candidacy interview. This is why we noted earlier that understanding does not always require numbers and why the search for quality improvement does not always require measurement. It does require curiosity and the investment of time and caring.

Other illustrations on the application of TQM in college and university settings may be found in the books by Seymour and Lewis/Smith and in a host of journal articles. At the University of Tennessee, TQM analysis was utilized in reframing the MBA program in the early 1990s and in the creation of the Management Development Institute, which has trained thousands of both corporate and service sector managers in the principles of TQM.[24] One of the authors (Bogue) is a graduate of that institute. TQM principles were also applied in setting long-term performance goals and benchmarks for the University of Tennessee Institute for Public Service.

Institutionalwide ventures in TQM have been initiated at large public universities, such as Oregon State University[25] and Pennsylvania State University,[26] at smaller private schools such as Samford,[27] and at two-year schools such as Delaware County Community College.[28] Applications of TQM have included a wide variety of both academic and administrative services: classroom management, admissions processes, response time to dormitory mechanical and engineering problems, mail services and redesign of student food services. In an article appearing in the 1992 issue of *Quality Progress,* over 200 colleges and universities were reported as engaged in some form of TQM.[29] In our concluding conversation of this chapter, we will explore the question of whether "farewell" or "fanfare" can describe the movement and impact. At this point, however, we need to examine the fourth accent of TQM philosophy. As previously noted, Lewis and Smith entitle this accent or pillar as "respect for people." Several of the ideas advanced by Seymour—quality is leadership, quality is fear reduction, quality is recognition and reward—would fall under this fourth accent, which we are inclined to label "leadership philosophy."

AN ACCENT ON CIVILITY, CANDOR, AND RESPONSIBILITY IN HUMAN RELATIONS

Several of the fourteen principles articulated by Deming and outlined earlier in this chapter center on a change in management philosophy. The call to institute leadership, drive out fear, develop training and development programs, eliminate slogans, and remove barriers to pride of workmanship are directions for rethinking the way in which we create leadership climates in any organization.

When we examine the evolution of thought and theory about the nature of leadership in our organizations, whether profit or service sector, it is clear that at the opening of the twentieth century, we worked primarily from a "tell and compel" vision of leadership role in which the leader resided at the apex of the organizational pyramid, gave orders, and solved problems brought to him or her by subordinates. This was a highly satisfying arrangement for a number of reasons. We knew whom to blame when things went wrong; for the most part subordinates, those who give voice and meaning to any organization, were not called to responsibility and were often deprived of the opportunity to have a major voice in their own working conditions. This inhibition of self-governance is injurious to quality of workmanship and pride of workmanship.

Employees were treated like interchangeable parts in the "machine" and "structural" configurations of the organization. Then along came the "Hawthorne" studies of Mayo and others and we discovered that efficiency engineering gave us an insufficient frame for looking at both productivity and satisfaction. Men and women who enter the front door of our workplaces, we discovered, have dreams and pains, intersecting group memberships and interests, and are not as lazy and irresponsible as we might have assumed. Management scholars Bolman and Deal have given us a useful conceptual map in the evolution of our understanding of both leadership and organizations in their concept of the four frames of organizations: the structural, the human relations, the political, and the cultural.[30]

The newer conception of effective management philosophy we describe as the "inquire and inspire" model in which the leader listens as much as talks, and calls colleagues to be responsible for the identification and resolution of their own problems and challenges. This newer view is less about driving our colleagues than calling them, less about giving orders than asking questions, less about suspicion and checking than expecting the best from each and every talent whose promise and performance is entrusted to our care, less about directing than about designing. We cited earlier Mary Parker Follett's vision of leadership role as that of calling colleagues to responsibility; and it is interesting to note that Follett was writing about these ideas some thirty to forty years in advance of TQM.[31] Former corporate executive turned author Max Depree also offered a crisp and clear definition of leadership role in 1989 when he suggested that "The first responsibility of the leader is to define reality. The second is to say thank you."[32] The leader's ideals and values define and design a climate and a culture, a reality, if you will, in which men and women do their work. The voices of these and other writers would affirm the value of civility, which requires us to treat our colleagues with respect and dignity; the value of candor, which calls us to put information on the table and to open communication. Writing in *Leadership by Design,* Bogue details several other values designed to enhance effectiveness and integrity in collegiate organizations.[33]

A DERIVATIVE PROGRAM: THE MALCOLM BALDRIGE AWARD

Congress was so taken with the fanfare of TQM and quality initiatives that seemed to be emerging that it created in 1987 the Malcolm Baldrige National Quality Improvement Act. This national recognition was initially created to encourage quality initiative in manufacturing, service, and small business sectors. Named for Malcolm Baldrige, secretary of commerce from 1981 until his death in 1987, the award is designed to stimulate performance excellence and to promote sharing of information on performance enhancement practices.

Earlier corporate winners read like a "Who's Who" of corporate America: Cadillac, Eastman Kodak, Motorola, Texas Instruments, and the Ritz-Carlton Hotel, though at least one of the winners has filed for bankruptcy protection. This note notwithstanding, the award was expanded to include an Educational Division and national awards are now being made to schools and colleges electing to compete for the award. The goals of the award in this division are to improve school performance with result-oriented performance expectations, to facilitate sharing of best practice, to foster partnerships among schools and businesses.

Writing in an article that appeared in the January/February 1994 issue of *Change* and entitled "The Baldrige Cometh," Seymour noted that the Baldridge Award could lead to serious soul searching in higher education.[34] In a later two-volume work entitled *High Performing Colleges,*[35] Seymour and others further explicate the theory and concepts underlying the award, evidence of its success in corporate enterprise, criticism of the award, and experience of some twenty colleges involved in pilot work. Competing for the Baldrige Award in the Educational Division requires an extensive internal self-study and application. Competing institutions will be evaluated by an external visiting panel on the following criteria:

Criteria and Point Values for Baldrige Award Educational Division

1.0 Leadership—90

2.0 Information and Analysis—75

3.0 Strategic and Operational Planning—75

4.0 Human Resource Development and Management—150

5.0 Educational and Business Process Management—150

6.0 School Performance Results—230

7.0 Student Focus and Student Stakeholder—230

Will the Baldrige Award become something akin to national accreditation? Will winners continue to improve or rest on their laurels after receiving the award? Will some winners go into educational bankruptcy, repeating the results in the corporate award sector? In 1997, business commentator James Byrne asked: "What's dead as a pet rock? Little surprise here. It's total quality management. TQM, the approach of eliminating errors that increase costs and reduce customer satisfaction, promised more than it could deliver and spawned mini-bureaucracies charged with putting it into action."[36] In higher education, it would be revealing to learn how many directors of TQM, CQI, and Strategic Quality Improvement (SQI) have been created around the nation. Indeed what was once the intelligence work primarily of directors of institutional research, a professional field itself of relatively new origins in the latter half of the twentieth century, we can now find a growing new array of administrative appointments in directors of assessment, directors of planning, and directors of quality assurance. Minibureaucracies may just as surely be found in collegiate as in corporate settings. Well, this commentary leads us nicely to our final reflections of this chapter, which center on the passage taken by TQM in colleges and universities.

FROM FANFARE TO FAREWELL?

No two journal titles could possibility capture the journey of TQM in American higher education better than the two authored by long-time higher education scholar and commentator Ted Marchese. In a May/June 1993 article appearing in *Change* magazine, Marchese titled his comments "TQM: A Time for Ideas." In his commentary, Marchese noted that "One of the ideas TQM has put in the air is that organizations should be driven by the intrinsic motivation in all of us to do our best work."[37] In an editorial appearing in the May/June 1996 issue of *Change,* Marchese's title is "Bye, Bye, CQI for Now." In this piece appearing just three short years after his opening fanfare on TQM, Marchese offers this note:

Since 1991, hundreds of colleges and universities—complex universities and community colleges in the lead—have attempted to implement quality management. Among them, there are wonderful stories to be told of big gains in customer service, cost reduction, curricular effectiveness, and employee morale. Does CQI work in higher education? Absolutely.

Even so, it's also the case that a couple thousand institutions decided to sit this one out. Dozens of institutions that began a quality journey ended it; others persisted but have little to show for it. And most of the gains one can point to have been on the administrative side, not the academic. In sum, the most talked-about management development of the past two decades has so far had only modest impacts on American higher education.[38]

Writing in *Management Fads in Higher Education,* long time higher education scholar Robert Birnbaum refers to TQM/CQI as one of those fads.[39] He details the fanfare associated with the emergence of TQM as one of the most widely heralded management paradigms in the twentieth century, a revolution in management thought; and he chronicles its entry, passage, and at least partial departure in higher education. The commentaries by both Marchese and Birnbaum remind us of an unfortunate tendency in higher education and perhaps in the corporate sector as well: to seize the latest management practice and associated acronym as the cure for all organizational ills of purpose and performance. Often management concepts acquired from corporate sector enterprise enter academia with much fanfare, make an initial splash of great visibility, experience uneasy digestive passage through higher education, and depart with quiet farewell. Those who thrived on the acronyms and buzz phrases of these concepts as symbols of being "in the know" and evidence of being in the conceptual avant garde are left awaiting arrival of the next wave.

Even while TQM was making a fanfare entrance into corporate America, not all was consensus even there. In an article appearing in the January 1993 issue of *Management Review* and entitled "Ten Reasons Why TQM Doesn't Work," Oren Harari noted that "TQM is only one of many possible means to obtain quality. In other words, quality is sacred; TQM is not. There's another difference: as we shall see, quality is about unbending focus, passion, iron discipline, and way of life for all hands. TQM is about statistics, jargon, committees, and quality departments."[40] Shapiro wrote that advocates of TQM in corporate America saw it as "manna from management heaven" and critics as "mania from management hell."[41]

Reflecting on the need to balance both fact and faith, passion and evidence in quality assurance for higher education, Bogue and Aper offer this note:

It is possible for an individual musician or an ensemble of any size, including a full orchestra, to play correctly. Meaning the orchestra plays with zero defects and, as the statistical process folks might say, "in control and capable." But this "correct" performance may not constitute musical quality. In the orchestra hall, customers are patrons, and patrons know that correct music is not necessarily quality music. If the music lacks passion and fire, inventiveness and imagination, "correctness" will not transform a dull and uninspired performance into a quality performance. In the orchestra halls of colleges and universities, our students will also be able to discern when we are correct, and especially when we care.[42]

We invite the reader to keep the ideas of passion and evidence as guarantors of quality in mind as we will revisit this relationship in our concluding chapter of this book.

TQM: A STORY WITH AN ENDING NOT YET TOLD

What, then, shall we make of TQM as a way of thinking about quality assurance in higher education? Is the story as exciting as the fanfare associated with its much-heralded entry into academia or as dreary as its predicted demise as a passing management fad? As the oft-cited folk expression cautions, it is not necessary to throw out the baby with the bath water.

Clearly it is important that those educational leaders holding our colleges and universities in trust understand the philosophical and cultural heritage of the enterprise. In an enterprise that searches for truth in the numbers and in the mist, celebrates and acknowledges the contributions of both fact and faith, holds argument and debate dear, searches for truth in conceptual contention, holds hands with the past even as it reaches for the future, celebrates the energizing power of human curiosity, and whose principal work is to assault the limits of common sense—in such an enterprise we believe it difficult and even inappropriate to ignore the four accents we have featured for TQM in this chapter.

An accent on the needs, aspirations, and satisfactions of our students as premier clients can be justified in our duty to care for and love our students. Who can argue that we listen enough to our students? And who can argue with the often aggressive and historically constructive role students have played in the unfolding of the American college? Taking positive steps to hear from our students, whether in the quantitative instrument of a questionnaire or the qualitative simplicity of interview or observer, denies neither faculty responsibility for educational design nor student responsibility for disciplined initiative and investment in their own education.

An accent on continuous improvement in both administrative and educational services keeps us from a comfortable arrogance that can be prevalent among some faculty and administrators. This principle does not require us to rip up the roots of tradition every day, but it does call for us to tend and to balance the call of tradition and the call of change. More importantly, it can bring the quiet pleasure of having made administrative and educational passage more effective and efficient. Disciplined expectation is not the enemy of love and educational growth, nor is efficiency the enemy of love and educational growth. A place of reflection and even of imaginative play can also be a place in which dysfunctional processes and policies that impede human development can be analyzed, evaluated, and improved.

An accent on process analysis and performance measurement, a call for evidence—surely these cannot be strangers in an enterprise in which science is celebrated for its contribution to human welfare and understanding, even though we do not have venerable science as the only mode of legitimate inquiry. How can we discern what our students know, think, and feel and how can we know what has happened to them in their passage through the halls of ivy are questions that invite and encourage the acquisition of evidence beyond an occasional anecdote.

An accent on civility, candor, and responsibility in management style and philosophy can be as easily justified in collegiate organization as corporate organization. Indeed, one may argue that such concepts are even more essential in an organization designed to advance on truth, to promote human learning and development, and to prepare leadership for every sector of our society. In the opening chapter to this book we argued that questions of quality cannot be separated from questions of integrity. Nor is it possible to believe that we may create climates of quality without treating both students and colleagues with due respect, without honoring the principle of public forum and candor on questions of both personal and institutional performance, and without calling both students and colleagues to responsibility in designing and nurturing learning climates.

In summary, our reflection is that TQM has made useful conceptual contribution to the way in which we think about quality assurance in higher education and that while the initial excitement over the promise of TQM may now be more subdued and guarded, there is still constructive promise in TQM philosophy and method. How to thoughtfully and effectively integrate these ideals with other quality assurance systems is not a small challenge and one that we hope to engage further in our closing chapter of this book.

NOTES

1. Seymour, D. (1992). *On Q: Causing Quality in Higher Education.* New York: American Council on Education/Macmillan.
2. Ibid., x.
3. Lewis, R., and Smith, D. (1994). *Total Quality in Higher Education.* Delray Beach, FL.: St. Lucie Press, ix.
4. Walton, M. (1986). *The Deming Management Method.* New York: Perigee.
5. Deming, W. E. (1986). *Out of the Crisis.* Cambridge: Massachusetts Institute of Technology, 23–24.
6. Graham, P. (ed.). (1996). *Mary Parker Follett: Prophet of Management.* Boston: Harvard Business School Press.
7. Seymour, *On Q*, 13–20.
8. Lewis and Smith, op. cit., 91–101.

9. Seymour, *On Q*, 15

10. Bogue, E. G. (1994). *Leadership by Design.* San Francisco: Jossey-Bass.

11. Block, P. (1993). *Stewardship.* San Francisco: Berrett Koehler.

12. Bogue, E. G., and Aper, J. (2000). *Exploring the Heritage of American Higher Education.* Phoenix, AZ: Oryx Press, 94.

13. Mingle, J. (1994). "Colleges Must Think of the Customers." *Roanoke Times and World News,* Tuesday, January 25, A7.

14. Browne, N. (1989). "Students Are Too Important to Be Treated as Customers." *At BG,* Bowling Green State University, Summer, 16.

15. Imai, M. (1986). *Kaizen: The Key to Japan's Competitive Success.* New York: Random House.

16. Senge, P. (1990). *The Fifth Discipline: The Art and the Practice of the Learning Organization.* New York: Doubleday.

17. Thomas, L. (1974). *The Medusa and the Snail.* New York: Viking Press.

18. Drucker, P. (1985). *Innovation and Entrepreneurship.* New York: Harper and Row.

19. Harrington, H. J. (1987). *The Improvement Process.* New York: McGraw-Hill, 103.

20. Deming, *Out of the Crisis.*

21. Senge, *The Fifth Discipline.*

22. Goldratt, Eliyahu. (1984). *The Goal.* Great Barrington, MA: North River Press, Inc.

23. Seymour, *On Q*, 89.

24. Foggin, J. (1992). "Meeting Customer Needs." *Survey of Business,* 28(20), Summer, 6–9.

25. Coate, L. E. (1990). "TQM on Campus." *NACUBO Business Officer,* November, 26–35.

26. Marchese, T. (1992). "TQM at Penn." *AAHE Bulletin,* 45(3), November, 3–14.

27. Harris, J., and Sylwester, D. (1991). "The Top Down Approach to Quality Improvement Really Works." *Proceedings of the American Statistical Association: Section on Quality and Productivity,* 67–72.

28. Entner, D. (1993). "DCC Takes the TQM Plunge . . . And Tells How." *Educational Record,* 74(2), Spring, 29–34.

29. Axland, S. (1992). "A Higher Degree of Quality." *Quality Progress,* 25(10), October, 33–38, 41–46.

30. Bolman, L., and Deal, T. (1997). *Reframing Organizations.* San Francisco: Jossey-Bass.

31. Graham, *Mary Parker Follett.*

32. Depree, M. (1989). *Leadership Is an Art.* New York: Doubleday.

33. Bogue, *Leadership by Design.*

34. Seymour, D. (1994). "The Baldrige Cometh." *Change,* 26(1), January-February, 16–17.

35. Seymour, D., and Associates. (1996). *High Performing Colleges.* Maryville, MO: Prescott Publishing Company.

36. Byrne, J. A. (1997). "Management Theory—Or Fad of the Month." *Business Week,* June, 47.

37. Marchese, T. (1993). "TQM: A Time for Ideas." *Change,* May/June, 10–13.

38. Marchese, T. (1996). "Bye, Bye, CQI for Now." *Change,* May/June, 4.

39. Birnbaum, R. (2000). *Management Fads in Higher Education.* San Francisco: Jossey-Bass.

40. Harari, O. (1993). "Ten Reasons Why TQM Doesn't Work." *Management Review* 82(1), January, 33–38.

41. Shapiro, E. C. (1995). *Fad Surfing in the Boardroom: Reclaiming the Courage to Manage in the Age of Instant Answers.* Reading, MA: Addison-Wesley.

42. Bogue and Aper, *Exploring the Heritage of American Higher Education,* 96.

Chapter 9

Performance Indicators and Performance Funding

Systems of Accountability

In the previous chapters, we have concentrated on the "evidences" of quality in college and university settings and explored the strengths and limitations of quality assurance systems designed to develop and demonstrate quality. In some ways, this chapter is a bridging chapter. The emergence and utilization of performance indicator policy systems could be seen as yet another approach to quality assurance. However, performance indicators are also a central feature in performance funding policy systems, which are intended to use fiscal policy as both incentive and reward for performance improvements.

For public institutions, state policies related to performance indicators and performance funding have been under active development and debate over recent years and remain so at this writing. In this chapter, our aspirations are to describe the emergence, the elements, and the application of both performance indicator and performance funding policy systems and to further examine the contributions and liabilities of these two policy concepts.

PERFORMANCE INDICATORS: A FORM OF OPERATIONAL INTELLIGENCE

One useful way to gauge the birth and emergence of a concept is to date the literature that carries the dialogue. If the decade of the 1980s centered heavily on the assessment movement in higher education, then perhaps we might suggest that the decade of the 1990s was the dominant period of dialogue for performance indicators. Early in the 1990s, for example, Linke in Australia was publishing on the development and use of performance indicators in Australian higher education,[1] and throughout the 1980s other countries outside the United States were also working with the concept. In the March 1992 of the *NACUBO Business Officer* journal in the United States, we find a story on "Key Success Indices" at the University of Miami.[2] NACUBO is an acronym for National Association of College and University Business Officers.

In 1993, the Southern Regional Education Board (SREB) released a report by Bogue, Creech, and Folger entitled *Assessing Quality in Higher Education: Policy Actions in the SREB States.*[3] This report detailed state legislation requiring accountability and assessment reporting in the form of performance indicators. Two important monographs centering on the theme of Performance Indicators appeared in 1994: "Using Performance Indicators to Guide Strategic Decision Making" edited by Borden and Banta[4] and *Measuring Up: The Promises and Pitfalls of Performance Indicators in Higher Education* authored by Gaither, Nedwek, and Neal.[5] Also appearing in 1994 was a major report detailing the development and application of performance indicators at the state level. This report was released by the Education Commission of the States (ECS) and was entitled *Charting Higher Education Accountability: A Sourcebook on State-Level Performance Indicators.*[6] In 1997, an issue of *Assessment Update* carried an article entitled "Performance Indicator Systems as Instruments for Accountability and Assessment."[7]

We may glean several understandings just from the titles of these pieces. One is that performance indicators may serve several purposes: as evidence of quality, as guides for decision making, as instruments of accountability, as intelligence to track the progress and health trends of an operation, and as signals of goal achievement. Second, it is clear that performance indicators are a policy instrument used at both the campus and state level. Perhaps, however, it is appropriate to determine exactly what a performance indicator is, how it may be defined. Then we will furnish examples of performance indicator systems at campus, system, and state levels and conclude with an analysis of strengths and limitations of indicator systems.

An Approach to Definition. Peter Ewell and Dennis Jones of the National Center for Higher Education Management Systems (NCHEMS) organization in the United States offer this definition: "a concrete piece of information about a condition or result of policy action that is regularly produced, publicly reported, and systematically used for planning, monitoring, or resource allocation at the state or system level."[8]

This definition is a useful beginning but neglects the application of performance indicators at the program and institutional levels. Cave, Hanney, and Kogan offer a concise definition as follows: A performance indicator is "an authoritative measure—usually in quantitative form."[9] From this quick definition, we garner another essential feature: Indicators are "quantitative." There is a number to express some value for the indicator. Taylor, Meyerson, and Massy suggest that performance indicators are "ratios, percentages, or other quantitative values that allow an institution to compare its position in key strategic areas to peers, to past performance, or to previously set goals."[10]

Borden and Bottrill add additional clarity to the concept of performance indicator when they suggest that a performance indicator implies a worth, a value, a point of reference.[11] Perhaps this would be a good moment to return to an idea ventured in our opening chapter, where we used a medical analogy to think about quality. There we suggested that a patient does not go to a physician and expect to be plugged into a "healthometer" that yields a single indicator of patient health. What happens is that the physician acquires a range of health indicators that, when evaluated collectively and holistically, enable the physician to make some judgment on the patient's state of health. The important matter, however, is that each indicator—whether blood pressure or blood chemistry, x-ray or EKG—has reference levels that enable an informed judgement. A temperature of 98.6 degrees carries little meaning without some well-understood reference point. Reference points for performance indicators in higher education may be found in previous program, institutional, system, or state performance benchmarks; in competitive benchmarks garnered from similar institutions; in comparison to some stated goal or objective. Here is our venture in definition: A performance indicator is a publicly reported quantitative measure or evidence of educational resources, activity, or achievement (1) that furnishes intelligence on strategic operating conditions, (2) that facilitates evaluation of operating trends, goal achievement, efficiency, and effectiveness in benchmark relation to historic, comparative, or criterion standards, and (3) that informs decision making on resource allocation and program/service improvement. Performance indicators may be developed at the program, institutional, system, state, regional, national, and international levels.

Let's consider a simple yet informing example. If the department chair of a graduate academic program can report to his or her dean and provost that the graduate credit hour production in the department is the same in the current year with eight full-time faculty as it was ten years ago with sixteen full-time faculty, then all have a performance indicator or measure of program efficiency. The production efficiency has doubled over ten years. By itself, this may be a limited point of program intelligence. If, however, peer and program evaluation reports of the graduate program reveal that the program has remained nationally recognized in scholarship, enjoys strong student and graduate endorsement, then this department chair has one important performance indicator at his or her disposal, and perhaps two if one is willing to consider the evaluation report as a form of qualitative performance indicator.

It may be appropriate to enlarge further on definition and to explore questions of what performance indicators systems are designed to accomplish. In 1992, Sizer, Spee, and Bormans suggested that performance indicator systems serve five functions: monitoring, evaluation, dialogue, rationalization, and resource allocation.[12] Most of these functions will be relatively obvious, but we should probably briefly elaborate on two. What the authors suggest under the function of "dialogue" is that the presence of common definitions and measures facilitates conversation and communication among different policy stakeholders. The concept of "rationalization" refers to a coherent policy process in which performance indicators play a central planning role. Also writing in 1992, Linda Darling-Hammond pointed to these purposes of performance indicator systems:

- Monitoring the general conditions and contexts of education
- Identifying progress toward specified goals
- Illuminating or foreshadowing problems
- Diagnosing the potential sources of identified problems[13]

In their monograph entitled *Indicators of "Good Practice" in Undergraduate Education,* authors Ewell and Jones point to these purposes of indicator systems:

- to quickly *compare* relative performance across units, institutions, or settings
- to monitor what is happening within a particular unit, institution, or setting *over time*
- to explicitly examine the *effects of intervention or policy change*–either across settings or over time[14]

Indicator Profiles at Different Levels of Interest. Let's explore the application of performance indicator systems by examining performance indicators profiles at different levels of interest. One of the earlier journal pieces on campus management use of performance indicators was an article by Sapp and Temares on "key success indices" at the University of Miami.[15] We should note that the terms/phrases "critical Success Factors,"[16] "key Success Indices," and "key Performance Indicators"[17] usually make reference to the same concept. The monthly management report at the University of Miami, according to Sapp and Temares, contained data points on over 100 indicators. Readers interested in the complete listing will find that in Exhibit 3 of the original article.

A more concise profile of campus-based indicators may be found in an article by Dolence and Norris.[18] (See Table 9.1.) This indicator profile for the University of Northern Colorado at once indicates a strength and liability. The measures of activity and productivity found in this profile are certainly needed sources of intelligence at the campus level. What is most obviously missing, however, are achievement data on students. In this profile, we have performance indicators on entering student aptitudes; but beyond graduation and retention rates, the only outcome indicator might be "placement of graduates." There are no measures on value added or criterion measures of student knowledge and skill, for either major fields or general education, nor are there any data on percentage of eligible programs that are accredited. Extensive examples of performance indicator profiles can be found in Borden and Banta,[19] in the Peterson's/Association of Governing Boards report on strategic indicators,[20] and in the Ewell and Jones *Indicators of "Good Practice" in Undergraduate Education.*[21]

Illustrating another perspective on the value of performance indicators at the campus level is the experience of one of the authors in accepting appointment as

Table 9.1
Performance Indicators for University of Northern Colorado

1. Undergraduate FTE enrollment	8,271	9,250	10,000	Number units attempted divided by 15
2. Graduate FTE enrollment	1,435	1,600	2,000	Number units attempted divided by 12
3. Off-campus cash funded enrollment	834.8	1,150	1,500	Number units attempted divided by 15
4. Academic quality of entering freshmen	97.7	100	103	CCHE index combining SAT, ACT, and GPA
5. Minority share of UNC graduates	7.9%	15%	20%	Percentage of minority bachelor's degree recipients
6. In-state resident students	89%	85%	79%	Percentage of students who are Colorado residents
7. Six-year graduation rate	41.2%	50%	60%	Percentage of full-time first-year students who graduate within six years
8. Undergraduate fall-to-fall retention rate	77.2%	80%	85%	Percentage of students who enroll the following fall
9. Doctoral degrees awarded	55	75	100	Number of doctoral degrees awarded annually
10. Alumni attitude audit	85%	85%	85%	Percentage of alumni rating UNC Good or Very Good
11. Faculty quality				To be determined by faculty evaluation task force
12. Faculty teaching contribution	63%	TBD	TBD	Percentage of lower-division courses taught by full-time faculty
13. Teacher certification ratio	23.1%	25%	25%	UNC students as a percentage of all students recommended for teaching certification
14. Placement of graduates	93.8%	93.8%	93.8%	Percent of graduates employed or in advanced study one year after graduation
15. Instructional cost	$2,840	TBD	TBD	State general fund for instruction divided by student FTE
16. Funds generated by research corporation	$6.4 million	$10.3 million	$15 million	Total dollars generated by sponsored programs
17. Funds generated by UNC foundation	$1.8 million	$2.7 million	$4 million	Total dollars generated by annual giving
18. Institutional grant and scholarship aid per FTE	22.5%	25%	30%	Percentage of institutional aid of total aid
19. On-campus student support services cost	$683	TBD	TBD	Expenditures for student services divided by student FTE
20. Meeting authorized state appropriation	$30.7 million	TBD	TBD	Annual appropriated dollars from all sources

interim chancellor at Louisiana State University and Agricultural and Mechanical College in 1989. Author Bogue had been serving for eight years as chancellor at LSU Shreveport, a campus of approximately 5,000 students and awarding bachelor's degrees and three master's degrees, and then was called to be interim chancellor at Baton Rouge, the state's research university with extensive doctoral and research programs and an enrollment of approximately 26,000. There was a need to get a quick feeling for the heritage and challenge of this campus, the size and shape of the enterprise, so to speak. A major piece of intelligence acquisition took the form of early personal visits to offices of major administrators of colleges and research institutes and in informal and unannounced visits at all times of the day and evening throughout the university—to the music building at 7:00 A.M., the office of the LSU Press at noon, the biology department at 4:30 P.M. and the physical plant office at 9:00 P.M. As we will reflect in our concluding remarks on the value of performance indicators, not all the meaning of an organization as complex as a college or a university can be carried in the numbers.

To acquire some grasp of the campus in another way, however, the author asked the Office of Institutional Research to prepare ten-year trend profiles in such areas as enrollments, student admissions aptitudes, facilities value and utilization, revenue and expenditure profiles, faculty rank/ tenure/salary profiles, library and computer profiles, and intercollegiate sports profiles. These indicator profiles were of immense value in gaining quick perspective of heritage and leadership challenges.

Beyond the campus, performance indicator systems have emerged at system and state level. Sanders, Layzell, and Boatright furnish an illustration of accountability indicators used at the University of Wisconsin System.[22] Among the accountability indicators employed by the UW system, according to this 1996 report, were these (see Table 9.2):

The State University of New York (SUNY) system also developed a performance indicator system and those indicators are shown in Table 9.3.[23] Here we can begin to see an interest in a comprehensive set of questions that treat fiscal context, undergraduate access, undergraduate quality, state needs and goals, graduate education and research, and management efficiency and effectiveness. These tables illustrate a purpose of indicator systems that may have been neglected or at least insufficiently emphasized in previous conversation, which is the accountability function.

Performance indicators are a crisp and quick means of furnishing civic/political stakeholders and educational leaders with information on two important questions: How are resources being applied and with what results, and what progress is being made in achievement of goals (minority enrollment increases, improved retention, etc.)? Moreover, other questions of interest may also be examined: Are senior faculty being used in teaching undergraduate courses or just graduate teaching assistants/adjunct faculty?

Similar policy interests may be found in state systems of performance indicators. Indeed, in the 1993 SREB report previously cited, Bogue, Creech, and Folger describe the emergence of state-mandated performance reporting systems in southern states. At that time, only two of the fourteen SREB states did not have some form of mandated accountability reporting. Performance indicator profiles for each of the twelve states may be found in this report and Table 9.4 furnishes a sample from the state of Tennessee.[24] This annual performance indicator report is required by law in Tennessee, as in many other states. Actually the full report of performance indicators is presented in an annual publication

Table 9.2
Performance Indicators for University of Wisconsin System

*Research Funding and Doctoral Universities
*Sophomore Competency Tests
*Four-Year and Six-Year Graduation Rates
*Post Graduation Experience
*State Funding for Instruction-Related Activities
*Admission Rates and Access
*Hiring, Retention, and Tenure Data for Women and Minority Faculty/Staff
*Minority Student Enrollment and Graduation Rates
*Sexual Harassment Complaint Data
*Faculty Retention and Development
*Facilities Maintenance
*Workplace safety
*Employer Satisfaction with UW System Graduates
*Continuing Education/Extension Enrollment.
*Faculty Retention and Development
*Facilities Maintenance Data
*Workplace Safety
*Employer Satisfaction with UW Graduates
*Continuing Education/Extension Enrollments

entitled *Challenge 2000,* which contains an extensive current and ten-year trend report on a range of indicators that describe current enrollment and financial conditions, as well as data on achievement of state goals.

A June 1994 report of the Education Commission of the States furnishes case study analyses of performance indicators in ten states over the United States.[25] By no means, however, is the use of performance indicators restricted to the United States, as our opening commentary in this section made plain. Additional information on other countries may be quickly gleaned from the two monographs previously cited, the 1994 monograph by Gaither, Nedwek, and Neal and the 1994 monograph by Borden and Banta.

We have mentioned the publication of institutional "fact books" as compilations of performance indicators at the campus level, and publications such as Tennessee's *Challenge 2000* as compilations of performance indicators at the state level. At the regional and national levels, two publications are the SREB's *Fact Book on Higher Education*[26] and the U.S. Office of Education's *The Condition of Education.*[27]

Table 9.3
SUNY Performance Indicators

Fiscal Context

1. Six-year trend of tuition as a percent of SUNY revenues, compared to national public institutions and SUNY peers.

2. Six-year trend of percentages of SUNY income from tuition, state, federal, hospitals, and other sources for state-operated campuses (excluded community colleges).

3. Five-year trend of percentages of income from students, state, local sponsor and other sources for SUNY community colleges.

4. Five-year trends in total student costs for SUNY four-year campuses compared to those at public institutions in New England and the Middle States for commuter and residence students.

5. Ten-year trend of tuition increases by SUNY compared with the trend in New York State median family income.

6. Five-year trend in educational and general expenditures per FTE student compared with national public, SUNY peers, and New York private institutions.

7. Four-year trend in system funding as a percent of modeled need, based on national peers.

8. Seven-year trend in New York State appropriations for higher education.

9. Six-year trend in state allocations to public higher education as a percent of state tax revenues.

Undergraduate Access

1. Applications and percent of acceptances of first-time and transfer students in SUNY state-operated campuses.

2. Six-year trends in first-time enrollment compared to trends in high school graduates.

3. Ten-year trends in enrollment by age and gender.

4. Seventeen-year trend in racial and ethnic enrollments.

(Continued)

Health and Progress: A Summary Assessment. What we have seen in these reflections is that the use of performance indicators as an instrument of collegiate quality assurance began to emerge in some other countries in the 1980s but took full root in the United States in the 1990s. A variety of higher education interest groups have played an important role in the development of suggested core indicators. These would include aforementioned organi-

Table 9.3
(Continued)

5. Four-year graduation rates and positive outcomes by race, ethnicity, gender, and high school averages for SUNY two-year campuses.

6. Six-year graduation rates and positive outcomes for SUNY baccalaureate campuses compared with national public peers and by race, ethnicity, and gender.

Undergraduate Quality

1. Percent of campuses with approved assessment plans for student learning outcomes.

2. Percent of campuses with assessment plans for fundamental skills, general education, academic programs, and students' personal and social growth.

3. Percent of campuses with active assessment committees with faculty and student representation.

4. *ACT* Student Opinion Survey of the quality of educational experiences and services at SUNY two- and four-year campuses.

5. UCLA Higher Education Institute's faculty opinion survey on educational goals, institutional priorities, faculty/student interactions, interests in undergraduate students, and students' academic preparedness.

State Needs, especially Workforce Development

1. Percent SUNY represented in total college enrollment for the state and its major regions.

2. Percentages of New York State's undergraduate and graduate degrees conferred by SUNY, CUNY, and independent institutions.

3. Percent of degrees conferred by SUNY in critical fields: agriculture and natural resources, business, management, and law; education, engineering, and technologies; biology and health sciences; mathematics; physical sciences.

4. Number of non-credit courses and enrollment in critical subject areas.

Graduate Education and Research

1. Percent of doctoral degrees for the state and each of its regions conferred by SUNY.

2. Six-year trend of New York State funding for graduate studies and research in SUNY.

(Continued)

zations such as NCHEMS, NACUBO, ECS, SREB, and also the American Association of Community Colleges, which sponsored a special task force that developed core indicators of effectiveness for two-year colleges.[28] In addition, the movement of state government onto the higher education accountability scene was often made explicit by means of mandated accountability report-

Table 9.3
(Continued)

3. Eleven-year trend of increased expenditures for research and sponsored programs and comparison SUNY's rate with national peers and with New York State institutions.

4. SUNY's percent of the national scholarly awards for faculty and graduate students in New York State.

5. Number and percent of SUNY medical residencies in primary care fields.

Management Efficiency and Effectiveness

1. Five-year comparison of actual enrollment with budget plans.

2. Comparison of the number of courses taught by SUNY faculty by campus type with national averages.

3. Comparisons of the time allocation of SUNY faculty by campus types to teaching, research, and service responsibilities with national averages.

4. Five-year loss of positions in SUNY to budget cuts, with statistics on faculty, academic support, and institutional support.

5. Comparisons of SUNY staffing to student ratios for faculty, non-teaching professionals, and support staff with national public and New York private averages.

6. Comparisons of SUNY costs for maintenance and operations of physical plant to regional and national averages.

7. Percentages of SUNY building conditions evaluated as good to excellent, fair, and poor.

8. Five-year trends for private fund raising in SUNY.

9. Eight-year trends in woman and minority staffing in faculty, professional, and support positions.

10. Six-year trend in reallocation of faculty positions among academic programs with increasing and decreasing enrollments.

ing systems involving performance indicators. Finally, higher education systems, individual campuses, and programs have developed performance indicator profiles.

The use of performance indicators to convey useful intelligence on the operation, health, and goal achievement of higher education at any level would appear to be not only reasonable but essential for educational leaders who want to know, and should know, what the condition of the enterprise may be. Thus, performance indicator systems may build on and complement other quality as-

Table 9.4
Accountability Performance Indicators for the State of Tennessee

- Number and percentage of accredited programs and programs eligible for accreditation
- Percentage of students accepted from those applying; percentage meeting admissions standards; average ACT scores of admitted students
- Number and percentage of students completing their degree programs within specified time limits
- Number of degrees awarded by discipline
- Percentage of lower division courses taught by full-time faculty, part-time faculty, and graduate assistants
- Number of students in remedial courses
- African-American enrollment and course completions
- Pass rates on professional licensure exams
- Job placement rates for vocational students
- Alumni satisfaction indices
- Student transfer data

surance systems described in previous chapters—such as accreditation, student/alumni feedback, and outcomes assessment information. Intelligence on resources and results—current conditions and trends—that reflect the distinctive heritage and mission of a campus would appear to be such a fundamental management and educational decision tool that we might wonder why it has taken so long for such a policy system to emerge. And to be fair to higher education scholars and administrators, higher education "fact books" have been around since the emergence of institutional research. The data points found in these early fact books may be seen as the forerunners of today's performance indicator systems.

Perhaps there are two other notes we may insert in closing this discussion. One is that there is no performance indicator that cannot be manipulated for false or misleading purpose if decision makers lack integrity, and this shortcoming of public management reports may be found in every organization, whether collegiate or corporate. For colleges and universities, we saw evidence of this back in chapter 3 on rankings and ratings; and there is certainly no lack of similar evidence in American business organizations such as manufacturing, tobacco, asbestos, and savings and loan. Second, we must not believe that the full reality of our colleges and universities—whether in the reality of their purpose or their performance—will ever fully be captured in the numbers. Years ago, American higher education scholar and president Harold Enarson caught the heart of this idea: "In measuring things that can be counted or expressed in quantifiable terms, we are led unawares to the grand illusion—that only the measurable really matters."[29]

Performance indicators are the foundation for another emerging system of higher education accountability, that of performance funding, and it is to that policy system that we now turn.

PERFORMANCE FUNDING POLICY SYSTEMS

As we noted in the opening to this chapter, performance funding policy systems have emerged as an instrument to link institutional budgets and their educational performance, serving as both incentive and reward for performance achievement and improvement. As with performance indicator policy systems, the emergence of performance funding policy has been dominantly a policy development of the 1990s, with one major exception to be noted later in this discussion.

Burke and Serban in their 1998 monograph entitled *Performance Funding for Public Higher Education: Fad or Trend?*[30] note that the accent on higher education accountability moved from an emphasis on assessment in the 1980s to the linkage of funding and performance in the 1990s. In 1994 Ruppert reported that 44 percent of state government chairs of higher education committees indicated that their states were likely to link funding and performance in the coming years.[31] In a 1997 national survey, Burke found that ten states had adopted some form of performance funding policy and another eighteen had such a policy under consideration.[32]

These descriptive notes notwithstanding, there is considerable policy "volatility," which is the term Burke employs to tag the often rapid movement into and away from performance funding. Texas, for example, has been discussing the concept for over a decade but has yet to put a policy into action. Arkansas moved into a policy and just as quickly back out. In the late 1990s, a legislative mandate moved South Carolina into a policy intended to allocate 100 percent of funds to South Carolina's public universities on a performance basis. The state has since concluded that this is not working. The first state to adopt a performance funding policy was Tennessee in 1979–80 and that policy is still in effect.

In this section, we will first briefly visit performance funding policy systems in selected states and then concentrate on Tennessee's policy as an example of the first and longest-standing policy of performance funding, ending with summary notes on those factors that associate with stable and effective policy systems. As a quick note, two of the most informing references on performance funding policy systems are the aforementioned monograph by Burke and Serban and a 2002 book entitled *Performance Funding for Public Higher Education: From Fad to Trend,* edited by Joseph Burke, published by SUNY Press, and featuring the results of case studies conducted in five states.[33]

State Vignettes on Performance Funding. Let's just be alphabetical in this venture. Higher education in Arkansas adopted a performance funding policy in 1994 and abandoned the policy in 1997. The policy was developed by the State Board of Higher Education and the Arkansas Higher Education Department and involved institutional reporting on some twenty performance indicators that included such data points as retention, graduate rates, licensure exam performance, rising junior exam performance, and diversity issues. The indicators were assaulted by both two-year and four-year campuses for a variety of imperfections and only a modest sum of the total state appropriation (about $5 million in 1995–97) was involved.

In Colorado, a performance funding policy was adopted by the state legislature in 1993 and was suspended in 1996, a short policy life. In Florida two competing systems of performance funding were introduced, one championed by Governor Lawton Chiles and the other by the state senate. In fiscal year 1998, about $12 million was made available to community colleges for performance funding but only $3.3 million for universities. In Kentucky, Governor Bremerton Jones implemented a performance funding policy in 1993 and Governor Paul Patton discontinued the policy in 1997. Only about $3 million was to be allocated on this policy in 1996–97, which has to be "much ado about nothing." In Louisiana, a performance funding mandate was legislated in the 1997 legislative session and that state's higher education system is still grappling with how to get the system into place. In Minnesota an initial policy foray was legislated in 1994 and suspended in 1998. Ohio and South Carolina are two additional states working under legislative mandates related to performance funding.

The South Carolina policy is of particular interest because it required 100 percent allocation of state appropriations on nine success factors and thirty-seven performance indicators. The implementation of this 1996 law was passed to the South Carolina Commission on Higher Education, and the commission inherited a policy nightmare of the first order. Are you going to have a policy that ignores differentials in enrollments by program and degree level? Are you going to set performance goals that are easily achievable and thus guarantee receipt of performance funds or are you going to set performance goals that are going to challenge the institution? How are your performance indicators going to recognize differences in mission and context between community colleges and four year institutions? No doubt many a lively conversation on ethics passed between campus presidents and their institutional research officers in this venture. A legislative panel report issued in 2001 suggested that the policy had not had the performance improvement impact anticipated in the original legislation.[34]

Twenty Years of Performance Funding in Tennessee. Representatives from the higher education and government community in Tennessee began exploring the technical and philosophic feasibility of a performance funding policy in 1974, and Tennessee was the first state to formally implement a performance funding policy in 1979–80. The developmental story of the Tennessee Performance Funding Policy is told more fully in a project monograph by Bogue and Troutt[35] and in a *Harvard Business Review* article by Bogue and Brown.[36] And a twenty year descriptive tour of the policy can be found in a chapter by Bogue appearing in the previously cited volume by Burke.[37] For Tennessee, performance funding policy, then and now, involves the allocation of a modest portion of state appropriations to public campuses based on a small number of performance indicators

The intent of the pilot and development work on performance funding was to explore the feasibility of allocating some portion of state funds on a performance criterion. Anticipating the emergence of accountability interests in all of American education, certainly at the elementary and secondary level, another purpose of the policy was to demonstrate the initiative of the Tennessee higher education community in engaging performance issues. The hope was that this initiative might forestall the imposition of performance measures and assessments by political action, which had occurred for elementary and secondary education and for higher education in many states in the form of legislation and regulation requiring different forms of assessment and accountability. On this criterion the Tennessee policy could be counted a success, as there are no current legislative curricular or assessment mandates for public colleges and universities in Tennessee. The one exception is one previously cited in this chapter. There is legislation requiring an annual report on a selected field of performance indicators.

The leadership initiative for development of performance funding policy in Tennessee came from the Tennessee higher education community. The Tennessee Higher Education Commission (THEC), the state's coordinating agency for higher education and the agency having responsibility for developing policies for the equitable distribution and use of public funds, took the initial policy design lead. However, campus and governing board officers and faculty were also involved early on in the design of pilot work. In the two opening years of the pilot work on the policy (1974–76) approximately $500,000 in grants was secured from the Fund for the Improvement of Postsecondary Education, the W. K. Kellogg Foundation, the Ford Foundation, and one anonymous Tennessee foundation. These funds supported five years of pilot and developmental work on performance funding policy during the years 1974–79. This five-year developmental work involved (1) the creation of pilot policy research projects at ten campuses, (2) the advice and review of a state-level advisory committee composed of both faculty and staff from campuses and their governing boards and government officials (two legislators and the state commissioner of finance), and (3) the advice and review of a national advisory panel of higher education scholars and experts on fiscal policy.

Launched in pilot form in the budget year 1979–80, performance funding policy in Tennessee has now been in operation for twenty years. During this twenty-year history, the policy has been revised every five years, these revisions producing a variety of policy shifts that we will explore later in this discussion. The policy shifts have included (1) changes in the nature and number of performance indicators, (2) changes in acceptable measures and evaluation standards for several of the performance indicators, and (3) a change in the proportion of stated appropriation assigned on the basis of performance funding.

Over the past thirty years, Tennessee has employed formula funding as the basic instrument for the equitable and objective allocation of state appropriations to its colleges and universities. Most funding formulas utilize enrollments by degree level and program field as the basic elements in developing an appropriations request for various public campuses in a state. Funding policy variations, such as peer-based formula funding, allow consideration of faculty salary demands as a function of institutional mission (community college vis-à-vis research university, for example). While satisfying the public policy criteria of equity and objectivity, enrollment driven formula funding does not involve any consideration of performance or quality. In other words, the emphasis is on the educational question of "how much" and not "how good."

The purpose of the Tennessee performance funding policy development phase was to ascertain whether a "performance" or "quality assurance" feature might be built into state funding policy. The result of the five-year developmental work resulted in a policy whose architecture has remained relatively stable over a twenty-year period. Campuses may have their basic enrollment driven appropriations recommendation enhanced by their record on several performance indicators. In the 1979–80 pilot implementation of the policy, a campus could earn up to 2 percent additional funds in its appropriation recommendation. This percentage is now up to 5.54 percent additional. To understand the policy in action see the illustration of Exhibit 9.1.

An important feature of the Tennessee policy is that the performance amount is not technically an "add-on." In a word, the performance feature of the policy is imbedded in an institution's appropriation recommendation and has effect or "grip" regardless of what appropriation level is finally funded by the state. For the case of Exhibit One, for example, if the state funded the formula appropriations request at a 100 percent level, then First Rate College would receive $20.22 million. If, however, the revenue and priority picture for the state permitted funding higher education appropriations requests at only 90 percent, then First Rate College would receive 90 percent of $20.22 million or $18.198 million. Thus, the performance feature is in effect whether state appropriations are increasing, decreasing, or remaining stable.

A second and important distinguishing feature of the policy is that it does not pit one campus against another in a "zero-sum" competition for funds. Essentially campuses are competing against their own record, and one campus is not advantaged by the poor performance of another campus. While the basic policy architecture has remained the same over its twenty-year history, what has changed is the nature and number of the performance indicators, to which we now turn.

The Evolution of Performance Indicators in Tennessee. In the opening of this chapter, we indicated that performance indicators form the basis for most performance funding policy systems. A summary analysis of the nature of performance indicators or standards over the twenty-year history in Tennessee might be described as follows:

- The number of indicators has grown from an initial five indicators to ten indicators.
- The profile of indicators moved from an initial set of five indicators that were common to all institutions to a set that acknowledged different campus mission and goals.
- The nature of the evaluation or scoring protocols on the performance indicators moved from a prescribed set in which evaluation standards were largely self-referential to policy expectations wherein the standards of evaluation encouraged comparison of performance with institutions similar in mission, but outside of Tennessee.
- The percentage of the state higher education appropriations dedicated to performance funding grew from 2 percent to 5.54 percent.
- The performance indicators or standards moved from an occupation with indicators common to all institutions to a position that allowed variation by mission (four-year and two-year, for example), and to an assessment of campus contributions to its own strategic goals and to state strategic goals.

These changes to the policy and its standards reflected primarily the values and interests of higher education representatives from campuses, governing board staffs, and coordinating commission staff, and did not emerge from political interests pressures. The change in the profile of the performance indicators from the original pilot indicators to those in effect 2000-2004 may be seen in Exhibit 9.2.

In the year 2000, clearly, Tennessee higher education had in place an extensive system for assessing higher education performance that was not in place in 1980, and an extensive system of performance intelligence and trend lines on a wide range of indicators that was also not in place in 1980. In 1979 campuses were doing almost nothing in the way of performance assessment. In 2001, the challenge is choosing among a variety of assessments and encouraging decision application of results.

Exhibit 9.1
The Initial Implementation of Performance Funding

Assume that First Rate College, a hypothetical public college in Tennessee, has an educational and general appropriation recommendation of $20 million derived from an enrollment-driven formula funding policy, which recognizes enrollment by level of program and type of program.

During the pilot implementation of the Tennessee performance funding policy, five performance indicators were identified and standards of performance for each of those five indicators were also developed. (Scoring protocols for the various indicators are outlined in the next section of this chapter.)

The maximum performance funding amount available to First Rate College would be 2 percent of $20 million, or $400,000. In other words, in First Rate College had absolutely perfect scores on each of the five performance indicators its final appropriation recommendation to the Tennessee Legislature and governor would be $20.4 million. Consider now this score profile for First Rate College on the five indicators:

Performance Indicators	Maximum Points	Assigned Points
Accreditation	20	10
General Education Outcomes	20	15
Major Field Outcomes	20	0
Peer Evaluation	20	10
Optional Variable	20	5
Total	100	55

Added to the basic formula appropriations recommendations of $20 million for First Rate College would be an amount equal to 55 percent of $400,000 or $220,000, making the total appropriation recommendation First Rate College $20.22 million.

It will be important to note that the principal policy accent in the pilot phase was to use the power of fiscal policy to call institutions to more assertive performance assessment efforts—*without the state specifying or mandating an assessment instrument.* This policy accent may be seen in the general education evaluation standards of the pilot phase shown in Exhibit 9.3. Within three years of the pilot phase, all twenty-one institutions in the state had *voluntarily* selected the ACT COMP as a measure of general education outcomes. Let us move forward on the same indicator of general education outcomes to the 2000–2004 cycle. In this most recent cycle the number of points awarded on the general education indicator is now fifteen, compared to the twenty in the pilot cycle twenty years earlier, and more importantly there is some prescription in the acceptable measurements of general education: the California Critical Thinking and Skills Test, the College BASE test, and the Academic Profile Assessment. As contrasted

Exhibit 9.2
Performance Funding Standards Pilot Cycle 1979–80

Performance Standard	Points Awarded
Standard One - Program Accreditation	20 Points
Standard Two - Graduate Performances in Major Field	20 Points
Standard Three - Graduate Performance on General Education	20 Points
Standard Four -Evaluation of Institutional Programs/Services by Students/Alumni	20 Points
Standard Five - Peer Evaluation of Academic Programs	20 Points

****

Performance Funding Standards Fifth Cycle 2000-2004

Performance Standards	2 Year	Univ.
Standard One - Academic Testing and Program Review		
A. Foundation Testing of General Education Outcomes	15	15
B. Pilot Evaluations of Other General Education Outcome Measures	5	5
C. Program Accountability		
Program Review	5	10
Program Accreditation	10	15
D. Major Field Testing	15	15
Standard Two - Satisfaction Studies		
A. Student/Alumni/Employer Surveys	10	10
B. Transfer and Articulation	NA	5
Standard Three - Planning and Collaboration		
A. Mission Distinctive Institutional Goals	5	5
B. State Strategic Plan Goals	5	5
Standard Four - Student Outcomes and Implementation		
A. Output Attainment		
1. Retention/Persistence	5	5
2. Job Placement	15	NA
B. Assessment Implementation	10	10
TOTAL POINTS	100	100

with the early history of performance funding, the ACT COMP general education assessment has gone out of existence.

Another performance indicator that has remained relatively stable over the twenty-year history of the policy is that of alumni surveys. Here again, we can see an interesting evolution in the performance measure and evaluation standard for this indicator. In the 1979 pilot cycle, an institution could earn points if it had taken any number of steps toward surveying its alumni. In the 1992–97 cycle, the entire state used a common survey instrument and the policy required alternating surveys of alumni and currently enrolled students.

The evaluation was based on comparison to state norms or to previous year's data. Again, for this indicator, we can discern a clear movement from the initial policy call to begin assessment to a more restricted instrumentation requirement and quantitative evaluation. An interesting addition to the 1997–2002 and 2000–2004 policy cycle was the recognition of campus performance in achieving its own educational goals and in achieving state strategic goals. This policy feature links campus performance to state strategic goals, a reasonable and appropriate policy accent, and also allowed campuses some flexibility in setting their own developmental goals. The 2000–2004 standard unites the program accreditation standard with the provision for academic program review, based on the reasonable argument that program accreditation can be seen as a form of program review. As an aside, it may be argued that one success associated with the Tennessee performance funding policy is that while in 1979 only two-thirds of eligible programs were accredited in public institutions, that percentage has approximated 100 percent for several years.

Another feature that found its way into the new standards is an "implementation" requirement, a "decision utility" expectation (see Standard 4B in Exhibit 9.2). This feature asks not only what an institution found from its various assessments but also what program or student decisions were influenced by the results. This is a policy change to be admired, because it may reduce cosmetic and adaptive responses to the various performance indicators and encourage educational application of performance indicator data. Some institutions satisfy the requirement of the general education standard by administering one of the aforementioned assessments, but the results of the assessment have little or no decision effect on either the general education program or student progress or performance.

Table 9.5 furnishes a twenty-year summary profile of institutional points and dollars earned on the Tennessee policy. These profiles are global profiles of institutional performance in any given cycle, but do not furnish direct evidence on educational performance. A more extended treatment of educational performance trends on the various indicators may be found in the chapter by Bogue.[38] What this table does illustrate, however, is that close to $350 million has been allocated to performance funding over its twenty-year history, not a small investment.

High and low performances may be found among all Carnegie classifications, so that the Tennessee policy has not appeared to favor, for example, the research university over community colleges, nor vice versa. This characteristic of the Tennessee policy, equity in application, was one of the principles that the policy attempted to honor from the earliest stages of planning. For one of the cycles, the University of Tennessee, the state's public research university, was high scorer, but for the other cycles, the high scorer was to be found in the community college sector.

Table 9.5
Twenty Year History of Performance Points and Dollars

Institution	1978-79	1981-82	1982-83	1986-87	1987-88	1991-92	1992-93	1996-97	1997-98	1998-99
	Pts	Dollars	Pts	Dollars	Pts	Dollars	Pts	Dollars	Pts	Dollars
APSU	56.0	$352,428	93.8	$2,592,534	77.8	$3,263,365	90.4	$5,189,253	92.0	$2,182.790
ETSU	43.8	$568,984	85.6	$4,632,841	81.0	$6,811,325	84.4	$8,570,113	92.0	$3,706,955
MTSU	60.5	$878,976	90.0	$5,948,048	76.4	$8,181,453	90.2	$12,788,952	91.0	$5,599,720
TSU	45.0	$521,661	83.8	$3,592,708	51.2	$2,978,562	80.2	$5,622,167	86.0	$2,549,006
TTU	71.8	$789,099	98.2	$5,136,264	83.8	$6,525,823	92.6	$8,050,890	94.0	$3,324,818
UM	61.3	$1,578,081	91.4	$10,743,739	80.0	$14,238,431	89.8	$18,502,259	90.0	$7,419,428
Subtotal		*$4,689,229*		*$32,646,134*		*$41,998,959*		*$58,723,634*		*$24,692,771*
UTC	62.8	$560,278	86.8	$3,557,180	78.8	$4,670,112	92.2	$6,533,513	96.0	$2,837,793
UTK	74.8	$3,261,881	99.0	$19,137,613	84.2	$23,710,066	89.0	$28,970,873	95.0	$12,392,866
UTM	64.5	$477,541	91.0	$2,925,204	77.2	$3,470,876	87.4	$4,751,459	92.0	$2,041,926
Subtotal		*$4,299,700*		*$25,619,997*		*$31,851,054*		*$40,255,845*		*$17,272,585*

(Continued)

Table 9.5
Twenty Year History of Performance Points and Dollars (Continued)

Institution	1978-79	1981-82	1982-83	1986-87	1987-88	1991-92	1992-93	1996-97	1997-98	1998-99
	Pts	Dollars	Pts	Dollars	Pts	Dollars	Pts	Dollars	Pts	Dollars
CSTCC	50.0	$193,008	91.2	$1,627,585	84.4	$2,685,522	87.0	$3,694,427	95.0	$1,652,619
CSCC	57.3	$161,2460	90.0	$1,013,639	72.8	$1,129,126	88.2	$1,674,507	92.0	$701,611
COSCC	62.0	$125,458	93.4	$813,589	84.8	$1,424,127	96.4	$1,922.715	97.0	$857,492
DSCC	26.8	$30,097	94.4	$527,284	82.2	$725,757	86.4	$980,122	92.0	$444,246
JSCC	69.0	$146,442	97.2	$891,125	76.2	$1,131,219	85.6	$1,614,382	82.0	$646,410
MSCC	67.0	$114,264	95.2	$704,247	85.2	$1,055,179	95.0	$1,576,937	94.0	$631,947
NSTCC	12.0	$14,700	88.4	$637,644	84,2	$948,277	90.2	$1,584,319	91.0	$869,291
NSTI	58.0	$191,770	100	$1,455,401	82.2	$1,633,040	85.4	$1,910,020	91.0	$700,892
PSTCC	34.3	$58,493	84.2	$695,753	81.0	$1,759,759	89.4	$3,089,343	94.0	$1,358,153
RSCC	64.0	$166,456	97.2	$1,209,117	92.0	$2,120,846	89.8	$2,797,022	91.0	$1,154,515
SSCC	60.3	$286,733	96.4	$1,726,959	81.6	$2,056,157	87.4	$3,219,541	76.0	$1,101,673
STIM	38.5	$182,910	98.2	$2,006,850	79.8	$2,601,385	87.4	$3,643,838	99.0	$1,645,199

(Continued)

Institution	**1978-79**	**1981-82**	**1982-83**	**1986-87**	**1987-88**	**1991-92**	**1992-93**	**1996-97**	**1997-98**	**1998-99**
	Pts	Dollars	Pts	Dollars	Pts	Dollars	Pts	Dollars	Pts	Dollars
VSCC	72.0	$175,103	100	$1,069,624	88.6	$1,572,782	93.6	$2,547,349	94.0	$1,197,530
WSCC	47.5	$136,710	94.4	$1,198,726	92.4	$1,920,956	91.2	$2,644,351	95.0	$1,218,347
Subtotal		*$1,983,390*		*$15,577,543*		*$22,764,132*		*$32,898,873*		*$14,179,925*
Grand Total		$10,972,319		$73,843,674		$96,614,145		$131,878,352		$29,439,495

Exhibit 9.3
General Education Standard—Pilot Cycle 1979

1. The institution has assessed the performance of a representative sampling of graduates for its major degree—associate or bachelor's—on a measure of general education outcomes at least once during the past four years.
2. The institution has during the last four years assessed the general education performance of a representative sampling of its graduates by major field and has begun a program of interfield or intercollege analysis.
3. The institution has an ongoing program to assess the general education performance of its graduates on a measure of general education outcomes and has data available, preferably on the same measure, for representative samples of two or more classes of graduates during the previous four years.
4. The institution meets the requirement of Standard Three and can further demonstrate for the most recent assessments that the development of its graduates—that is, the change in performance from freshmen to graduation—is equivalent to or greater than the development of students for at least one institution whose freshman performance is on a comparable level.

Note: Meeting each standard results in progressively more points awarded. An institution meeting Standard One receives five points, meeting Standard Two ten points, Standard Three receives fifteen points, and meeting Standard Four twenty points.

RECONCILING IMPROVEMENT AND STEWARDSHIP: A SUMMARY

Over its twenty-year history, the Tennessee Performance Funding Policy has reflected that inevitable tension found in any accountability policy, the tension between the call for educational improvement and the call for financial stewardship, between the use of quality assurance exercises to improve programs and the use of quality assurance exercises to demonstrate that public monies have been applied effectively and efficiently. In the original pilot indicators or standards of the policy, the accent was clearly on improvement. In latter years, the standards featured comparative evaluations based on national or peer norms. In the latest policy iteration (2000–2004), the comparative feature remains, but there is an acknowledgment of educational decision utility, in the application of results for educational improvement.

More extended evaluative treatments of the Tennessee policy may be found in articles by Banta,[39] Burke,[40] and Bogue.[41] The two later reports chronicle the results of an extensive survey of administrators at different levels in Tennessee colleges and universities and the results of five case studies that probed more deeply and specifically policy impact at three universities and two community colleges. From these evaluative studies, we may first note that the presence of an important accountability system is not necessarily a guarantor of enhanced financial support for higher education. In the decade in which the policy was developed in Tennessee (1970s) and in the first decade of the policy's operation (1980s), financial support for higher education was reasonably strong and at least regionally competitive. In the decade of the 1990s, however, Tennessee's financial support of its higher education slipped seriously, with per student appropriation support declining by about $1,300 per student, the most serious decline among SREB states.[42]

It might be argued that America's investment in its educational systems has always been as much faith based as fact based, and thus we might not be surprised at this lack of coupling between the presence of accountability systems and level of financial support. Moreover, there are other obvious factors that constitute major influences on financial support for higher education. These include the economic condition of the state, the architecture of its revenue system, the commitment of a state's governor concerning higher education priorities, and the ability of a governor and state legislature to create a political partnership. If, then, we ask in our policy evaluation whether the implementation of performance funding has resulted in continuous strong financial support for Tennessee higher education, the answer is no.

If, however, we probe other evaluative criteria, the answers are more affirming. The fact that this public policy has been in operation for twenty years and has entered another five-year cycle is one signal, though not an infallible signal, of its utility, as seen through both educational and political lenses. Second, over this twenty-year history, the policy has been subjected to review and evaluation by a panel of campus, governing board, and coordination commission representatives, which may have served to enhance the reservoir of ideas and allegiance associated with the policy and contributing to its relatively long policy life. Third, the proportion of state budget dedicated to the policy has risen from 2 percent to 5.45 percent.

Moreover, the State of Tennessee now has in place an extensive system of performance indicators and trend lines that was not in place in 1980, furnishing the state and its higher education community an important source of operational intelligence and strategic intelligence on both campus and state goals. While some of the direct performance assessments, general education assessments as an example, do not reveal improvements in student performance, they do reveal performance that is favorable when compared to national norms. On at least one other measure considered central as an indicator of both institutional and program quality, that of accreditation, the improvement to virtually 100 percent accredited programs at both community colleges and universities has allowed the state to consider modifying and perhaps dropping that indicator in favor of others that might continue to move the state forward. In other words, here is one qualitative goal that may be considered achieved, and it is now time to look for other improvement goals.

It may also be noted that whereas in 1979–80, the pilot year of the policy, few campuses were doing any educational assessment, there is clearly an active assessment process under way on most campuses. Only three campuses were assessing general education outcomes in 1979–80, but now all campuses are conducting some assessment of general education.

There are some important liabilities to the policy, however, and these suggest improvement possibilities. Some assessments are clearly being conducted just to satisfy the policy and have little or no relation to either student or program decisions. There is a notable lack of penetration to the department and program level in terms of using assessment data for program improvement decisions and for decisions related to student placement and progress. This must be counted one of the more important disappointments in the impact of the policy. Thus, for most campuses, energy and attention to the policy centers at the executive administrative levels and very little at the department chair and faculty level. And more recent campus emphasis has been on maximizing points and dollars and not on utilizing assessments for educational improvement. This liability, however, has been at least partially recognized in the 2000–2004 policy revision, which offers some recognition for application of assessment results. And given the financial context for higher education funding for Tennessee in the 1990s, we should not find it too surprising that campus executives are more interested in maximizing dollars earned than emphasizing educational improvements.

In his book *Speaking Truth to Power,* Wildavsky[43] suggested that one way to think about the contribution of a public policy is to ask what problems are being addressed following policy implementation as compared to before policy implementation. The problems being addressed by the Tennessee higher education community now are certainly not about whether there are any assessments in place or any performance intelligence available. Nor is the problem whether Tennessee educational programs bear the well-recognized imprimatur of accreditation. The problems now turn on enhancing the decision utility of an impressive assessment effort.

THE NEED FOR INTELLIGENCE AND INCENTIVE: A SUMMARY

Perhaps we should loft this reflective note into the discussion as we close. As we will note on more than one occasion in this book, there is no single indicator of quality in American higher education that cannot be faulted for some philosophic or technical imperfection. And there is no system of quality assurance, whether accreditation or total quality management, and so on, that cannot be criticized on some philosophic or technical basis. And there is no policy of any kind, and especially a quality assurance policy, that does not depend upon the values and skills of those administrators and faculty who implement the policy and that cannot be manipulated for purposes both noble and self-serving. Policies are limited in their ability to compensate for lack of caring, competence, or courage at any level in an institution. Occasionally, therefore, we may ask whether criticisms lofted at policy might be more properly directed to the values and skills of those who implement policy.

From a summary perspective, however, performance indicator policy systems offer an informing approach to the acquisition and presentation of intelligence reflecting activity and achievement at campus, system, state, regional, and national levels. And as we noted earlier, performance indicator policy systems can convey useful intelligence on the operation, the condition, and the achievement of higher education at every level. To have such performance intelligence would appear not only reasonable but essential for educational leaders. Thus, the acquisition and application of intelligence on resources and results, on conditions and trends that reflect the heritage and mission of a campus may be counted a fundamental management and decision instrument.

Some cautions are in order. A performance indicator policy system that contains so many indicators that it tends to be clumsy and to fall over of its own weight will not prove helpful. Second, leaders in higher education do well to understand the nature and complexity of the enterprise and to remind themselves that not all of the beautiful reality of that enterprise can be found in the numbers. Third, there is no system of performance indicators that cannot be manipulated by the unscrupulous so that everything "looks good." Fourth, an extensive performance indicator system having no decision utility is of little or no value.

As for performance funding policy systems, properly conceived and designed, performance funding policy systems may offer a useful linkage between funding and performance and an incentive to focus on performance questions. As we noted in our opening chapter, it would seem reasonable even in collegiate organizations to keep before us questions of purpose (what is our intent) and questions of performance (how good a job did we do and how do we know). However, performance funding systems may also prove distracting and destructive to higher education purpose if ill conceived in either design or process.

There is, for example, going to be a tendency to shape the numbers to produce the dollars. And there is going to be a tendency to select performance goals easy in attainment but not worthy in challenge. There is going to be a tendency to have "much ado about nothing" at the executive and administrative level, but little penetration of performance issues to the faculty and program level. Small rudders, however, can move big ships. If both academic and civic/political officials are involved in the design of the policy ship and its rudder, we are more likely to birth effective performance indicator and performance funding policy systems.

NOTES

1. Linke, R. D. (1990). "Australia," In *The Development of Performance Indicators for Higher Education: A Compendium for Eleven Countries,* ed. H. R. Kells. Paris: Organization for Economic Cooperation and Development. ED 331 355, MF-01.

2. Sapp, M. M., and Temares, M. L. (1992). "A Monthly Checkup: Key Success Indices Track Health of the University of Miami." *NACUBO Business Officer,* 25(9), March, 24–31.

3. Bogue, G., Creech, J., and Folger, J. (1993). *Assessing Quality in Higher Education: Policy Actions in the SREB States.* Atlanta, GA: Southern Regional Education Board.

4. Borden, V. M. H., and Banta, T. W. (eds.) (1994). Using Performance Indicators to Guide Strategic Decision Making [Special issue]. *New Directions for Institutional Research,* No. 82, Summer.

5. Gaither, G., Nedwek, B. P., and Neal, J. E. (1994). *Measuring Up: The Promises and Pitfalls of Performance Indicators in Higher Education.* ASHE-ERIC/Higher Education Report No. 5, Washington, DC: George Washington University, Graduate School of Education and Human Development.

6. Ruppert, S. S. (ed.). (1994). *Charting Higher Education Accountability: A Sourcebook on State-Level Performance Indicators.* Denver, CO: Education Commission of the States.

7. Gaither, G. (1997). "Performance Indicator Systems as Instruments for Accountability and Assessment." *Assessment Update,* 9(1), January-February.

8. Jones, D. P., and Ewell, P. T. (1994). "Pointing the Way: Indicators as Policy Tools in Higher Education. In *Charting Higher Education Accountability: A Sourcebook on State-Level Performance Indicators,* ed.S. Ruppert. Denver, CO: Education Commission of the States.

9. Cave, M., Hanney, S., and Kogan, M. (1991). *The Use of Performance Indicators in Higher Education: A Critical Analysis of Developing Practice* (2nd ed.). London: Jessica Kingsley, 24.

10. Taylor, B. E., Meyerson, J. W., and Massy, W. (1993). *Strategic Indicators for Higher Education: Improving Performance.* Princeton, NJ: Peterson's Guides, x.

11. Borden, V. M. H., and Bottrill, K. V. (1994). "Performance Indicators: History, Definitions, and Methods." In Borden, V. M. H., and Banta, T. W. (eds.), Using Performance Indicators to Guide Strategic Decision Making [Special issue]. *New Directions for Institutional Research,* No. 82, Summer, 11.

12. Sizer, J., Spee, A., and Bormans, R. (1992). "The Role of Performance Indicators in Higher Education," *Higher Education,* 24(2), 133–156.

13. Hammond, L. (1992). "Educational Indicators and Enlightened Policy." *Educational Policy,* 6(3), September, 237.

14. Ewell, P., and Jones, D. (1996). *Indicators of "Good Practice" in Undergraduate Education: A Handbook for Development and Implementation.* Boulder, CO: National Center for Higher Education Management Systems, 10.

15. Sapp and Temares, "A Monthly Checkup: Key Success Indices Track Health of the University of Miami."

16. Rochart, J. (1979). "Critical Success Factors." *Harvard Business Review,* 57(2), March-April, 81–93.

17. Dolence, M. (1989). "Key Performance Indicators." *Planning for Higher Education,* 18(1), 1–13.

18. Dolence, M., and Norris, D. (1994). "Using Key Performance Indicators to Drive Strategic Decision Making." In Borden, V. M. H., and Banta, T. W. (eds.), Using Performance Indicators to Guide Strategic Decision Making [Special issue]. *New Directions for Institutional Research,* No. 82, Summer, 75.

19. Borden and Banta, "Using Performance Indicators to Guide Strategic Decision Making."

20. Peterson's Incorporated and Association of Governing Boards. (1992). *Survey of Strategic Indicators.* Princeton, NJ: Peterson's, Inc.

21. Ewell and Jones, *Indicators of "Good Practice" in Undergraduate Education.*

22. Sanders, K., Layzell, D., and Boatright K. (1996). "University of Wisconsin System's Use of Performance Indicators as Instruments of Accountability." In *Performance Indicators in Higher Education: What Works, What Doesn't, and What's Next? Proceedings from the Pre-Conference Symposium,* ed. G. Gaither, June 8–9. Bryan: Texas A&M University System, 22.

23. Burke, J. (1996). "Performance Indicators in SUNY: An Imperfect Beginning, An Uncertain Future." In *Performance Indicators in Higher Education: What Works, What Doesn't, and What's Next? Proceedings from the Pre-Conference Symposium,* ed. G. Gaither, June 8–9. Bryan: Texas A&M University System, 28–30.

24. Bogue, Creech, and Folger, *Assessing Quality in Higher Education,* 9.

25. Ruppert, *Charting Higher Education Accountability.*

26. *SREB Fact Book on Higher Education, 2000–2001.* Atlanta, GA: Southern Regional Education Board.

27. *The Condition of Education, 2000.* (2000). Washington, DC: United States Office of Education.

28. American Association of Community Colleges. (1994). *Community Colleges: Core Indicators of Effectiveness. A Report of the Community College Roundtable.* AACC Special Reports, Number 4. Washington, DC.

29. Enarson, H. (1973). "University or Knowledge Factory." *Chronicle of Higher Education,* June 18, 16.

30. Burke, J., and Serban, A. (eds.) (1998). Performance Funding for Higher Education: Fad or Trend? [Special issue]. *New Directions for Institutional Research,* No. 97, Spring.

31. Ruppert, *Charting Higher Education Accountability.*

32. Burke, J. (1998). "Performance Funding: Present Status and Future Prospects." In Burke, J., and Serban, A. (eds.), Performance Funding for Public Higher Education: Fad or Trend? [Special issue]. *New Directions for Institutional Research,* No. 97, Spring, 5–13.

33. Burke, J., and Associates. (2002). *Funding Public Colleges and Universities for Peformance.* Albany: The Rockefeller Institute Press.

34. Schmidt, P. (2001). "Performance Based Aid Has Had Little Effect on Colleges in South Carolina, Report Says." *Chronicle of Higher Education,* June 6.

35. Bogue, E., and Troutt, W. (1980). *Allocation of State Funds on a Performance Criterion.* Nashville: Tennessee Higher Education Commission.

36. Bogue, E., and Brown, W. (1982). "Performance Incentives for State Colleges." *Harvard Business Review,* 60(6), November-December, 123–128.

37. Bogue, E. (2002). "Twenty Years of Performance Funding in Tennessee." In *Performance Funding for Public Higher Education: From Fad to Trend,* ed. J. C. Burke and Associates. Albany: State University of New York Press.

38. Ibid.

39. Banta, T., Rudolph, L., Van Dyke, J., and Fisher, H. (1996). "Performance Funding Comes of Age in Tennessee." *Journal of Higher Education,* 67(1), 23–45.

40. Burke and Serban, *Performance Funding for Higher Education: Fad or Trend?*

41. Bogue, op. cit, 2002.

42. *SREB Fact Book on Higher Education, 2000—2001,* 173.

43. Wildavsky, A. (1993). *Speaking Truth to Power: The Art and Craft of Policy Analysis.* New Brunswick, NJ: Transaction Publishers.

Chapter 10

Beyond Systems

Moral Outrage and Other Servants of Quality

As made clear in the earlier chapters, one can find several theories of quality in current literature; and American higher education has fashioned diverse systems to define, develop, and demonstrate quality. There are the traditional approaches of accreditation and program review; instruments built heavily on the concept of peer evaluation. Rankings and ratings accent the competitive and "limited supply" theory of quality. There is the assessment movement, built around the concepts of valued added and multiple evidences. Emphasizing continuous improvement and customer/client satisfaction, the concept of total quality management has found acceptance in some college and university settings. Finally, some campuses, systems, and states have developed performance indicators and performance funding reporting as a way of learning about their operations and achievements.

Quality assurance in our colleges and universities, however, is more than systems and technique, more than ciphers and computers. A faculty member with a caring touch and high standards may be more directly potent in the cause of quality than a pleasant ranking in *U.S. News and World Report,* a well-oiled TQM system, or a positive performance indicators report. An academic administrator with courage, compassion, and integrity may more directly affect quality than any system of quality assurance. Let us illustrate.

Earlier in his career, one of the authors found himself in the office of Memphis State University Graduate Dean John Richardson, a splendid educator known throughout Tennessee as a man of integrity, high standards, and personal caring. Dean Richardson was on the phone with a state senator who wanted a student who did not meet regular admission standards admitted to graduate school. Perhaps the senator surmised that a touch of political pressure might ease the dean to a satisfactory response. Dean Richardson's visage assumed a grim and determined fix, and he spoke over the phone as follows: "Son, are you threatening me? Because if you are, I will come to your district and campaign against you next year. And, son, I will defeat you." And he would have.

Did this exchange reflect a quality issue? Certainly! But it had little to do with the traditional approaches of accreditation and program review, little to do with outcome assessments and reputational rankings, little to do with TQM and customer satisfaction, and little to do with accountability reporting. It was about caring, courage, and character. It was about a college administrator who knew what was right and was willing to act. And it was an exemplary lesson in ethics.

In our opening chapter, we took the position that questions of quality in our colleges and universities cannot be separated from questions of integrity. In this chapter, we hope to further reveal why we take this position. In a word, a complete and effective approach to quality assurance in higher education must go "beyond systems" and embrace those personal behaviors of faculty, staff, and administrators that advance or impede the cause of quality.

MORAL AND ETHICAL DIMENSIONS OF QUALITY

The current ferment over quality and productivity in higher education may have as much to do with the level of integrity and caring exemplified in the daily behavior of college and university officials as with our ability to design systems of quality assurance. Thus, all those who hold our colleges and universities in trust—board members, administrators, faculty—must look beyond such systems to the principles and standards manifested in the behavior of faculty and administrators. The cause of quality may be advanced or damaged in a thousand "moments of truth" that occur in exchanges between faculty, administrators, and students.

As we noted in an earlier chapter, the phrase "moment of truth" comes from Jan Carlzon's book of the same title.[1] As president of Scandinavian Airlines, Carlzon noted that the qualitative reputation of the airline derived not so much from customer awareness of aircraft performance specifications or the airline's financial ratios but from each moment of truth that occurred when a customer encountered an employee of the airline.

Is there a lesson here for colleges and universities? Here's one student's story: A dean of students received a call from a student who had the flu and missed a chemistry exam. Having contacted the professor in advance to explain her absence, she spoke with the professor upon her return to see if she might arrange a makeup examination. He explained that he was only on campus two days a week to teach his one class, while he devoted the remainder of his time to his research in a nearby research park. His principal responsibility to the university, he said, was to keep his research moving. He had neither the time nor the inclination to arrange a makeup exam, and she would have to accept the scores on her other exams for the course. When the dean of students called to see whether any compromise might be reached, the professor informed her that if he attended to every little problem and excuse offered by hysterical undergraduates, he would hardly have time for his research. A crabby, arrogant, or dishonest spirit can destroy in a moment the good built over a long period of time.

An exception, you may say, to the reality of caring that may be found in most of our classrooms, studios, and laboratories. As noted, however, just one story or instance of our failure to treat students with dignity, with civility, has the potential to outweigh a thick accreditation report, a formidable set of performance indicators sent to the state, or a slick annual report from the president's office. Moral outrage on the part of a department chair or a college dean would be an appropriate response to this unhappy case where arrogance of spirit and narrow vision of role prevented a faculty member from celebrating the nobility of the call to teaching.

Here is a news clip that appeared in *USA Today:* A community college had canceled almost two-thirds of its summer school classes on the second day of the term. Students were given no advance notice or any reasonable explanation, except the president's statement that he had ordered the classes canceled to meet the budget.[2] The story carried a photo of angry students besieging administrative offices. Is this a quality issue? Well, if you think about students as clients, the answer surely must be "Yes."

Might we expect an accreditation team to arrive and investigate this situation? Not likely. Will the assessment plan for this campus address this situation? Improbable. May we expect to find the director of total quality management in the middle of the fray, tending to the concerns of student customers? We doubt it. And will the institution's accountability and performance indicators report to the state reflect this incidence? Absolutely not.

How any college president could enter a summer session and not know enough about his or her budget to avoid such behavior is beyond comprehension. Something is missing here. That something is competence and caring. Moral outrage would be an appropriate response to what happened to these students.

Here's another media report of college shenanigans and dreary behavior; this story found its way into the *Wall Street Journal* after appearing in several other papers.[3] A professor of engineering apparently engaged in a shady entrepreneurial venture, exchanging his endorsement of shoddy and short work on plagiarized master's and Ph.D. degrees for students who, from the vantage point of their industrial appointments, shuffled lucrative consultant contracts to their major professor. We can only hope these students will not work on our bridges, aerospace systems, or nuclear power facilities. And save us from their obtaining faculty appointments in our colleges or universities.

At least responsible faculty, administrators, and trustees on this campus engaged in a speedy piece of "due process"—arranging a prompt departure for this entrepreneurial but morally bent professor and recalling the faulty degrees from students, who surely must have harbored a flawed notion of educational quality. The reports on this incident do not indicate that the accreditation, assessment, total quality management, and performance indicators systems of the campus were active elements in this quality assurance drama.

Consider this illustration of offense to quality: Here is a private college launching a new master's program, an initiative designed to reach a new market of students. Nothing wrong with initiative. However, here are the program's unhappy conditions following two years of operation and the graduation of the first class: only one-fourth of the graduating class of approximately twenty-three students met the admissions requirements stated in the college catalog and accreditation-candidacy prospectus for this program. More than two-thirds of the graduates have been given credit for courses that cannot be found in the institution's catalog, that were not in the original graduate prospectus, that have little or no relation to the program's mission, and that were not authorized for acceptance in the program as originally outlined in the program prospectus.

Only one of the half-dozen full-time faculty in the program area listed in the institutional catalog has taught in the graduate program, while the remaining courses have been delivered by adjunct faculty of marginal qualifications. A review of course syllabi files reveals at least one syllabus from another university. This syllabus is supposed to describe a course taught in this new program, but the name of another university has not even been changed. A cross-check reveals that this university is the same university that granted a doctorate to the graduate program's administrator. A good argument can be made that not one but two colleges have something to think about here. For this program and this campus, any reasonable sense of academic standard has fallen before the seductive call of numbers and tuition trend lines.

This campus scenario, like those preceding and others to follow, unfortunately is real. A potentially happy ending is that apparently some faculty and administrators on this campus are exhibiting moral outrage over these conditions. How can we measure the damage already inflicted on the ideal of quality—and on the competence and character of students who have graduated from this program? These graduates had to know they were being cheated, or else they were allowed to nurture a shallow sense of educational standard.

Well, here's another sad case: Reaching the conclusion that credit hour production was, not surprisingly, a factor in the number of faculty that might be authorized for a department, the chairman of a research university philosophy department had all of his master's students enroll in a readings course that required no readings. This mandatory course enrollment was a subterfuge for pumping up the department's enrollment and credit hour production numbers. The ultimate irony of this case was that the chair was also lead professor in the department's course on ethics. Since there is no specialized accreditation agency for philosophy, it is unlikely that this dark venture will be caught by accreditation as an instrument of quality assurance. *U.S. News and World Report* rankings and ratings will never dig deep enough to spot this offense, nor is this likely to be found in the department's list of improvement objectives for the total quality management system.

A curious assistant vice president for academic affairs office, however, smelled something fishy while browsing through curriculum and course enrollment records one day, and with a modest amount of detective work involving informal conversation with department graduate students ferreted out this curriculum facade. A courageous vice president and helpful dean arranged for the appointment of a new chair.

A friend sent us a news clip appearing in the morning issue of a major urban newspaper of a western state:

> Why is Wendy Router standing there looking puzzled? Because she registered at City College by phone—a new system—and then mailed in the fees for two courses, plus $10 for a campus parking sticker. Simple, no? Not. Back came a receipt but no parking sticker. However it did show $10 overpayment so all is well? Well: she went out to the campus and stood in line for an hour to get the parking sticker. "That'll be $10," said the bureaucrat, at which Wendy triumphantly presented the credit slip, to no avail. "You'll have to give me $10 if you want the sticker now, and then you may apply for a refund, which will take about eight weeks," he said, not unkindly. Defeated, Wendy asked for a refund form. "Here you go," he said, handing her one, "but you won't get any money back. There's a $10 fee for processing a refund."[4]

Do you suppose they have a director of total quality management at City College? This little venture sounds worse than a Keystone Cops or Three Stooges movie clip. And since we are talking about movies, perhaps we can further accent our point here. A few years, a movie starring William Hurt and titled *The Doctor* was produced. It profiled the fictional experience of a physician diagnosed with cancer and his subsequent treatment. He experienced treatment from the other side of the stethoscope, so to speak. A similar theme may be found in the movie *Patch Adams,* starring Robin Williams, which chronicles the experience of a medical student who challenges the culture of physician training, a culture in which the physician was cast in the hero role of treating and curing the patient, who was seen as an object but not a person with a name. The emotional links with health care may also be found in Norman Cousins's books *The Anatomy of an Illness*[5]and *Head First: The Biology of Hope.*[6]

Effective quality assurance, one more time, moves "beyond systems" to the culture of caring and courage in our colleges and universities, to the acquisition of performance intelligence that may be derived from informal as well as formal sources.

In the middle of the 1990s, the University of Kansas Medical School came under scrutiny by legislative audit committees and a special study committee on charges that the medical center was accepting patients for heart transplants while refusing to accept donated hearts.[7] In a story appearing in the September 27, 1995, issue of the Kansas City (Missouri) *Star* is this note:

The audit was prompted by articles in the Kansas City *Star* that found that KU's heart transplant program performed no transplants for 10 months but continued to accept patients. Patients were not told that during that time KU refused every heart offered to it. The program was shut down in April after inquiries by the *Star*.[8]

A September 26, 1995, issue of the *Star* indicated that "University of Kansas Medical Center administrators knew about problems with the center's heart transplant program and that hearts were being turned down for nonmedical reasons but failed to respond, a state audit to be released today concluded."[9]

No doubt considerable complexity may be uncovered in this extraordinary case of mismanagement. However, if we were patients on the receiving end of this mistreatment, the behavior of the medical center and its personnel would be counted as more than a modest dysfunction. If you are a member of a profession that has taken an oath to prevent and treat disease, to save lives and do no harm, if you are a faculty member in a university whose mission is to train exemplary leadership for every sector of our national life, you could argue that we have a quality issue of majestic proportion.

There is no record in the news stories surrounding this event, this divorce of competence and conscience, that an aggressive medical accreditation team arrived, that an academic program review had apprehended the culprits wearing white coats, or that the performance indicator report indicated a surplus of income or donor hearts and a deficit in treated patients.

THE CALL OF COURAGE AND COMPASSION

Courage and compassion among faculty and staff are just as surely instruments of quality assurance as all the systems profiled in previous chapters. Why do some leaders, corporate and collegiate, wilt under criticism, run before the shifting winds of popularity, and sacrifice their honor while others stand to principle and maintain the conviction of solitude when thrust into the company of critics and into the caldron of political and social, economic, and ethical pressures? In another essay, one of the authors identified this leadership virtue as "The Vital Badge of Courage."[10] Manifestations of professional courage are to be found in the willingness to discharge one's acknowledged duty, to endure and persist in noble cause, to reach and risk, and to insist on responsibility from our colleagues. These are moral calls and not systems calls.

Duty means that we face our responsibilities on those days when we are targeted and tired as well as on those days when we are filled with energy and cheer, that we face our responsibilities when frustration and failure thwart our efforts as well as when achievement and accomplishment furnish an elevating reinforcement. Not always a colorful and dashing affair, duty is a grit-your-teeth and carry-on matter, in which one puts one foot in front of the other every day in standing for what is right and good.

What does one do as faculty, chair, or dean when a school superintendent, who is also a doctoral student in education, announces on public billboards and public relations pamphlets in an election campaign that he holds a doctoral degree from a state university, but the true status of the student is that he has not yet completed course work and is not yet in candidacy status? Such PR tactics may be a useful way to gain an edge in a hotly contested election for the superintendency, but they also constitute a blatant lie on the part of an educational leader who hopes to hold principals, faculty, and students in trust. And there is more than one question to be engaged here. Do the billboards come down and are the retractions printed? And if not, what action on the part of the program, college, and university is appropriate and effective? And does this student remain in the doctoral program? In this instance, the misguided educator is no longer superintendent and does not hold a doctoral degree.

Patience and persistence are among the more difficult virtues to acquire and cultivate but among the more powerful when deployed in the service of noble purpose. We live in an "instant world," where our expectation is that we can mix most any substance with a little water, put it in the microwave, and have the finished product in a moment or two. Colleges and universities serve a tensioned mission in our society as cultural curator and cultural critics. They respond slowly to change, as they should; and nurturing quality requires patient educational craftsmen committed to the long run.

In chapter 2 we featured accreditation as a system of quality assurance with a long and unique heritage in American higher education. One of the authors was involved with specialty field accreditation of a College of Business at LSU Shreveport. Many human motives are compounded of both noble and selfish elements. In the case of this academic quality goal, we were convinced that the American Association of Collegiate Schools of Business (AACSB) would be a mark of distinction for our program, as we were a "teaching university" of primary strength with four master's degree programs. This more noble aspiration, however, was reinforced by a selfish motive, one traced to a policy of the Louisiana Board of Regents requiring that every master's program in business in the state would become accredited by 1990 or be terminated. We may become swift because we want to run fast, and we may become swift because we are being pursued!

And so we had the vision and the plan to become AACSB accredited. We labored with many disappointments as the recessionary economic conditions of the 1980s in Louisiana greased the steep slope we were trying to climb—producing leadership challenges in recruiting and retaining doctoral qualified faculty in a tight market. The leadership character of the dean and his faculty was reflected not only in their dreams but also in their determination. They stayed the course, standing to duty over a ten-year period, and the college was finally accredited. This is a quality assurance story depicting the useful intersection of a system (accreditation) and value commitments (the courage to persist).

Perhaps at a more fundamental level, acts of courage are acts of compassion, of caring and love. When collegiate faculty and administrators exemplify in their lives a quiet but persistent passion for basic virtues, they are trustees of nobility and custodians of quality. If one examines management, leadership, and organizational behavior texts of the first half of the twentieth century, it is improbable that the word "love" would be found in tables of contents, in the body of the books, or in their indexes. Not so, however, for more recent works. Those who give leadership to our colleges and universities love soul, standard, and system. They care for the welfare and promise of students entrusted to their care. They care for a standard of quality and excellence. And they care for the social, cultural, and technical systems in which we do our work.

A NEW VICE PRESIDENT?

If we surveyed the administrative directories of American colleges and universities, we probably would find a growing number of directors of assessment and vice presidents of continuous improvement. Do we need a vice president for moral outrage? Perhaps not. However, we might make use of a position suggested in Robert Townsend's 1971 book *Up the Organization*,[11] a vice president for "antibureaucratization." Anytime the vice president finds tangled processes, four-stage signature approvals, five-part forms, or other performance nonsense within an organization, the vice president would, according to Townsend and in his words, take position outside the offending office and yell "horse shit!" as loud as possible until the situation was corrected.

We are only half joking. Accreditation, assessment, total quality management, and performance indicators are "head first" solutions. Nurturing quality in our colleges and universities, however, must go beyond such systems. We need presidents and professors, deans and directors who have a keen sense of standard and right behavior, who answer the call to honor and are willing to use moral outrage as an instrument of quality assurance, who create a climate of quality via the influence of their ideals as well as their ideas.

What unites the systemic and moral guarantors of quality? In our minds, the uniting element is a habit of mind and heart that creates a community of caring. In a community of caring, the values of courage and compassion create a climate in which a respect for diversity of mission and talent is matched with a scorn for shoddy work, whether individual or institutional. A community of caring responds not only to the intellectual call of advancing the truth but also to the ethical and personal call of honoring dignity, excellence, and responsibility. Again, in a community of caring, quality does not and cannot live apart from integrity.

A trustee willing to leave the boardroom and walk around campus may find such "walking about" a promising vehicle of qualitative discovery. A president, vice president, or dean willing to leave the power tower and sit on a bench outside the student center may find such passive but open behavior a discovery option of premier value. Faculty and administrators can contribute to the ethical and the qualitative climates of their campus by exemplifying personal and professional ethical conduct in their own lives. They can encourage the identification of core values by which a campus community can hold itself accountable. They can support any student, professor, or administrator taking courageous and thoughtful stands on points of principle and standard. They can attend carefully to systematic approaches to quality assurance and to performance indicators that offer evidence of campus quality. But above all, they will hold close to heart the recognition that when students exit our institutional portals, they will remember not our quality systems but whether they were inspired, challenged, and encouraged by those who held their lives and their talents in trust.

NOTES

1. Carlzon, J. (1987). *Moments of Truth.* Cambridge, MA: Ballinger.

2. "Across the USA: News from Every State." (1994, June 2). *USA Today,* 7A.

3. Putka, Gary. (1991, July 12). "Academic Barter: A Professor Swapped Degrees for Contracts, University Suspects." *Wall Street Journal,* A1.

4. Caen, H. (1993, August 25). "Gamut from Ho to Hum." *San Francisco Chronicle,* 6.

5. Cousins, N. (1979). *The Anatomy of an Illness.* New York: W. W. Norton.

6. Cousins, N. (1989). *Head First: The Biology of Hope.* New York: Dutton.

7. Myers, R. (1995, May 12). "Study of KU Heart Program Ordered." *Topeka Capital Journal,* D1.

8. Thompson, C. (1995, September 27). "Review Vowed by KU Official." *Kansas City Star,* F9.

9. Thompson, C. (1995, September 26). "Audit Details Trouble at KU." *Kansas City Star,* D4.

10. Bogue, E. G. (1996). "The Vital Badge of Courage." *Planning for Higher Education,* 24(4), Summer, 53–57.

11. Townsend, R. (1970). *Up the Organization.* New York: Knopf, 84–85.

Chapter 11

Improvement versus Stewardship

Reconciling Civic and Collegiate Accountability Cultures

In the latter half of the twentieth century, Americans made, by any standard, a magnificent investment of faith and finance in higher education, expanding the number of colleges and universities in this nation from 1,900 to 4,000. American colleges and universities enroll fourteen million students, are staffed by 600,000 faculty, and operate on $200 billion in revenues. And in the most recent year for which statistics are available, Americans gave beyond tuition and government support just over $20 billion in voluntary support to their colleges and universities through alumni, corporate, foundation, and other gifts.[1]

Thus, one of the more obvious higher education policy accents in the latter half of the twentieth century was the accent on access. Beyond the increase of institutions just cited, Americans dramatically expanded expensive professional and graduate programs, built extensive community college systems, developed state and federal aid programs to make college more affordable, and via law and court rulings sought an end to barriers of gender, ethnicity, and physical handicap. In contrast to some predictions at midcentury, both private and public higher education flourished.

A second obvious policy accent was that of accountability. Changes in accreditation criteria from process indicators to educational outcomes and institutional effectiveness indicators was one manifestation of accountability.[2] The emergence of the assessment movement[3, 4, 5] was yet another expression of increased accountability expectations from within and without. State governments became a more assertive player in higher education policy as various regulations and laws mandated assessment practices,[6] called for reporting on various performance indicators,[7, 8] and created performance funding and budgeting systems.[9, 10]

The intent of this chapter is to examine the tensions of motive and method that have emerged between collegiate and civic/political expectations of accountability and to explore ways of strengthening the partnership between academic and civic/political leaders. As preface, it may prove informing to explore mission expectations for higher education, as questions of performance might reasonably be anchored to some common vision on the purpose of the enterprise.

CULTURAL CURATORS AND CULTURAL CRITICS

Posing questions of mission and purpose is not surprisingly a venture of majestic complexity, as American higher education is a system of both privilege and opportunity in which our elitist and egalitarian impulses contend. It is a system in which the principle of autonomy, so essential in the search for truth and in the nurture of democracy, is in dynamic tension with the principle of accountability, which is antidote to professional arrogance and intellectual narrowness.

We herald our colleges and universities as organizational instruments of our curiosity and wonder, as forums of discovery and dissent. We cherish our colleges and universities as citadels of reason and persuasion. We assign them the mission of advancing on enemies of ignorance, arrogance, and prejudice. We hold them as repositories of value, beauty, and standard—calling student and society to excellence in the arts, in the sciences, and in the professions. We fashion them as guardians of liberty and democracy.

We mark them as engines of cultural and economic development, making it possible for individuals and society to reach the far edge of their circle of promise. We place with them the responsibility of putting knowledge and wisdom to work—grappling in the dirty trenches of the nation and the world to battle those problems that beset mind, body, and spirit; engaging issues of both soil and soul erosion.

We expect them to be cultural curators and cultural critics. Conserving the past, critiquing the present, constructing the future—this is a mission expectation that destines our colleges and universities to remain always in the crucible of public conversation and one that guarantees a continuing tension in civic expectation and evaluation of higher education. Indeed, Peters[11] argues that educational goals are deeply political and that this constitutes one of the more important reasons that many approaches to accountability fail to persuade stakeholders that they are getting a good "bang for their buck" or that the effects of college are worth the costs. This need for consensus on goals will be a theme to which we will return later in this chapter.

AN EROSION OF TRUST AND A LOSS OF SANCTUARY

What Americans esteem and salute they may also depreciate and criticize, however. There has been an arresting and critical perception in the closing years of the twentieth century, years marked by frequent critical assault for a range of perceived and real shortcomings. These years are hardly the first season of criticism, however. Never without its critics, history suggests that American higher education lives in a state of chronic crisis, if we may entertain this oxymoron.

Each of the closing years of the twentieth century has seen at least one book-length treatment critical of higher education. Bloom's 1986 *The Closing of the American Mind,*[12] Sykes's 1990 *Profscam,*[13] Smith's 1990 *Killing the Spirit,*[14] Anderson's 1992 *Imposters in the Temple,*[15] Roche's 1993 *The Fall of the Ivory Tower,*[16] Patterson's 1996 *When Learned Men Murder,*[17] Kors and Silverglate's 1998 *The Shadow University,*[18] and Lewis's 2000 *When Power Corrupts*[19] are just a few among those critical reviews. These books and other critical coverage in the media have not advanced the cause of public trust in higher education.

Critical accounts in *USA Today,* the *Wall Street Journal,* and other newspapers tell a story of faculty and administrators taking themselves, their students, and their institutions in harm's way, forsaking both personal and professional integrity. As illustrated in the 1993 monograph *An American Imperative,*[20] concern with the "moral compass" and "moral vocation" role of higher education appeared more frequently in public discourse.

The disappointing display of values in American higher education can be found in individual and institutional dramas of unfortunate and dark texture.[21] We cited in chapter 10 a major university medical center admitting patients for heart transplant surgery, with the full knowledge that the probability of these surgeries actually taking place was virtually zero. Patients and insurance companies were billed for large sums. Those aware of this cruel charade included medical staff and the dean of the medical school; it appears that upper-level administrators in the university were also aware. The depressing state of health for both patients and university was brought to light in a legislative audit.

We are not talking here about the mismanagement of research, the degradation of academic credentials, or the careless stewardship of public resources. We are talking about a callous disregard for human life and dignity in an academic and professional field whose purposes are to revere and enhance human life and dignity. From this and a hundred other sad stories, is it any wonder, then, that civic and political friends may question whether those who give voice and means to our colleges and universities have severed the precious link between mind and heart, between competence and conscience?[22]

We should not believe that the aberrant personal and institutional leadership accounts described here and in other disappointing records constitute the dominant reality in either corporate or collegiate America. There is a reality of nobility and goodness manifest in quiet lives of devotion among faculty and administrators over this nation every day, exemplars who show us courage and conscience in action, who elevate our vision of what is possible for our lives and for our society.

The difficulty is that just one departure from nobility and integrity is one too many in an organization whose avowed purpose is to prepare leadership for every sector of our national life. A May 1997 monograph published by the Education

Commission of the States suggested that current accountability pressures might be traced to "declining public resources and the sense that colleges and universities are ill-prepared to meet the needs of the 21st century."[23] We do not argue the validity of these two points, but we do believe that acts of personal and institutional duplicity have not helped the public cause of American higher education.

We are, not surprisingly, no longer perceived as places of sanctuary, where values *other* than the purely financial and selfish might prevail, where commitment to truth and unfettered inquiry nurtures a standard of conduct marked by nobility and integrity. Thus, in the opening of the twenty-first century, American higher education faces a serious question of public trust, which brings a call for accountability.

Public disaffection with some of the values being modeled in higher education has added force to other pressure vectors faced by higher education in the closing years of the twentieth century: cost containment pressures and reduced revenue regimens, political leaders expecting sharper mission focus and less across-the-board mentality in dealing with fiscal retrenchment, parents and students expecting their college tuition investment to yield a good-paying and satisfying job upon graduation, civic and collegiate policymakers relying increasingly on market mechanisms to define public goals and priorities, civic dissatisfaction with attention to teaching, competitive pressures from an emerging privatized sector, impressions of organizational obsolescence and recalcitrance to change, egalitarian discomfort with higher education as a haven for a protected and privileged class, and a clash of liberal-conservative values in our society and within academia.

Surely there is much about American higher education that deserves reform and renewal, but questions of higher education purpose and performance are not necessarily a sign of pathology. An institution whose mission embraces the unswerving search for the truth, whose methods include the adversarial testing of ideas in public forum, whose spirit embraces a certain irreverence, and whose best work is done when its graduates exit with a sustained curiosity and with the competence and courage to ask "Why?" may count it a measure of success when those graduates turn their curiosity to the academy itself.

ACCOUNTABILITY: CONTENDING CULTURES

As we noted earlier, one of the commanding changes in climate for higher education is the more assertive posture of agencies external to the campus—coordinating agencies, legislators, executive branches of government, accrediting agencies—insisting on a more public engagement of quality and performance issues. As Ted Marchese noted in a 1994 editorial in *Change* magazine: "Most accountability enactments call for public information about performance. So 'what's the big deal?' the legislator asks. In her workplace, technology-based information systems routinely make available to every employee key facts about unit and corporate performance. Why haven't you similar systems on campus? Do performance and improvement matter to you?"[24]

Beyond legislators and executive officers of government, trustees and board members have become more vocal and active in their concern for institutional purpose and performance issues. Consider these policy developments having an accountability emphasis:

1. The increased state regulation of higher education to include such heretofore unregulated policies as curriculum, assessment, and faculty workload.
2. The growing number of states mandating some form of assessment and testing.
3. The growing number of states having some form of consumer protection regulation to protect their citizens against fraudulent private institutions.
4. The growing number of states requiring some form of performance indicator reporting by campuses.
5. The number of states adopting and experimenting with some form of performance funding/budgeting.
6. The ferment over the effectiveness and reform of accreditation.
7. The increased curiosity of boards of trustees with curricular issues and faculty personnel issues such as tenure.

Many of these developments in such areas as assessment, performance indicators, and performance funding have been explored in previous chapters. A more recent accountability development has not. We refer to the development of "report cards," designed to evaluate and "grade" campuses, systems, and even states. One of the best-known and widely discussed/debated "report card" initiatives is the one launched by the National Center for Public Policy and Higher Education. The homepage for the policy center describes *Measuring Up 2000* as "the first state-by-state report card for higher education. This report grades states on their performance in five categories: preparation, participation, affordability, completion, and benefits."[25]

The "grade" given to states in each of the five categories is derived from an evaluation of performance on several indicators within that category. For example, the "Preparation" category covers the following indicators:

- High School Completion—percentage of residents who earn a high school diploma or GED
- K–12 Course Taking—percentage of students taking upper-level math and science courses
- K–12 Student Achievement—percentage of eighth graders scoring at proficient levels on National Assessment of Education Progress in such areas as math

Similar indicators are scored for all five categories. Readers interested in more in-depth treatment of *Measuring Up 2000* will find extensive data presentations by state with accompanying visuals on the website/homepage previously cited.

The Oklahoma State Regents have published *Report Card on Oklahoma Higher Education*[26] that presents comparative data for Oklahoma against national data and benchmarks set for the state in categories that are similar to the National Center for Public Policy report card, but it also includes a section on "Resources and Funding." The Oklahoma report card, however, does not assign "grades" to the various performance categories.

With whatever benefits and liabilities that may have attended thereto, most Americans are familiar with the report card as a simple and prevalent educational accountability expression for the student. The report card concept has also enjoyed some use in the annual Phi Delta Kappa/Gallup Poll on public schools.[27] The emergence of the report card as an accountability instrument for American higher education, however, is a relatively new venture, and one whose merit and utility have yet to be fully evaluated.

These contemporary expressions of accountability notwithstanding, accountability is not a new idea or term in the lexicon of higher education. Mortimer[28] was talking about the emphasis on educational results in higher education almost thirty years ago. And we can even go back some 350 years to the founding of Harvard and read in a promotional document about the function of the "Overseers." "Over the college (sic) are twelve Overseers chosen by the general court, six of them are of the Magistrates, the other six of the Ministers, who are to promote the best good of it and (having a power of influence into all persons in it) are to see that every one be diligent and proficient in his proper place."[29]

Accountability may be defined as a formally expressed expectation—a campus or board policy, state or federal law, or formal policy of another agency such as an accrediting agency—that (1) requires evaluation of both administrative and educational services; (2) asks for public evidence of program and service performance; (3) encourages independent/external review of such performance evidence; and (4) requests information on the relationship between dollars spent and results achieved.[30]

The motives and methods of civic and collegiate accountability interests are sometimes contentious and adversarial and tend to create two cultures.

- Improvement versus stewardship
- Peer review versus regulation
- Process versus results
- Enhancement versus compliance
- Consultation versus evaluation
- Trust versus evidence
- Interpretation/holistic versus measurement/specifics

Living on the tensioned boundary where these motives intersect is a daily engagement of collegiate faculty and administrative officers, who understand the delicate negotiation between public support/benevolence and public trust. More importantly, collegiate educators know the beneficial promise that resides in the partnership between higher education supporters, who give financial support and serve as custodians of civic allegiance, and faculty, who give voice and meaning to the enterprise and serve as custodians of standard and quality.

Are collegiate and civic accountability cultures destined to remain contentious and adversarial, or is there promise for partnership and for reconciliation? We believe that partnership is not only possible but also essential in designing a system that serves both educational and political decision utility.

SOBERING REALITIES: STUDIES IN POLITICS AND POWER

Reconciling civic and collegiate accountability requires an examination of both attitude and method. First to matters of attitude. There are sobering realities to be entertained before we venture ideas on how to bring civic and collegiate accountability cultures closer together. The first of these is that no accountability system will negate the unhappy fruits of poor economic and revenue conditions in a state, region, or nation. Second, there is no accountability system that will negate the attitudes of political officers who do not value higher education. Third, there is no accountability system that will negate the dark motives of faculty and administrators intent on abandoning their integrity. Fourth and finally, there is no accountability system that will negate the positions and perceptions of those who do not want to be bothered by the facts—whether academic or political officers.

Thus, we would be wise to understand in advance that favorable trend lines, factual evidence, statistical profiles, and public relations campaigns may not alter cherished positions of those who hold colleges and universities in trust. Indeed, important questions that have been raised about current accountability policy and systems is (1) whether they have had constructive decision impact at either the campus or the state level and (2) whether some campus responses to state policy have been more cosmetic and adaptive than substantive and constructive.[31]

While these notes may shake our faith in the power of rationality, they point to the importance of political alertness and astuteness on the part of college leaders. Politics is the art of influence and power is the ability to influence. And influence is heavily invested in our willingness to be personal. The accountability of higher education will be advanced, in our conviction, if academic administrators and political officers are willing to be more personal. Academic administrators will carry a special burden in the challenge of engaging civic and political friends in more personal dialogue.

THE MIND OF THE SCHOLAR

In an organization that prospects for truth in adversarial forum, in an organization holding that we have not understood a truth until we have contended with its challenge, would we feel comfortable if our policies and our practices, our assumptions and ways of doing business went unchallenged? The mind of the scholar is hospitable to dissent and disputation—and should remain so when the dissent and disputation touches and targets the heart of the collegiate enterprise.

Moreover, we should not be surprised that an organization like a college or university, whose principal work is to assault common sense, may itself come under assault. Today's truth was yesterday's heresy; and the harbingers of new truth, whether individuals or institutions, are not always greeted with warm and friendly embrace.

Might the mind of the scholar also accept the range and intensity of public criticism as an indicator of higher education's success, a pleasure measure of constructive moment? Enhanced access to a college and university education produces more minds equipped for and inclined to criticism. Have we not said in our catalogs and promotional brochures that we want our graduates to think critically? Did we believe that they would not also think critically about their intellectual homes? Gibran says that "I have learned silence from the talkative, toleration from the intolerant, and kindness from the unkind; yet strange, I am ungrateful to these teachers."[32] It is easy to be ungrateful to our critics, but we should resist that impulse.

A good college is a good argument. Dissent and disputation are inevitable and welcome outcomes of our inclination to curiosity, which is perhaps the most fundamental mark of the educated mind. Accompanying that curiosity should be the values of courage and persistence that enable a good mind to stay the course. Such a mind does not run and hide at the first sign of contention and criticism. Can an organization whose purpose is learning also learn? As noted in an earlier chapter, the concept of learning organizations has been much popularized by the works of Senge[33] and Morgan.[34] Among the attributes Morgan cites for a learning organization are (1) the ability to question, challenge, and change norms and assumptions, and (2) the inclination and skill in breaking the boundaries that separate it from its environment. These organizational attributes accord nicely with habits of the scholarly mind.

RECONCILING ACADEMIC AND CIVIC ACCOUNTABILITY CULTURES

Here are reflections on how we may realize additional complementary and partnership ventures between civic and collegiate accountability systems.

Continuing Use of Peer Review. The practice of laying performance before the judgment and experience of those external to an organization is in the best spirit of the concept of accountability. And this is precisely what colleges and universities have been doing for years in accreditation and academic program reviews. While the limitations and liabilities of these practices are by now obvious to both academics and civic friends, they reveal the willingness of academics to experience the discomfort and growth that can come from the evaluation of those beyond the walls of an institution. There are some changes we would commend. First, we would urge a stronger governance involvement of lay and civic voices in the management boards of accrediting associations. Second, we like the suggestion put forward by Graham, Lyman, and Trow in their monograph on accountability[35] that accreditation utilize the concept of audit. If an institution is meeting the conditions of accreditation, it could be argued that it should be meeting those conditions all the time and not just on a ten-year sampling. Perhaps accrediting groups would form their visiting committees from both peer reviewers and professional evaluators, similar to hospital accrediting groups, and make unannounced visits to campuses for purposes of auditing their conformance to accrediting criteria and standards. Self-study might continue as a second component of accreditation.

Third, we would urge the adoption of an evaluation disclosure that yields more public information and distinction than a simple pass/fail. The image and the reality of institutional and program excellence should match in such public reports. The insertion of a "commendation" status might be a helpful addition; and campuses must be willing to endure public scrutiny of less-than-favorable outcomes such as "warning" and "probationary" beginning.

And finally, we commend the merit of involving board members/trustees in selected accreditation and program reviews. In the early history of American higher education, board members often sat on baccalaureate examinations. Why not call board members to a more active participation in the quality assurance activities of a campus?

Performance Indicator Profiles. All but two states served by the Southern Regional Education Board required annual reporting on a series of performance indicators in 1993,[36] and it is clear that indicator reporting is increasingly expected in other states. For both collegiate and corporate organizations, performance profiles can be manipulated and camouflaged in various ways, but asking campuses to offer public evidence on performance indicators accenting their mission and distinctiveness does not seem unreasonable.

What might help to improve the decision utility and acceptability of these profiles would be to involve teams of academics, board members, and political officers/staff in their design and use. Instead of academics and political officers standing off in grand detachment and/or adversarial posture, let them join in ventures of design and evaluation. Understanding and appreciation are more likely to emerge from more intimate association than from polite political distance.

Performance Audits. Most public colleges and universities are already subject to financial and administrative audits from state auditors working from either executive or legislative base. What might be the benefits of expanding state audits to examine campus performance indicator reports and other quality assurance activities to ascertain what policy and practice decisions have been influenced by campus quality assurance efforts? Might there be professional development and renewal advantages in inviting selected faculty and staff to take paid leave from their campus to serve occasionally on audit teams with state professional auditors?

Strengthening Academic/Civic Evaluation Partnerships. Many campuses currently make provision for lay oversight and involvement in their academic programs via advisory committees or boards of visitors. These panels are often invited to campus to review performance plans and evaluation reports and to review proposed curricular changes. Eisner[37] accents a "connoisseurship" approach to educational evaluation in which a panel of evaluators rates performance (say of a written or other performance work) in a holistic fashion. There is no reason why some combination of professional/faculty judgment might not be combined with judgments of educated civic friends/alumni in evaluations of essays, senior theses, and so forth.

Guarding the Guardians. Since we have noted that there are few public policies that cannot be met with adaptive and cosmetic response, perhaps we would want to commend periodic external evaluations of accountability policy by evaluator panels external to a state—an accountability of accountability, if you will. Evaluator panels would examine data and interview principal campus and political officials to garner candid and open perception about the value and impact of accountability systems and policy in a state. Here are principles that might anchor and guide such evaluation. Accountability systems should accent:

- Decision—enhance and improve both academic and political decision
- Discovery—offer opportunity for both campus and government to learn
- Disclosure—require campus and state to place performance data in public forum
- Distinction—offer opportunity to accent campus distinction in mission/goal

Would these principles not be welcomed by faculty and academic administrators? We cannot see that they should prove offensive to academic or political conscience?

BEYOND SYSTEMS: THE MORAL ELEMENT OF ACCOUNTABILITY

As we noted in chapter 10, beyond a well-crafted accountability system, assuring quality in any organization, whether corporate or collegiate, is an activity as much personal and moral in content and tactic as it is systemic and technical. A campus or system officer defending the educational standards of a college or university against political meddling, a governor bringing visibility to shady or illegal financial work of a governing board, a faculty member calling a student to accountability for cheating on a test or plagiarizing a paper, a governing board recalling a degree for student misconduct, a dean standing against shallow curricular provisions in an academic program, a department chair holding a faculty member accountable for demeaning behavior toward students, a state-level agency calling an institution to account for false representation of its academic programs, a state newspaper exposing vested interest activity on the part of a college board of trustees member, an advancement officer refusing a gift having prejudicial overtones—yes, accountability is more than systems. It is a matter of conscience, compassion, and courage.

A culture of evidence must be linked to a culture of caring. In a culture of caring, high expectations call students and colleagues from the poverty of the commonplace and launch each to the far reach of his or her circle of promise. Courage and compassion create a climate in which a respect for diversity of mission and talent is matched with a scorn for shoddy and shallow work, whether individual or institutional. In a community of caring, quality cannot and does not live apart from integrity.

THE CONDITIONS OF PARTNERSHIP

Now this closing note. Widely respected by corporate America, management scholar Peter Drucker wrote of higher education in *Innovation and Entrepreneurship* that "No better text for a History of Entrepreneurship could be found than the creation and development of the modern university, and especially the modern American university."[38] Thus, the American college and university system is a product of both civic and collegiate imagination and invention. We see no reason why these pleasant attributes of mind cannot continue to shape our thinking as we search for ways to construct an accountability partnership.

Such a partnership is not possible, however, without strength among all parties. Neither arrogance nor ignorance is a friend of partnership. Those of us in higher education may not ignore the validity of criticism being lofted at the academy nor delay in responsive action. Nor may we target our society and culture with the probing light of our scholarship and remain unwilling to turn that light on the house of intellect. From an advancement perspective, we will not be found accepting gifts with hidden prejudicial promise or repressive promise for academic freedom.

In the same spirit, civic and corporate friends looking down the barrel of the criticism cannon at higher education should make sure they are not living in glass houses. The financial, personal, and civic costs of duplicity disasters such as the savings and loan debacle, insider trading scandals, creative corporate billing on government contracts, shady behavior in energy companies, and political character fissures offend our sense of decency and justice, sear the public conscience, and create a climate of cynicism dangerous to democracy.

Profit is a human motive and an impulse engine of notable power. This is one real world. Service is a human motive and a constructive force of majestic import. This is also a real world. In a democratic society, these two motives are essential and complementary. Neither exists without the other. And public accountability on issues of quality and integrity is central to the real but different worlds of profit and service.

THE INSTRUMENT OF OUR WONDER

A beautiful line found in Gibran's *Sand and Foam* observes that "Your mind and my heart will never agree until your mind ceases to live in numbers and my heart in the mist."[39] A captivating dimension of the inner life of the American college and university is that here are places where some minds live in numbers and some hearts live in the mist—and there are truths to be found in both places.

Here are expressions of nobility and beauty—of art, music, poetry, literature—that furnish inspiration to elevate and enrich our lives. Here is the home of our hope—enclaves of social and physical science and engines of search for solutions to those pains and problems that rob men and women of their promise and dignity. Here is the cradle of leadership development—professional schools attempting to link technical and ethical and delivering men and women who will in every field serve us not so much with direction and structure as by calling us to responsibility and integrity, who in both solitude and teamwork seek to enlarge our repertoire of ideas and perspective. Well and carefully tended, these are mission elements that will earn the trust of civic friends and continue to encourage the philanthropic impulses that have so enriched American higher education's ability to serve our nation and world.

Here are found the "Dreamers of Day," if we may borrow a phrase from T. E. Lawrence, faculty men and women living in the interrogatory mood and exemplifying colleges and universities as instruments of our capacity and inclination to wonder. Honoring the heritage of this enterprise is to recognize and celebrate the energizing power of our curiosity. If there is dissent over purpose and performance of the institutions we hold in trust, let us embrace that dissent, for it may be seen as evidence that higher education is meeting its most fundamental responsibility for asking what is true, what is good, what is beautiful and for equipping its graduates in both motive and skill to ask obnoxious questions and to challenge conventional wisdom.

NOTES

1. Lively, K. (2000). "Giving to Higher Education Breaks Another Record." *Chronicle of Higher Education*, 46(35), May 5, A41.
2. Bogue, E., and R. Saunders. (1992). *The Evidence for Quality*. San Francisco: Jossey-Bass.
3. Banta, T., and Associates. (1993). *Making a Differences: Outcomes of a Decade of Assessment*. San Francisco: Jossey-Bass.

4. Astin, A. (1993). *Assessment for Excellence.* Phoenix, AZ: Oryx Press.

5. Messick, S. (ed.). (1999). *Assessment in Higher Education.* Mahwah, NJ: Lawrence Erlbaum Associates, Publishers.

6. Ewell, P., Finney, J., and Lenth, C. (1990). "Filling in the Mosaic: The Emerging Pattern of State-Based Assessment." *AAHE Bulletin,* 42(8), April.

7. Borden, V. M. H., and Banta, T. (eds.). (1994). Using Performance Indicators to Guide Strategic Decision Making [Special issue]. *New Directions for Institutional Research,* No. 82, Summer.

8. Gaither, G., Nedwek, B., and Neal, J. (1994). *Measuring Up: The Promises and Pitfalls of Indicators in Higher Education.* ASHE-ERIC/Higher Education Report No. 5, Washington, DC: George Washington University, Graduate School of Education and Human Development.

9. Bogue, E., and Brown, W. (1982). "Performance Incentives for State Colleges." *Harvard Business Review,* 60(6).

10. Burke, J., and Servan, A. (eds.). (1998). Performance Funding for Public Higher Education: Fad or Trend? [Special issue]. *New Directions for Institutional Research,* No. 97, Spring.

11. Peters, R. (1994). "Accountability and the End(s) of Higher Education." *Change,* November/December, 16–23.

12. Bloom, A. (1987). *The Closing of the American Mind.* New York: Simon and Schuster.

13. Sykes, C. (1988). *PROFSCAM.* Washington, DC: Regnery.

14. Smith, P. (1990). *Killing the Spirit.* New York: Viking Press.

15. Anderson, M. (1992). *Imposters in the Temple.* New York: Simon and Schuster.

16. Roche, G. (1993). *The Fall of the Ivory Tower.* New York: Regnery.

17. Patterson, D. (1996). *When Learned Men Murder.* Bloomington, IN: Phi Delta Kappa Foundation.

18. Kors, A., and Silverglate, H. (1988). *The Shadow University.* New York: Free Press.

19. Lewis, L. (2000). *When Power Corrupts.* Somerset, NJ: Transaction Publishers.

20. *An American Imperative: Higher Expectations for Higher Education.* (1993). *A Report* of the *Wingspread Group on Higher Education.* Johnson Foundation.

21. Wilshire, B. (1990). *The Moral Collapse of the University: Professionalism, Purity, and Alienation.* Albany: State University of New York Press.

22. Boyer, E. (1987). *College: The Undergraduate Experience.* New York: Harper Collins.

23. *Refashioning Accountability: Toward a Coordinated System of Quality Assurance for Higher Education.* (1997). Denver, CO: Education Commission of the States.

24. Marchese, T. (1994). "Accountability." *Change,* November/December, 4.

25. *Measuring Up 2000.* (2000). San Jose, CA: National Center for Higher Public Policy and Higher Education. Available on-line: http://measuringup2000.highereducation.org.

26. Oklahoma State Regents for Higher Education. (2001). *Report Card on Oklahoma Higher Education.*

27. Rose, L., and Gallup, A. (2001). "The 33rd Annual Phi Delta Kappa Gallup Poll on the Public's Attitudes Toward Public Schools." *Phi Delta Kappan,* 83(1), September, 41–58.

28. Mortimer, K. (1972). *Accountability in Higher Education.* Washington, DC: American Association for Higher Education.

29. Hofstadter, R., and Smith, W. (eds.). (1961). *American Higher Education: A Documentary History, Volume I.* Chicago: University of Chicago Press, 7.

30. Bogue, E., and Aper, J. (2000). *Exploring the Heritage of American Higher Education: The Evolution of Philosophy and Policy.* San Francisco: Jossey-Bass.

31. Bogue, E., Creech, J., and Folger, J., (1993). *Assessing Quality in Higher Education: Policy Actions in the SREB States.* Atlanta, GA: Southern Regional Education Board.

32. Gibran, K. (1926). *Sand and Foam.* New York: Alfred A. Knopf, 58.

33. Senge, P. (1990). *The Fifth Discipline: The Art and Practice of the Learning Organization.* New York: Doubleday.

34. Morgan, G. (1997). *Images of Organization.* Thousand Oaks, CA: Sage.

35. Graham, P., Lyman, R., and Trow, M. (1995). *Accountability of Colleges and Universities.* New York: Columbia University.

36. Bogue, Creech, and Folger, *Assessing Quality in Higher Education.*

37. Eisner, E. (1985). *The Art of Educational Evaluation.* Philadelphia: Falmer Press.

38. Drucker, P. (1985). *Innovation and Entrepreneurship.* New York: Harper Collins.

39. Gibran, *Sand and Foam,* 30.

Chapter 12

Decision and Discovery

Developing a Strategic Vision of Academic Quality

For anyone who writes, a 1990 book titled *Rotten Rejections* will prove a delightful companion. It is a compilation of rejections received by authors great and small. One of the more interesting entries comes from a Chinese economic journal: "We have read your manuscript with boundless delight. If we were to publish your paper, it would be impossible for us to publish any work of lower standard. As it is unthinkable that in the next thousand years we shall see its equal, we are, to our regret, compelled to return your divine composition."[1]

Surely there is no lack of clarity in the quality assessment presented in this rejection letter. In the daily life of our colleges and universities, however, the quest for quality is a more complex venture. Previous chapters make clear that American higher education has fashioned a diverse cluster of quality assurance systems and instruments, systems that possess interesting theoretical and value foundations. Whatever allowances we may make for the philosophical and technical liabilities associated with any one of these systems, we must remain impressed with the energy and the thought devoted to quality assurance systems—and to the finding that American higher education is one enterprise in our national life that enjoys a favorable balance of attention when it comes to international exchange.

However, we can identify a number of systemic liabilities to our current approaches to quality assurance. First, there is not always clear and effective linkage among our different systems of quality assurance. What contribution, if any, do rankings and ratings make to accreditation studies, and vice versa? Second, we have a variety of stakeholders interested in quality assurance, stakeholders not always united in motive and tactic. Third, we have a range of perspectives on the purpose of quality assurance efforts. Some look on quality assurance with an eye to civic accountability, others for the improvement of teaching and learning, others as a means for student development, others as a tool for management, and still others as an occupation for research—all legitimate purposes. Fourth, our concerns for quality may be myopic, an occupation of the moment. And finally, there can be a serious question on many campuses as to whether the concern for quality has penetrated the institution, residing not in the depths, in the hearts and minds of the faculty who give life and meaning to the institution but too often floating lightly on the administrative surface.

The title of this chapter anticipates our hope and intent. We want to accent the "decision and discovery" potential of quality assurance systems, and we want to accent the need for a more integrated approach, the development of a more philosophical perspective and strategic vision. To achieve these purposes, we first propose to glean from our review of existing quality assurance practices a set of principles or governing ideals by which we may build a philosophy of quality. Second, we will present a minimal-element quality assurance model that we think will help deliver on the quality definition offered in chapter 1 and also offer some promise of a closer integration of quality assurance exercises. Third, we intend to describe the renewing and learning outcomes that can associate with our search for quality. Finally, we want to dwell on the special and precious nature of the collegiate enterprise and the implications there in our quest for quality.

GOVERNING IDEALS: A PHILOSOPHY OF QUALITY

As we reflect on the quality assurance approaches described in previous chapters, several principles or governing ideals may be identified for constructing an effective "decision and discovery" quality assurance system. These governing ideals constitute a useful test for building quality assurance systems and for evaluating those already in place.

Partnerships

To the important quality concerns of purpose and performance in our opening chapter, we add the concept of partnership. Effective quality assurance is a partnership journey of caring and daring. In *When Giants Learn to Dance,* Kanter[2] tells of the leadership styles and attitudes that American corporate executives need for competing in today's international business Olympics—the need for teams and partnerships rather than corporate cowboys and corporate czars. We believe that team efforts and partnerships are important to collegiate quality as well.

No one who has taken the journey toward improved quality concludes that journey without acknowledging the need for partnership. In his book describing the development of a new core curriculum and associated assessment system at King's College, D. W. Farmer noted: "A condition of trust is the first ingredient required on a college campus to create a positive attitude toward change. Trust is not simply the result of rhetoric but more importantly the result of deeds. Actions are what help to define interpersonal relationships and expectations. Faculty and administrators need to see themselves as partners in higher education, not as adversaries."[3]

What is true for parties within the academy is also true for those external to the campus. Governing boards, state coordinating agencies, legislative and executive officers, and media professionals—the list of stakeholders in the quality of colleges and universities has been growing over the past few decades, particularly in the last quarter century. We have noted in earlier chapters the more assertive voices of those external to the campus and the potential discomfort and liabilities that can associate with the entry of these new external partners. In chapter 11 we pointed to the tensions that can emerge between civic and collegiate accountability interests.

Without partnership within and without, we may predict continued and perhaps unproductive conflict because stakeholders have not engaged in the hard work of building consent over educational purpose and over what will be accepted as legitimate performance evidence. If, to borrow a phrase from Neal Postman, civic and corporate friends believe that colleges are to serve primarily the "God of Economic Utility"[4] while faculty are centering on the civic mission of educating students for intelligent participation in democracy, and if there is no conversational traffic between these two different but important visions of purpose, would we be surprised if the two stakeholder groups disagreed over evidences of quality?

We believe that in their best and most effective expression, the quality concerns of those external to the university constitute acts of friendship rather than enmity. In no way, however, do we intend to diminish the premier role of the faculty in defining, evaluating, and improving quality in our colleges and universities. Any quality assurance system that does not directly affect the quality of teaching and the quality of what happens in our classrooms, studios, laboratories, and other learning settings is an empty exercise. Any quality assurance program that does not command the active allegiance of the faculty will be more facade than substance. This leads nicely to our next governing ideal.

Linkage to Teaching and Learning

Having commended the merit of quality assurance partnerships, we emphasize a second principle: the importance of tying quality assurance efforts to teaching and learning. Reporters for *U.S. News and World Report* or *USA Today* will, for the most part, not be teaching in our classrooms, nor will members of governing boards or legislators. A moment's reflection and a search of our memories will remind us of who is the premier architect of quality. As students, we will not remember the policy studies and critiques that have swirled about American colleges and universities. We are unlikely to remember anything about *U.S. News and World Report* rankings or accreditation visits. Except in the smaller enrollment institutions, we are unlikely to recall who was the provost or president. We will, however, remember faculty members who cared about us, who lifted our spirits and our vision, who challenged our intellectual apathy and fired our curiosity, who helped us escape the poverty of the commonplace and lifted us to new horizons of discovery and meaning. The quality of a college or university is to be found most fundamentally in the quality of its caring for students.

Improvement-Centered Culture

Colleges and universities that care for their students are interested in ascertaining the impact they have on students and society and in improving that impact. As stated in our opening chapter, our first accountability is to our students. Admission, placement, retention, graduation, and certification—each educational decision we make and assist our students to make is fundamentally an act of caring. It is not an act of caring when low standards and unimaginative teaching allow our students to cheat their own promise. In this sense, then, our quality assurance instruments should tell us something about the climate of caring in our colleges and universities.

In an early configuration of its quality assurance policy, Louisiana State University in Shreveport used the ACT Student Opinion Survey to obtain the reactions of a random sample of currently enrolled students to university programs and services. This survey provided a means to obtain structured responses on a five-point scale to many dimensions of services and support. In addition, however, students had the opportunity to furnish open-ended comments at the end of the form. Students were invited to comment on "what they liked best" and "what they wanted to see improved."

The open-ended comments yielded easily to analysis. The quality of advising services, the quality of support services available to evening and part-time students, and the attitude and spirit of service on the part of some faculty and staff stood out as lively improvement targets. In its planning and goal-setting activities, the university committed itself to "The Dignity Test:" to the principle of treating its students with dignity and rendering instructional and administrative service marked by courtesy and competence. The student comments offered useful evidence about the extent to which the university honored that commitment and identified specific places where improvement work could be undertaken.

Unobtrusive Practices

In 1966, Webb, Campbell, Schwartz, and Sechrest[5] wrote a book called *Unobtrusive Measures,* suggesting in that work that assessment of performance and quality can often be approached along novel paths. To measure the attractiveness of art exhibits, for example, one can measure the wear on floor tiles in front of those exhibits. However, what we have in mind with this term is that our quality assurance programs should be so woven into the educational fabric of the institution that their influence on the quality of what happens to teaching and learning is guaranteed. For example, faculty members from all disciplines can be involved in the evaluation of the written essay called for in the Academic Profile Test (ETS), the College Base (University of Missouri), or the Collegiate Assessment of Academic Proficiency (ACT). This sharing of evaluative responsibility can create a sense of community among these interested faculty members and can enhance their sensitivity to the importance of good writing as they return to their classrooms in different departments over the campus. The assessment is linked to improvement through the faculty.

Unobtrusive quality assurance practices are not heavily laden with publications and reports that burden our storage shelves, nor are they of interest to institutional research officers only. Unobtrusive systems do not necessarily require a director or office of quality assurance. What they do require is an intellectual and emotional commitment on the part of everyone in the collegiate community. This commitment will ensure that the concern for quality is expressed as much in the passions as in the policies of the institution.

Varieties of Excellence

No principle is more central to our philosophy of quality than this one. Beginning with the definition of quality presented in chapter 1, we have continued to affirm the importance of recognizing and rewarding diversity of institutional mission and individual talent. Quality is not a single-factor attribute of personal or organizational performance. Every dimension of collegiate life sings to the beauty and power of diversity. Begin with the cold chills that run up and down our spines when we sit in the recital hall of the music building and know that we are in the presence of a great talent singing or playing. Experience the touch of wonder as we perceive the power and inspiration carried in a short poem penned by a student and carried in a literature review published by the English faculty. Marvel at the integrating power of the mind that has just produced a new history. Stand amazed at the biology graduate student who has replaced a complex machine for splitting embryos (costing several thousands of dollars) with a razor and microscope slide roughened by diamond dust (costing just over a dollar). Be impressed with the physicist and the theologian discussing the nature of reality, each recommending to the other Zukav's *The Dancing Wu Li Masters*[6] and Jastrow's *God and the Astronomers.*[7] The hallway linking science and religion may be shorter than we thought. Nor are other academic hallways so distant. Economists, ethicists, and environmentalists will find common cause in the globalization arguments of Thomas Friedman writing in *The Lexus and the Olive Tree.*[8] Who can stand next to this exciting array of ideas and inquiry—

to say nothing of the diversity of institutional climates that furnish homes for them—and say that quality can be captured in a single factor or indicator? Creating a larger vision of excellence is a theme to which we will return in our closing comments in this chapter.

Multiple Indicators

We have emphasized throughout the book that no single indicator or measurement of quality can stand without some criticism. There is no indicator or evidence of quality that may not be assaulted for some philosophical or technical frailty. Outcome measures may not tell us about the value-added contributions of the collegiate climate. Student opinions and satisfaction indices do not tell us whether students have learned anything. Students can be happy and ignorant. Reputation and ranking studies are sometimes viewed as "quantified gossip" and often do not furnish useful information for improving programs and policies. Accreditation can be an exercise in professional back-scratching, a cost-and-time burden serving only the interests of various professions and disciplines. Licensure examinations can be subject to the changing interests and standards of a profession and the profession's own self-interests. Academic program reviews can become paper producing burdens and busywork for administrators needing occupation. Alumni opinions can mellow and modify with time.

Obviously, then, we need multiple indicators for this conceptual challenge and for other reasons as well, because individual and institutional performances are, as we have noted, too complex and too precious to be captured in a single point of evidence. The artist/scientist physician does not look at a single indicator of our physical or emotional condition to ascertain our state of health. Diagnosis and prescription are built on analysis, evaluation, and interpretation of multiple indicators. We will suggest an educational diagnostic profile in this same spirit later in the chapter.

Public Disclosure

Colleges and universities are built to stimulate and sustain a search for truth. An essential feature in that search is our willingness to expose both our ideas and our convictions to the test of public disclosure, both within and outside the institution. The transmission and the testing of ideas confer upon publication an essential role in the academy. How can we lay claim to a concept or to a value until we have tested that idea or that value in the crucibles of practice and publication, debate and dissent? The student of science or music will have his or her knowledge of both science and music greatly enlivened by reading the biographies of Galileo and Stravinsky. Both of these creative minds were exposed to unhappy public receptions of their works, as is true with so many scholars. Today's heresy is tomorrow's common sense, and new knowledge often makes ragged and raw entrance into conventional wisdom. See Thomas Kuhn's classic

The Structure of Scientific Revolutions for a probing excursion into the nature of knowledge and its advancement.[9]

In a recent visit to a state university, we had the opportunity to examine the progress of a faculty struggling with the adequacy of its general education curriculum and the appropriate means to assess the effect of the general education core. The institution had employed a director of assessment and had appointed a representative committee of faculty and staff to work with the director of assessment. The minutes of the committee were instructive; at one point, the committee debated the merit of any assessment, because assessment would offer the prospect of the results becoming public and perhaps being published in local newspapers. The minutes recorded no commentary on the contrast between this apprehension about public disclosure and a value disposition on which the academy is built: the sharing of perspective, process, and products with those external to the community as a means of testing our advance on truth. To the credit of this faculty, we can report that the initial suspicions and concerns were overcome, and the campus has moved forward in the best spirit of the decision-and-discovery journey we are trying to emphasize in this chapter.

What we expect our students to learn about the search for truth can also be found in our search for quality. How can we furnish effective models of curiosity and courage for our students unless we are willing to submit the nature of the collegiate enterprise to the test of public scrutiny? The journey from knowledge to wisdom begins with performance—when we lay open the workings of mind, heart, and hand to the critical review and standards of others. The journey of institutional learning begins in the same fashion, in a performance test that brings us to our next principle.

External Standards

The ideal of public disclosure also assumes that we are willing to place the performance of our students and services against standards external to the campus. When we seek accreditation and conduct academic program reviews, we are making use of this principle. When we use assessment instruments that offer comparative performance profiles from other institutions and student populations, we recognize the merit of an external standard. When we make use of student performance on licensure examinations, we use this standard.

A philosophic tension is inherent in the concept of external standard. Is it a misplacement of responsibility and trust to insist on an independent check on performance? We believe not, and for reasons just cited in our discussion of the "public disclosure" principle. An essential nature of the collegiate enterprise, in the search for truth, is the testing of conviction and findings against the community of scholars, for there may be elements of insulation and solitude in creative acts of scholarship. Whether emerging from the creative impulse of a solitary mind or the synergistic outcome of many minds, the results of creativity must come into public forum and public test at some point.

Learning by Doing

In our roles as teachers, we embark daily upon the delicate obligation of judging human talent. As consultants we are willing participants in the task of judging organizational performance in cultural, civic, and corporate settings. For our students, we conceive performance tests that will give us public access to private mastery and growth. Our students must demonstrate concept or skill mastery through some behavioral and overt expression.

Thinking about quality is certainly a reasonable first step in its delivery—no matter what the organizational setting. But thinking must be linked to action if we are to realize the full fruits of learning about quality. In a paraphrase of Ralph Waldo Emerson, thinking about writing will not release that parade of friendly thought that will march across the page when we begin the "doing" of writing, when our fingers hit that first key or our pen carries that first word to paper. Similarly, only those institutions that have married argument to action will experience the discovery potential of the search for quality.

A POSTSCRIPT: UNRESOLVED TENSIONS

We are not sure whether this next reflection qualifies well as a governing ideal, but it is surely a matter of reality and merits our attention. We speak of certain tensions among the principles cited. In the previous discussion, for example, we cited the tension between internal responsibility and external standards in our search for quality. The call for recognizing diversity of talent and variety of excellence will argue with the call for minimal standards for our credentials and degrees. It seems reasonable to ask that the musician, the engineer, the accountant, and the teacher master certain communication skills as a requirement to earn the bachelor's degree—but at what level and standard?

The role of competition in human development and learning argues with the role of cooperation/collaboration in learning, but where is the balance point? The best of competition calls us to stand on our tiptoes and the worst calls us to a dog-eat-dog mentality. The best of collaboration calls on the intelligence and imagination of many good minds and the worst of collaboration fondles mediocrity and allows a dumbing down of standard. We emphasized in our definition of quality the essential requirement of tying quality judgments to the mission of a campus. How can we reconcile this emphasis on internal standards to the use of external standards? We hold up for salute the premier role of faculty in quality assurance but admit to legitimate roles for other partners external to the campus. We offer both reflection and action as sources for learning. Living with ambiguity and paradox is a legitimate learning exercise in our search for quality.

It would be perhaps both unwise and arrogant to suggest that "good practice" in quality assurance may be conveniently summarized and adequately described in these "bulleted" ideals or principles. We intend these "governing ideals," however, not as some exhaustive evaluative template but as a reasonable philosophical background against which to consider the effectiveness of current quality assurance practices, as a basis for asking questions of effectiveness and utility of our quality assurance policy and system.

An Integrated Quality Assurance Model

As we reflect on the various tests of quality presented in the previous chapters and the principles cited in the opening reflections of this chapter, we are led to another question: Is it possible to conceive a model of quality assurance that would furnish a minimal base for a campus thinking about its students and its programs—a model that would speak to both improvement and accountability motives?

One liability of presenting such a model is that it might prove limiting in its effect. We do not want to encourage a dependent spirit that can be linked to "looking in the back of the book for answers" before we try to solve the problem. We believe, however, that this potential liability is a modest one and that there is merit in thinking through this question. Reflected in our definition of quality and in the principles we have outlined is our intent to encourage individual campuses and their faculties to define and describe their own varieties of excellence—the features of purpose and performance that mark the perimeters of distinction for a given campus.

Tables 12.1 and 12.2 present the suggested elements of this model. The elements of Table 12.1 center on student performance and attitude indicators, whereas the elements of Table 12.2 describe program and service assessment. In Table 12.2 we want to draw attention to a cluster of performance indicators associated more with the quality of leadership and support than the quality of educational programs and services. Here we list the acquisition and evaluation of media coverage profiles and financial/performance audit reports.

These evidences of performance reflect our earlier stated conviction that the educational and leadership integrity of a campus is also related to its quality. We recognize the danger of depending upon newspaper and media coverage, for example, as a reflection of campus performance. However, a campus that is frequently cited in the press and media for integrity questions related to its personnel, its policies, and its programs invites questions about quality. We do not believe that quality exists independent of integrity. A campus periodically cited by the inspector general or legislative auditor for poor judgment, sloppy practice, or obvious criminal activity will at the very least have a more difficult time keeping public attention on its educational quality.

The final element in this model commends the use of benchmark studies and total quality management studies in the evaluation of administrative services. Examining the budget and performance of such services as admissions, regis-

Table 12.1
A Minimal Element Quality Assurance Model of Student Assessment

Assessment	*Decision focus*
Upon admission	
College readiness skills inventory	To ascertain student readiness for college work
Interests inventory	To explore student personal and career interests
Values inventory	To establish baseline student values disposition
End of sophomore year	
General education knowledge skills Communication skill Problem-solving/analytical/ critical-thinking skill Reading skill Familiarity with modes of thought Cultural/historical awareness Health/nutrition/exercise awareness	To ensure that each student has mastered acceptable skill knowledge To ascertain changes (value-added) in student knowledge and skill
At graduation	
Major field assessment	To ensure that each student has achieved acceptable mastery of concepts in major field
Value inventory	To chart major changes in values disposition
Senior thesis/project portfolio	To ensure student ability to conceptualize, implement, and report on inquiry
Postgraduation	
Alumni follow-up surveys	To obtain alumni evaluation of programs/services and establish baseline and trend data on satisfaction

Table 12.2
(Continued)

Annual	
Review and evaluation of newspaper/media coverage	To evaluate evidence of educational/ management integrity
Review and evaluation of governing board/executive/ legislative audits or other special reports	
Periodic	
Sampling survey of enrolled students (phone, interview, questionnaire)	To evaluate programs and services as seen by "customers and clients" of the campus
Sampling survey of alumni	
Sampling survey of service area constituents	
Sampling survey of employers and schools receiving graduates or transfers	

(Continued)

tration, financial aid, maintenance, and parking against performance benchmarks from other campuses similar in size and mission and in probing the process flow and effectiveness of these services should also be an element in a comprehensive quality assurance system. Student feedback and satisfaction with these services, suggested in previous data points, can be one "trigger" for such evalu-

Table 12.2
(Continued)

Regional accreditation	To ensure that program service units and institution reflect on goals and performance
Professional accreditation	To subject programs and services to external perspective/standard
Academic program reviews by peer teams, advisory boards, or board of visitors	To encourage renewal moments
As desired	
Benchmark/total quality management studies	To evaluate effectiveness and efficiency of administrative services such as admissions, registration, financial aid, maintenance, parking, etc.

ations, and external consultant reviews similar to academic program reviews can be another "trigger" mechanism.

There are models of discovery in American higher education, institutions that are exemplars of the "governing ideals" we have elucidated in the opening of this chapter. Those exemplars are well and fully portrayed in more complete works. Perhaps there is no institution more frequently cited for its thoughtful integration of instruction and assessment than Alverno College, and the story of that quarter-century journey of leadership and response at Alverno is thoroughly recounted in the 2000 work *Learning That Lasts: Integrating Learning, Development, and Performance in College and Beyond.*[10] Several institutional exemplars of quality assurance integration and accent on decision and discovery may also be found in the 1992 book *The Evidence for Quality* by Bogue and Saunders[11] and in the 1996 book *Assessment in Practice* by Banta, Lund, Black, and Oblander.[12]

The Renewal Outcomes

Quality assurance efforts constitute a discovery venture, an adventure in learning. Learning about the nature of our goals (what we thought they were, what they really are, what we want them to be), learning about the nature of performance and how to define performance so that it adequately reflects both individual and institutional diversity, learning about the nature of truth and more about how we access truth—these are renewal outcomes worthy of an educational enterprise. Here are other renewal outcomes.

Discovering Purpose

To suggest that we can evaluate the quality and effectiveness of any educational program without knowing the goals of that program seems the height of illogic. There is, however, more than a little merit in a "goal-free" evaluation. As faculty and staff ask questions about results (How good a job are we doing?), they are inevitably forced to address questions of intent. Asking questions of ends forces us to address questions of beginnings. Readers interested in the philosophic and technical bases for different models of educational evaluation will find a work on that theme by Blaine, Worthen, and Fitzpatrick worth investing time and study.[13]

Academics are fond of the notion that one of the purposes of a college education is to develop in students the ability to think critically. Now how do we go about developing that facility? Do we simply throw students into a smorgasbord of courses from different disciplines and trust—not really know—that this feast will, in fact, develop the capacity to think critically?

Suppose that developing critical thinking skill is a legitimate goal for our general education program and we decide to assess the extent to which that skill is being developed in our students. Does critical thinking involve more than just problem solving? Does it involve the ability to exercise judgment? What about the ability to analyze, synthesize, and evaluate—the higher order intellectual skills of Bloom's cognitive taxonomy?[14] What about the practical intelligence suggested by Sternberg, to which we referred in chapter 7? What instrument might we employ to assess the mastery of critical thinking skill: The Watson Glaser Test of Critical Thinking, the California Test of Critical Thinking? The Academic Profile Test of ETS claims to measure reading and critical thinking skill as does the Collegiate Assessment of Academic Proficiency published by the American College Testing Program. Will a historian, a literature scholar, a musician, an engineer, an economist, and a chemist agree on whether these instruments do, in fact, measure this skill?

In his preface to Richard Paul's 1990 book *Critical Thinking*,[15] Gerald Nosich describes critical thinking as more than the acquisition of knowledge and skill. It involves the ability to examine without prejudice points of view that are directly opposed to those we hold. The person who thinks critically does not just entertain differing points of view; he or she actively seeks opposing perspectives and ideas. The key point to this partial definition of critical thinking is that it involves elements of mind and heart. Will critical thinking exist in the absence of a passion—a sustaining and driven curiosity harnessed to habits of judgment and evaluation? Paul's book proposes that critical thinking is not just cognitive but also moral and affective.

Do the commercially designed assessments of critical thinking previously mentioned meet this measurement challenge? To engage the question of how to assess the presence or absence of critical thinking in our students takes one on an interesting and exciting conceptual journey concerning learning goals, concept definitions, and measurement.

Defining Priorities

Putting first things first is an act of leadership. When Robert Hutchins took over the presidency of the University of Chicago, he found that "The great depression conferred marked benefits upon the university, for it forced a reconsideration of the whole enterprise. The first thing I had to contend with was the demand that I cut everything 25 percent. This made no sense to me. I thought what was important should be supported and what was trivial should be dropped."[16] We take a brief diversion in this narrative to note that programs and services do not have to be of low quality or "trivial" to warrant their discontinuance in difficult financial moments, and we will return to that idea in a latter discussion of this chapter.

We now know enough about mind-body interaction and the importance of nutrition and exercise in our lives that it would be reasonable to find some moment in our general education programs for knowledge of our physical selves. We should also consider new knowledge emerging as biologists explore the genetic factors related to disease. Is it important for this kind of self-knowledge—knowledge of nutrition and kinesthetic intelligence as described by Gardner—to be a goal of our general education programs? And will we recognize in the human quest man's search for meaning and spiritual yearning? If so, what priority position should it occupy? And should there be a value-added assessment here, just as we might embrace for communication and critical thinking skills?

A serendipity outcome of quality assurance exercises is that they often lead those working on the exercises—students, faculty, administrators, civic friends—to a more embracing sense of what is important in a college education.

Enlarging Our Vision of Quality

One of our more obvious convictions is that when faculty and staff begin to struggle with the philosophical and technical questions of quality, effectiveness, and evaluation, they will appreciate more fully the variety of meanings associated with quality. When faculty and staff begin the exercise of developing an applied philosophy of quality, new understandings will emerge. In a community of learning, this is an important and appropriate outcome to model before our students, because it demonstrates an institutional commitment to curiosity and courage.

The exercise before our students and our colleges exemplifies one other important idea. Of all the pleasures enjoyed by educated men and women—learning, loving, serving, creating—learning is perhaps one of the most fundamental. Our willingness to escape disciplinary boundaries—indeed, to apply the truth tools of our various disciplines—in a venture of common interest sends a happy message to our students, who learn not only from what we say but from what we model.

Extending Value Sensitivities

An extension of the previous renewal outcome is that the values of those who undertake journeys of discovery will be tested. As we confront questions of measurement and meaning, we discover again that not all that is meaningful, not all that is real, and not all that is important yields to measurement: the smile of an awakening mind, the satisfied grin of mastery, the courage of men and women with ideas in advance of their time, the payoff of perseverance, and the inventing force of knowledge in action.

A ray of sunlight falling through an early morning mist will reveal something about the nature of light that cannot be found or expressed in the physics of reflection and refraction. An orchestra performing Dvorak's *New World Symphony* will reveal something about music that cannot be found in the laws of musical intervals. The beauty of a painting or a poem can define the limits of the rational. Explorations in modern physics invite us to consider the reality of "antimatter" and "dark matter" and reveal again the short half-life of "common sense." Here is a note from now-deceased Harvard scholar Stephen Bailey: "I have a fairly simple theory: It is that what students take away in a positive sense from institutions of higher education is little more than the spillover of excitement and commitment they observe in the adult models about them. If administrators, faculty, and support staff are made up of contentious cynics and spiritual zombies, students will develop a notion of the life of the mind that is finally expressed in the phrase 'who needs it.' If, on the other hand, they find themselves surrounded by human beings who exude excitement about their own lives, an invaluable role model is created as young people are induced to recognize the possibilities of joy in the options of continued growth."[17]

Thus, in quality assurance efforts are to be found lovely discovery moments: wondering about the richness of human experience and talent, valuing a diversity of realities, experiencing humility and anxiety in the face of the unknown, and knowing the power of decision and daring.

Promoting Personnel Development

This renewal outcome is really embedded in a number of those already outlined. It is worth, however, a more specific mention. Rightly orchestrated, quality assurance efforts open yet another avenue for personnel development and growth, perhaps as useful as a good sabbatical.

Physicists will learn about the Delphi Technique. Historians will argue about normative and criterion standards. Accountants will debate not numbers but the merits of contrasting goals. Economists will stray from their regression analyses and explore adversary methods of evaluation. Literature scholars will examine the meaning of the standard error of measurement. Psychologists will teach literature scholars what the standard error means. All of this can take place on a journey of learning and developing.

In the decade of the 1970s, one of the authors directed a statewide quality assurance venture designed to explore the feasibility of allocating some portion of state funds to colleges and universities on a performance rather than an enrollment criterion, on a criterion of achievement rather than one of activity, and this policy venture has been previously described in chapter 9. A bright and energetic colleague in that policy journey was an accomplished literature scholar from the state's research university, who began the venture as the project's resident critic. This scholar, however, played no small role in keeping the entire five-year discovery process both honest and productive. He brought not only intelligence and a reasoned suspicion to the venture but also curiosity and intellectual stamina that other, more agreeable "friends" often lacked. No person participating in this statewide venture became a more informed and passionate advocate of quality assurance than did this friendly critic.

Quality assurance and evaluation ventures will present opportunity, then, for all to explore new conceptual and personal frontiers, to investigate and challenge biases, and to fashion friendships on a community venture. This last note carries us to a final renewal outcome.

Strengthening Community

Few instruments of human construct fail to have both positive and negative valence. We have cited what we believe to be the positive and the renewal outcomes of quality assurance ventures. There is intent. There is style. There is result. Obviously, poor or mean judgment in any one of these steps can work against all of the renewal outcomes cited here, can obscure purpose, can divert energy, can nurture cynicism and suspicion.

Rightly conceived and rightly prosecuted, however, the renewal benefits can strengthen community by bringing colleagues together in the spiritual strengthening that comes from working on a common goal, from translating difficulty and disappointment into achievement, and from fashioning consensus out of conflict. Why is this so important? We restate a point made in chapter 1. There can be no quality in any educational enterprise without caring, and there can be no caring without community. What kind of community? This is not a small query, and we intend now to probe that question more deeply.

THE NATURE OF THE ENTERPRISE

As we have noted several times, two of the more obvious policy accents in American higher education in the latter half of the twentieth century were accents on access and accountability. This book has centered its attention on issues of quality and accountability, which are not divorced from the issue of access in a democratic society. In recent years, there has also emerged an increasing accent on marketplace principles and ideology in higher education.

What does it mean to be "businesslike"? Does that mean to encourage imagination and risk, to accent efficiency, to insist on responsibility and accountability in the deployment of resources, to feel the exhilaration of competition, to enjoy the translation of product and service dreams into new realities? Or does it mean to seek the lowest common wages for those who produce our products and deliver our services and to cast them aside when we can find cheaper labor, to sacrifice quality and integrity in the relentless search for profit, to ignore longer-range destructive effects on human beings and environment for the sake of an assured quarterly profit record, and to collaborate with others in price fixing schemes, to serve ambition before loyalty?

Perhaps American colleges and universities should be pleased that we are "unbusinesslike" because that keeps us from excommunicating the musicians, the poets, the actors, and perhaps the physicists and historians as well. Of course there is everything to commend integrity, efficiency, and responsibility in the management of any academic enterprise and to encourage and reward initiative and imagination in new program ventures and in the attraction of revenues.

But there is a legitimate basis for financial subsidy and community in academic life as well. "Every tub on its own bottom" in academic life, as a point of unexcepted principle, makes about as much sense as eliminating from our culture every human activity that does not make money. And believing that human beings are motivated to effectiveness and efficiency only by profit makes about as much common sense as believing that we can sneak daybreak past a healthy rooster.

To carry the barnyard analogy a bit further, we would deserve a good flogging if we subscribed to profit as the only motivating force in life. In his informing and provoking work *The Hungry Spirit,* former Shell Oil Company executive and professor at the London School of Business Charles Handy notes that the lesser hunger in life is about the material possessions we seek and the greater hunger is about our search for meaning in life. In capitalistic societies, he notes, we have assumed that satisfying the lesser hunger will satisfy the greater hunger.[18] American higher education is about why that assumption is empty and false.

Our intent here is not to underestimate nor undervalue the importance and contribution of corporate culture and marketplace principles. Profit is a human motive and impulse engine of notable power. This is one real world. Service is a human motive and a constructive force of majestic impact. This also is a real world. Honest sweat may fall from the brow of the dreamer and the industrialist. Dreamers are indebted to the financial and faith investment of capitalists and entrepreneurs and pragmatists are indebted to the legacy of ideas that may flow from the dreamer and the researcher.

Our intent is, however, to argue for the distinctive nature of the collegiate enterprise. It is distinctive in its complexity of mission and purpose. As we have emphasized earlier, conserving the past, criticizing the present, constructing the future are mission elements of contradiction and complexity and represent an expectation of purpose destined to produce tension in the life of colleges and universities and to explain why there is continuing public ferment over issues of collegiate purpose and performance. The genius of the American system of education is that it is a system of multiple chances and multiple choices and that its intent is to educate the discretion of every citizen, to call each talent to the far edge of its circle of promise, to create what Barber calls *An Aristocracy of Everyone,* in a work of that title.[19] Holding in the same house a reverence for heritage while encouraging an irreverent and critical scrutiny of that heritage is a mission expectation of unusual complexity, but a mission of distinction and centrality for our democratic society.

Colleges and universities are further distinguished by their andante majesty, their commitment to longer-term pursuits, their slowness to change. A college or university wavering in the wind to every political breeze, management fad, or philosophical whim would not encourage confidence in its stability of mission or thoroughness of method. Nurturing truth and talent are occupations not of the moment but of the long run. And they are distinguished by complex governance processes that build heavily on consensus and deliberation. One gives few orders in a college or university and instead concentrates on calling colleagues and students to responsibility. This, however, is not a bad view of leadership in any organizational setting, whether corporate or collegiate.

Former president of Ohio State University Harold Enarson once noted that: "Universities are a very special kind of place. They are fragile as truth itself is fragile. They exist by public sufferance, and it is a marvel that the public at large supports with its dollar an institution that is independent, free standing. Openly critical of the conventional wisdom, enchanted with controversy, hospitable to those who 'think otherwise.' May it always be so."[20]

Critical of the conventional wisdom, friendly to disputation, enchanted with controversy, hospitable to those who think otherwise—we should be willing to model within higher education what we hold as a model before society. Asking questions of purpose and performance—the search for quality—offers an unparalleled moment to demonstrate the best features of a learning community.

THE PURSUIT OF PRESTIGE

A 2002 publication entitled *In Pursuit of Prestige* claims to take an "industry" perspective of American higher education, examines "how institutions serve customers," and centers on the competitive advantage sought by colleges and universities in the search for customers.[21] Reputation and prestige are defined as "assets that allow institutions of higher education to convey nonprice information to customers."[22] The extent to which an institution meets customer demands is taken as a definition of "reputation." "Prestige is more vaguely defined as the characteristics of an institution that has done a good job over some extended period of time."[23] *U.S. News and World Report*, however, is cited as source of "prestige" knowledge, even though the major variable in that ranking and rating is "reputation." The differences in definition tend to be both circular (reputation is an element of prestige) and without obvious conceptual anchor. We are not strongly impressed with this distinction between reputation and prestige. One useful contribution of this work, however, is its suggestion that the Carnegie classification of colleges and universities—originally intended as a "descriptive" taxonomy—has become an "evaluative" classification. Readers interested in this classification system will find the 1994 and 2000 classification systems more than interesting.[24, 25] We are led full circle back to chapter 1, in which we suggested a conventional wisdom about the pyramid of prestige in American higher education. In this conventional but flawed wisdom, Harvard, Yale, and Princeton may reside atop the qualitative heap while Bemidji State University floats in the middle and a lesser-known community college such as Motlow State Community College might come in dead last.

One of the factors that encourages the translation of the Carnegie classification system from a descriptive to an evaluative instrument and that encourages a marketplace mentality in American higher education is that colleges and universities are, as the aforementioned book suggests, in search for prestige and status and because we accept limited models of excellence and success.

The community college, a distinctive invention of American higher education, has a clearly defined mission and one that is well recognized and respected by campus and community, though the "reputation" of a community college will be more local than national. (Is this the difference between reputation and prestige?)

The second success model is the liberal arts college—seen as an enclave of modest size offering intimate connection between faculty and students and emphasizing learning in the liberal arts. Though many of our liberal arts colleges are private, a number of public institutions have embraced that prized but limited mission. When faced with declining enrollments and financial pressure, however, we will not be surprised to find such colleges more interested in the obvious market advantages of programs in business, teacher education, nursing, computer science, and health care management. In many cases, such professional studies may be located away from the main campus in more advantageous urban areas; and often there will be little evidence that the campus, if it has religious heritage, is as interested or as intense in making that religious and faith heritage obvious in these new "market-based" and "customer-driven" programs. One of the more surprising and not always happy developments is the movement of the liberal arts college into doctoral study. The popular and prevalent model is to begin by offering the doctor of education degree in educational leadership. Whether the credentials and scholarship of the faculty, the content of the curriculum, and the academic standards (a major paper instead of a dissertation?) mark such efforts as an adventure in excellence can be a discomforting but often ignored question.

A third success model, and the one most associated with "bracket creep," in the Carnegie classification system is the research university: the large doctorate-granting university featuring nationally and internationally recognized scholars, extensive externally funded research programs, and wide-ranging doctoral programs. Here, it appears, is the ultimate in higher education aspiration. The movement of an institution from offering master's degrees to even one doctoral degree is cause for celebration, an "arrival" of some moment, the ultimate prestige destination.

These models tend to leave a goodly number of splendid but confused institutions over the country. They are usually state universities often considered in a permanent state of academic adolescence because they do not know how to fashion distinction from limited mission and enrollment. They may be located in urban settings and thus look something like a community college, which indeed they are. They will offer bachelor's degrees and master's degrees, may participate in joint doctoral programs with other research universities (1994 Carnegie classification)/doctoral extensive (2000 Carnegie classification) and thus look something like universities, which they are. Given the unfortunate and inappropriate pecking order of prestige and quality that Americans can assign to the pyramidal pecking order just described, these campuses may be troubled about their image and unable to achieve a sense of identity or pleasure. Some will see expanded athletic programs (especially football) and enlarged arenas and stadiums as the key to enhanced status and prestige. Others will see a name change from a "directional" name—for example, Northeast Richland University—to a name with the appearance of more honorable heritage—for example, the University of Richland—as the cure for a perceived prestige pathology. The siren call of giantism in degrees and athletics is a temptation only the most stalwart of institutions and college presidents can resist.

A STRATEGIC VISION OF QUALITY

A strategic vision of academic quality will surely attend the governing ideals test offered in the opening reflections of this chapter, will recognize the renewing outcomes possible from "acting on the possible while awaiting perfection." Such a strategic vision will also celebrate the special and distinctive nature of the collegiate enterprise we have and rejoice in mission distinction that can be achieved if tended with patience and imagination over time. Here are other elements of a strategic vision.

Understanding Funding and Quality Linkages

Was the economist Ernest Schumacher right when he wrote his provocative economic treatise entitled *Small Is Beautiful*?[26] How many college presidents—even those who are economists—believe that small is beautiful? The relationship between funding and quality accents an observation once made that there is no subject so complex that careful examination and study will not render more complex.

Is quality positively and directly related to funding levels? If the answer is yes, then our arguments for additional support and revenue make sense, because any diminution of funding portends a decline in quality. There are mines in this attractive field, however. College presidents and campus lobbyists who passionately argue that quality will slip and suffer if there is less money for equipment, libraries, scholarships, and salaries are loathe to turn to graduates and friends on graduation day and say that the quality of the institution's educational credentials is diminished because the campus received a smaller state appropriation or suffered other revenue indignities. Is the quality of a bachelor's degree obtained while the per-student appropriation of a public university was $7,500 per student of greater moment that the quality of a bachelor's degree obtained when the per-student appropriation for that same university had dropped to $6,500?

We repeat: Is quality positively and directly related to funding levels? The answer can be yes or no. There are obviously limits to declining revenue regimens—levels of support where even the best intentioned and most servant-spirited faculty and staff can no longer carry the load and deliver a decent educational program. Indeed, many mobile faculty would have long departed the institution, which is one signal that quality may be slipping. When one-half of the accounting department of a state research university left the campus in an extended period of difficult financial support to take positions at comprehensive universities for significantly higher salaries, it is safe to say that a red flag concerning quality was an appropriate signal of distress.

On the other hand, if the campus has to make difficult priority decisions to retrench programs and services as a means of furnishing salary increases and operational support for programs and services retained, then quality is diminished only if we define quality in terms of bigness and comprehensiveness. We will return to this issue in a moment.

It would be hard to find any national or state report on higher education today that did not contain at least one recommendation for colleges and universities to more carefully define their mission, to do what they do best, to capitalize on their strengths, and to create a sense of distinctiveness. These are worthy goals for any campus, but often the policymakers use these lofty statements as euphemisms for "tighten up and get smaller." To borrow a corporate expression, the intent behind the mission advice is to downsize or, in military parlance, to "advance to the rear."

These civic/political calls for a more distinctive mission are often associated with other patently good advice to make differential cuts rather than fair-share or across-the-board cuts, which are suggested as cowardly strategies unworthy of real leadership. Such advice may be more often lofted at presidents by scholars and armchair administrators who have the advantage of dispassion and detachment than by academic administrators who have looked affected colleagues in the eye when delivering the news on how quality is to be improved with their termination.

The pressure on campus presidents and faculties to grow and to add programs and services is truly great. Growth is an easy performance signal—one that is most understandable and acceptable to both internal colleagues and external supporters, whether civic or corporate. A few institutions in this nation, perhaps the military academies and some private institutions, enjoy a stable sense of size and mission and a reputation for quality. The pressure on public institutions to look more like their larger and more mature counterparts is significant, however. A public college or university that deliberately chooses a moderate or small enrollment in association with a carefully chosen and constrained program profile can be subject to a double liability. The budgeting formulas of most states associate increased funding with enrollment growth—not an unreasonable linkage. In difficult financial times, however, the linkage can make life miserable for institutions electing or experiencing stable enrollments. Further, the spend-or-lose-it features of public budgeting policy do not encourage realistic priority settings.

The dilemma is described in the February 1991 issue of *Policy Perspectives*, "The Other Side of the Mountain":

> To ask for a reassignment of budget lines in this environment runs counter to all instincts of institutional self-preservation, for such a request is tantamount to admitting that an existing line was not necessary in the first place. Equally important is the fact that these budget lines are usually perceived as entitlements by departments and administrative units within the institution. It is far safer for a public institution to express its ambition in terms of new budget lines, seeking to expand the whole, rather than shifting resources away from ineffective units toward activities that show greater promise in effectively realizing the educational mission. Such colleges and universities know that accepting less from their state government implicitly gives power to other claims on public resources with which higher education competes for funding, such as roads, prisons, and public assistance programs.[27]

The second liability is that any president or faculty who deliberately approaches the budgeting process content to settle for the same or less support grants an advantage to other institutions that might not share the "small is beautiful" definition of quality. Indeed, they might be prone to body-count mentalities and turf-building definitions of "big is better." This is a leadership dilemma of majestic proportion.

Perhaps we may even cite a third political liability, both internal and external. Consider this hypothetical illustration in which fiction is not stranger than the truth. Faced with a multiyear budget scenario during which the campus had experienced several years of significant midyear budget cuts, ranging from 3 to 7 percent, and relatively stable or smaller state appropriations, the president of a state research university suggested that it made no sense to continue revenue starvation for the entire campus. She then suggested possible termination of the veterinary medicine school, on the theory that the needs for additional veterinarians were modest to questionable in the state, that large dollars would be freed for reallocation by this action, and that the educational heart of the campus would be less damaged by this action than by any other program deletion.

This president might be described as a courageous leader by those who campaign for the "small-is-beautiful" definition of quality and those who cheer for a more carefully drawn mission. These folks should be invited, however, to sit with the president as she receives sharply worded memos, phone calls, and personal visits accusing her of threatening the quality of the state's great "flagship" university, of diminishing the "comprehensive nature" of the university (another phrase meaning a diminution in quality). They might also find interesting the contacts from legislators and others who want their horses and dogs tended, the graduates of the veterinary school who are distressed at the possibility of losing their alma mater, and the practicing veterinarians who see the loss of a power base. Even members of the university's governing board accuse the president of undermining the university's regional and national status. Dire economic and status consequences are predicted. A short tenure for her presidency is promised. Is it not easier to be an academic hero by dashing up the legislative hill asking for more money?

Of course, this hypothetical scenario could be played out for the proposed reduction or termination of any program or service. The conversation would include observations something like this: What reputable college or university could make a claim to quality without a program in (you fill in the name) field? What are the limits to comprehensiveness? As we noted in an earlier chapter, no college or university—no matter its size or history—can hope to be completely comprehensive. All institutions will inevitably have limited missions.

Thus, a strategic vision of quality does not automatically assume that quality is immediately and linearly linked to swings, either positive or negative, in revenue and/or financial support. This vision does assume, however, that an effective retrenchment of programs and services is a priority exercise that must involve every partner in the higher education enterprise—the faculty and staff within and the governing and coordinating boards and legislature without. A strategic vision further assumes that quality is best served by stability and long-term commitment to funding support, funding that is reasonably predictable and not subject to the wild swings of boom-to-bust roller-coaster rides. This perspective is built on the simple realization that what takes a generation to build in a faculty can often be lost in a year or two. A strategic view of quality is also built on some sense of historical perspective. For example, institutions and states experiencing challenging financial moments would find sobering a review of financial-support patterns for higher education in most states during the Depression and World War II decade from 1935 to 1945. The history of faculty and staff devotion during those years might also prove inspiring and informing.

An Integrated and Systemic Approach

We suggest that a strategic vision of quality will be one in which a campus has an integrated and systematic approach to quality assurance. First there will be in this system perspective an allegiance to the governing ideals set forth in this chapter. All quality assurance efforts will be tied to the heart of the enterprise: the daily contact and interactions between those who teach and those who learn. The prime motivating force behind quality assurance efforts will be the desire to improve the impact of both instructional programs and administrative services. The style of these efforts will be relatively unobtrusive and woven into the daily fabric of practice and decision. Assessments and evaluation exercises will recognize and respect varieties of excellence for both individual talent and institutional mission and will shun pecking orders of prestige and status based on narrow notions of human and organizational promise. And expectations of quality will disdain shoddy and shallow work, whether personal or organizational.

A recognition of the power of diversity will call us to acquire multiple evidences of both personal and program performance, and we will try those evidences on standards involving internal and external judgments on the experience and values of peers within and without. We will be willing to learn by doing, modeling risk taking and discovery behavior before our students and our supporters. We will inform all management and educational decisions—personal, policy, and program—with information derived from our quality assurance efforts. And we will share the results of the journey in public forum as another expression of the spirit of the academy.

These principles will be put to work in a systematic approach to quality assurance in which every person, every program, and every service—educational and administrative—of the campus continuously asks these three questions:

- What is it that we hope to achieve?
- How good a job are we doing and how do we know?
- What improvements can be supported by the performance results?

The loop is closed by linking performance results to improvement.

A systematic approach to quality will be characterized by communities of partnership involvement so that performance issues reaching across program and organizational lines are thoughtfully engaged. Communications and publications of the institution will furnish a conceptual and philosophical map of the quality assurance program so that both the logic and the elements of the program will be apparent. These policy statements and/or other communication vehicles will outline the elements and evidences, the planning and decision purposes, the timing of assessments and evaluations, and the responsibilities for execution of the quality assurance program.

A Proactive and Risk-Embracing Perspective

Nothing is clearer from our review of the history of quality assurance initiatives in American higher education than this. The impetus for action has often come from outside the academy. This phenomenon, however, is not unique to higher education. A decent argument could be advanced that corporate America did not get serious about quality until all those foreign-built automobiles and electronics goods starting showing up on our shores and Americans started buying them.

There are, however, happy examples of more proactive collegiate histories in the country, at all levels. As we noted earlier Northeast Missouri State University (now Truman State University), for example, started its value-added program over two decades ago. Alverno College has been developing its competency-based program over three decades or more. The Tennessee performance funding project was an initiative emerging from the state's higher education system and not driven by legislative or executive threat. That policy and performance initiative now enjoys a quarter-century heritage.

A strategic vision of quality is one in which campuses and other higher education partners attempt to stay in front of the curve. We are not so naive as to believe that any organized enterprise, corporate or collegiate, might arrive at the point when it would not need and benefit from the stimulus of external review or competition. We are saying, however, that a campus with a strategic vision of quality will be one with an aggressive and imaginative program of quality assurance, attempting to lead and demonstrate initiative of thought and action, rather than follow and react.

In a 1989 book entitled *Head First: The Biology of Hope*, Norman Cousins explored the scientific relationships among human attitudes, the presence of hope, and our physiological well-being and health. Nestled midway into the book is this comment: "Life is the ultimate prize and it takes on ultimate value when suddenly we discover how tentative and fragile it can be. The essential art of living is to recognize and savor its preciousness when it is free of imminent threat of jeopardy."[28] This is an attitude with transfer potential. The work of collegiate educators is a precious work, and the essential mark of the true educator is a caring and compassion for students that emerges without the necessity of external threat. A strategic vision of quality, then, is characterized by an active caring, a "heart first" attitude, to which we now turn in our conclusion to this chapter and this book.

Quality: The Premier Leadership Call

The promise of quality can be realized in our colleges and universities with a strategic and unifying vision of quality, as outlined and expressed in this chapter. The vision begins with "head first" matters of knowledge. We need to know about the strengths and limitations of contemporary approaches to quality assurance, and we hope that this book has made some contribution to that goal. We need to know and to debate various definitions of quality, including those outlined in these chapters and the main definition offered in this book: *Quality is conformance to mission specification and goal achievement within publicly accepted standards of accountability and integrity.* We need to know about the kinds of evidences and indicators necessary to circumscribe quality and to understand that both individual and institutional performance is too complex to be captured in a single data point. We need to know about the standards that might be used to judge quality, and we need some understanding about who the legitimate judges of collegiate quality might be. We need to know about the kinds of decisions—whether improvement or accountability oriented—that furnish the motivating force for quality assurance exercises. We need to know about ways in which campus professionals and community and civic friends can fashion effective partnerships in the quest for quality, and we hope that this book has made some contribution to the concept of partnership. Finally, we need to know that our quest for quality is a powerful instrument of decision and discovery—a reflection of our commitment to curiosity. A compulsive curiosity is the first mark of an educated man or woman, and a willingness to learn is an important signal of campus health and spirit as well.

But the final guarantor in realizing the promise of quality is a "heart first" attitude in which a concern for quality constitutes the premier leadership call on the attitudes and actions of every person on the campus—from professor to president, from custodian to counselor, from director to dean. What we know will always be a servant to what we believe, and if we believe in the promise of quality, every action of the campus, whether educational or administrative, will serve that promise and be measured by that standard. Every policy, every personality, every practice, and every performance will stand muster before the call of quality. The technical competence and the ethical commitment of the people who give life and meaning to a campus will be linked to its quality and will either build or diminish it. A strategic and unifying vision of quality, then, will emerge when assessment is built not so much on the process and resource indicators that constitute conventional wisdom but on indicators that are results oriented. What difference have we made in the knowledge, skills, and values of those students entrusted to our care and in the communities that trust us with their support and expectations? Quality reflects not just our curiosity but our caring.

The promise of quality resides, then, in the plain of our passions. Do we care enough for truth, do we care enough for service, and do we care enough for human growth and dignity that our vision of quality permeates and penetrates the entire campus and touches the mind and the heart of every person who serves there? Will that vision yield standards and encouragement that call our students and our colleagues from the poverty of the commonplace, that salute the promise of each one on the campus (whether student or staff), and that launch each person to the far reaches of his or her potential? Will that vision reveal a happy curiosity and active compassion? Will that vision marry a respect for diversity or mission and talent with a scorn for shoddy work, whether individual or institutional? And will that vision respond not just to the intellectual call to advance the truth but also to the ethical call of justice, dignity, integrity, and nobility? The promise can only be realized in a community of caring, which ought to be an accurate descriptor of a quality college or university.

NOTES

1. Bernard, A. (ed.). (1990). *Rotten Rejections.* Wainscott, NY: Pushcart Press.

2. Kanter, R. (1989). *When Giants Learn to Dance.* New York: Simon and Schuster.

3. Farmer, D. (1988). *Enhancing Student Learning: Emphasizing Essential Competencies in Academic Programs.* Wilkes-Barre, PA: King's College Press.

4. Postman, N. (1995). *The End of Education.* New York: Vintage Books.

5. Webb, E., Campbell, D., Schwartz, R., and Sechrest, L. (1966). *Unobtrusive Measures: Nonreactive Research in the Social Sciences.* Skokie, IL: Rand McNally.

6. Zukav, G. (1979). *The Dancing Wu Li Masters.* New York: Morrow.

7. Jastrow, R. (1978). *God and the Astronomers.* New York: W. W. Norton.

8. Friedman, T. (1999). *The Lexus and the Olive Tree.* New York: Random House.

9. Kuhn, T. (1962). *The Structure of Scientific Revolutions.* Chicago: University of Chicago Press.

10. Mentkowski, M., and Associates. (2000). *Learning That Lasts: Integrating Learning, Development, and Performance in College and Beyond.* San Francisco: Jossey-Bass.

11. Bogue, E., and Saunders, R. (1992). *The Evidence for Quality.* San Francisco: Jossey-Bass.

12. Banta, T., Lund, J., Black, K., and Oblander, F. (1996). *Assessment in Practice.* San Francisco: Jossey-Bass.

13. Worthen, B., Sanders, J., and Fitzpatrick, J. (1997). *Program Evaluation.* New York: Longman.

14. Bloom, B., and Others. (1956). *Taxonomy of Educational Objectives: The Classification of Educational Goals, Handbook I.* New York: McKay.

15. Paul, R. (1990). *Critical Thinking.* Rohnert Park, CA: Center for Critical Thinking and Moral Critique, Sonoma State University.

16. Hutchins, R. (1966). "First Glimpses of a New World." In *What I Have Learned.* New York: Simon and Schuster.

17. Bailey, S. (1974). "People Planning in Postsecondary Education: Human Resource Development in a World of Decremental Budgets." In *More for Less: Academic Planning with Faculty Without New Dollars,* ed. J. N. Nesmith. Papers presented at a conference sponsored by the Society for College and University Planning, Nordic Hills, Itasca, IL, April 17–19.

18. Handy, C. (1998). *The Hungry Spirit.* New York: Broadway Books.

19. Barber, B. (1992). *An Aristocracy of Everyone.* New York: Oxford University Press.

20. Enarson, H. (1973). "University or Knowledge Factory." *Chronicle of Higher Education,* 7(36), 16.

21. Brewer, D., Gates, S., and Goldman, C. (2002). *In Pursuit of Prestige: Strategy and Competition in U.S. Higher Education.* New Brunswick, NJ: Transaction Publishers.

22. Ibid., 27.

23. Ibid., 28.

24. Carnegie Foundation for the Advancement of Teaching. (1994). *A Classification of Institutions of Higher Education, 1994 Edition.* Princeton, NJ: Carnegie Foundation for the Advancement of Teaching.

25. Carnegie Foundation for the Advancement of Teaching. (2000). *The Carnegie Classification of Institutions of Higher Education, 2000 Edition.* Princeton, NJ: Carnegie Foundation for the Advancement of Teaching.

26. Schumacher, E. (1973). *Small is Beautiful.* New York: Harper Collins.

27. PEW Higher Education Research Program. (1991). "The Other Side of the Mountain." *Policy Perspectives,* February, 1, 2, 3A.

28. Cousins, N. (1989). *Head First: The Biology of Hope.* New York: Dutton.

Index

About the Authors

E. GRADY BOGUE is Professor of Educational Leadership and Policy Studies at the University of Tennessee and Chancellor Emeritus of Louisiana State University in Shreveport. He is also the co-author of *Exploring the Heritage of American Higher Education: The Evolution of Philosophy and Policy,* published by the American Council on Education/Oryx Press.

KIMBERELY BINGHAM HALL is Vice President for Academic and Student Affairs at South College in Knoxville, Tennessee.